Contagious Metaphor

Related Titles

The Imagination of Evil, Mary Evans
Melancholy and the Archive, Jonathan Boulter
Milton, Evil and Literary History, Claire Colebrook
Palimpsest: Literature, Criticism, Theory, Sarah Dillon

Contagious Metaphor

Peta Mitchell

B L O O M S B U R Y
LONDON • NEW DELHI • NEW YORK • SYDNEY

Bloomsbury Academic

An imprint of Bloomsbury Publishing Plc

50 Bedford Square
London
WC1B 3DP
UK

1385 Broadway
New York
NY 10018
USA

www.bloomsbury.com

Bloomsbury is a registered trade mark of Bloomsbury Publishing Plc

First published 2012
Paperback edition first published 2014

© Peta Mitchell, 2012

British Library Cataloguing-in-Publication Data
A catalogue record for this book is available from the British Library.

ISBN: HB: 978-1-4411-3273-4
PB: 978-1-4725-2162-0
ePDF: 978-1-4411-9743-6
ePUB: 978-1-4411-0421-2

Library of Congress Cataloging-in-Publication Data
Mitchell, Peta.
Contagious metaphor/Peta Mitchell.
p. cm.
Includes bibliographical references and index.
ISBN 978-1-4411-3273-4 (hardcover) – ISBN 978-1-4411-9743-6 (PDF)
– ISBN 978-1-4411-0421-2 (ePub) 1. Metaphor–Social aspects.
2. Metaphor in literature. 3. Contagion (Social psychology) I. Title.

P301.5.M48M58 2012
808.032–dc23

2012011969

Typeset by Deanta Global Publishing Services, Chennai, India

For Alex

Contents

Acknowledgements

I am indebted to many individuals, groups and institutions, without whose support this book would not have been possible. First, I must thank my wonderful friends and colleagues in the School of English, Media Studies and Art History at The University of Queensland. In particular, I am incredibly grateful to Catriona Mills and Jane Stadler, who went beyond the call of duty both as friends and as colleagues to read drafts and offer encouragement, and to Angi Buettner, who helped me see it through to the end. I am also indebted to the Institute of Advanced Studies in the Humanities at the University of Edinburgh and to Graeme Turner and the Centre for Critical and Cultural Studies at The University of Queensland. My visiting fellowships at the IASH and the CCCS in 2009 provided me with vital time and space to develop this project. Just as importantly, they gave me access to two wonderfully interdisciplinary cohorts of scholars, with whom I could test out my ideas. Particular thanks are due to Richard Adelman, Tom Bristow, Will Christie, John Gunders, Greg Hainge, Eric Parisot, Mirjam Schaub and Andy Wells, all of whom contributed in important ways to the shape this project has taken.

A version of Chapter 2 appeared as 'Geographies/Aerographies of Contagion' in a special 'Aerographies' issue of *Environment and Planning D: Society and Space* (vol. 29, 2011, pp. 533–50). I gratefully acknowledge the issue editors, Maria Fannin and Mark Jackson, for the opportunity and incentive to write the original article, and Pion Ltd., London, for granting permission to reproduce it here. I am also, of course, exceptionally grateful to the editorial staff at Bloomsbury Academic: to Anna Fleming, who saw in my proposal something worth pursuing, and to Colleen Coalter, Rachel Eisenhauer and Laura Murray, who have all helped bring this book to fruition.

Finally, my deepest debt is to my loving and long-suffering family. Alex, Mum, Dad, Rhylla and Bruce: *sine quibus non*.

Introduction: Due Preparations

*Life no longer seems to be within us; it flows out, springs forth, is commu-
nicated as if by contagion, transmitted by a look, a tone of voice, a gesture,
impressing our will on others.*

Honoré de Balzac, 'Colonel Chabert', Comédie humaine. 1832.[1]

Contagion today is everywhere – it is in the financial markets, on the streets
and in our computers. It characterizes our use of social networking and the way
ideas spread through society. In public and cultural discourse, catchphrases such
as 'social contagion', 'emotional contagion', 'mental contagion', 'financial contagion' and even 'cultural contagion' have become prevalent, if not commonplace,
suggesting contagion has moved beyond our bodies and has begun infecting
our minds and our modes of interacting with and influencing others. We are
used to thinking of the word *contagion* as having a proper or literal meaning,
one that relates to the physical communication of disease. The *Oxford English
Dictionary*, for instance, gives the primary, denotative meaning of *contagion* as
'the communication of disease from body to body by contact direct or mediate'
('Contagion' 1989), and this is the meaning that has largely been retained in
contemporary medical-scientific discourse. When compared with this 'literal'
sense of contagion, the sociocultural formations noted above begin to appear
more metaphorical, more figurative.

Over the past decade, these extra-medical forms of contagion have flourished
in contemporary discourse. Many have crystallized around the growth of social
networking, with its attendant viral metaphors, and the global financial crisis
of the late 2000s. In the latter of these two examples, news services reported
not only upon the financial contagion spreading throughout Europe, but also
on dangers of 'contagious' protests and rioting in response to recession, unemployment and introduced austerity measures. Indeed, journalist Mallory Simon
(2011) went so far as to liken the financial and social contagion that characterized Greece's economic crisis to the plot of Steven Soderbergh's film *Contagion*
(2011), released the same year. Soderbergh's film is about a much more 'literal'

(i.e. biological) virus, but it also clearly emphasizes social or affective aspects of contagion. As Simon notes, both the Greek debt crisis and Soderbergh's film serve to demonstrate how affective contagion or panic spreads faster than the underlying virus (whether it be financial or biological) itself.

Soderbergh's *Contagion*, which I will return to in the final chapter, narrates the outbreak of a fictional virus that rapidly becomes a global pandemic. The virus, named 'MEV-1' (meningoencephalitis virus one), is a hybrid paramyxovirus that originated when 'the wrong pig met up with the wrong bat', and its epidemiology is, as microbiologist and biological warfare specialist Raymond A. Zilinskas has pointed out, similar to that of the sudden acute respiratory syndrome (SARS) outbreak of 2002 (2011, n. pag.). Like SARS, MEV-1 is contracted via contact with 'fomites' (surfaces that carry infection, such as telephones, door handles ATMs, etc.) or infectious airborne droplets caused by the sneezing or coughing of an infected person. Also like SARS, *Contagion*'s MEV-1 is depicted as originating in China and spreading globally out from the air transport network hub of Hong Kong. And yet, this literal (though fictional) virus is not the only one brewing in *Contagion*, for the film foregrounds the infectious fear, panic and collapse of social order that the MEV-1 virus invokes almost as strongly as the virus itself. Indeed, one of the film's theatrical release posters emphasizes affective contagion to such a degree that the physical nature of the virus is displaced from its central role. In this poster, images of the film's key characters – only one of whom appears to have physically contracted the virus – surround a tag line in red type: 'Nothing spreads like fear: Contagion'.

In a similar vein, José Saramago's 1995 novel, *Blindness* (*Ensaio sobre a Cegueira*), explores the complex physical, affective and social effects wrought by a mysterious, and unexplained, epidemic of blindness that takes over a city. A decade after the publication of *Blindness*, Saramago published a companion novel, *Seeing* (*Ensaio sobre a Lucidez*). *Seeing* is set in the same unnamed capital city as *Blindness*, but this time its inhabitants are struck by a different kind of contagion. In the city's elections, 70 per cent of the citizens cast blank ballots, a strange and inexplicable phenomenon that the government is quick to condemn as a 'moral plague that had infected a large part of the population' (2007 [2004], p. 37). This sickness of the body politic, the suspicious government determines, must have a cause, and so begins the administration's unrelenting and draconian search for an instigator, a kind of 'patient zero', of the moral contagion.

Where Soderbergh's *Contagion* and Saramago's novels play with notions of cultural, affective and moral contagion, three recent films have also explored and highlighted the related concept of thought contagion. In the opening scene of Christopher Nolan's *Inception* (2010), the protagonist, Cobb (Leonardo DiCaprio), poses a question to his soon-to-be employer, Saito (Ken Watanabe). 'What's the most resilient parasite?', Cobb asks. 'A bacteria? A virus? An intestinal worm?'. Perhaps sensing the rhetorical nature of the question, Saito remains silent, and Cobb furnishes him with an answer: 'An idea. Resilient, highly contagious. Once an idea's taken hold in the brain it's almost impossible to eradicate'. As a film, *Inception* plays with – indeed literalizes – what we might ordinarily consider a metaphor: the notion that ideas or emotions can be 'implanted' and that they are 'contagious' or 'viral' in nature.

In Charlie Kaufman's rather more cryptic *Synecdoche, New York* (2008), the thought contagion metaphor similarly enters in the first scene as the film's protagonist, theatre director Caden Cotard (Philip Seymour Hoffman), and his daughter, Olive (Sadie Goldstein), eat breakfast in front of the television in their Schenectady home. As they eat, Olive prompts her father to switch the television to a different station. Cotard does so, changing the channel to what is ostensibly a children's cartoon depicting a grazing sheep. Olive and Cotard appear to take little notice of the cartoon, but as the sheep grazes, an animated 'Mr. Virus' parachutes in to the pastoral scene, and the cartoon's voice-over ominously intones, 'There is a secret, something at play under the surface, growing like an invisible virus of thought'.

This brief scene at first seems peripheral to the film's narrative development. Yet, as the film continues, it becomes more significant in that it increasingly appears to explain Cotard's obsession with death, disease and decay. Cotard's name, indeed, invokes 'Cotard's syndrome', a psychiatric disorder that is also known as 'Cotard's delusion' or 'walking corpse syndrome'. Cotard's syndrome involves its sufferer believing that they are dead or dying, that they are missing vital organs or even that their body is putrefying. Also symptomatic of Cotard's syndrome is the sufferer's belief that ideas, thoughts and even the material world do not exist.[2] Kaufman's Cotard, too, believes he is dying and that his body is literally rotting away: for instance, he has blood in his stools and urine, he contracts the skin disease sycosis (pun intended) and he has a seizure that leaves him unable to salivate or cry. His doctor describes his seizure as 'fungal in origin', implying an infectious cause. And yet, Cotard's problems ultimately appear more psychosomatic – more psychosis than sycosis. That is, Cotard's problems seem to stem less from a biological infection or contagion, and more from what the cartoon tells us is a secret and sublimated 'invisible virus of *thought*', one that manifests in his monomania, hypochondria and death delusions.

The 'viruses of thought' depicted in *Inception* and *Synecdoche, New York* have no 'patient zero', no identifiable single origin. These films are less 'outbreak narratives' (to use Priscilla Wald's term) than they are narrative contentions that contagion is a basic and unavoidable, though often hidden, condition of thought. Moreover, it is not just the films' characters who exhibit signs of infection. The multi-strand narratives of *Inception*, *Synecdoche, New York* and even *Contagion* suggest a contamination, a destabilization of narrative structure. These films are 'infected' both in content and in form.

These recent outbreaks of the contagion metaphor in and across public and cultural discourse attest to the concept's potency and currency. They also mark, I would argue, the penetration of academic language and concepts into the popular consciousness, for the list of catchphrases I gave at the outset of this chapter have their origins in humanities and social sciences disciplines: 'social', 'affective' and 'mental' contagion are drawn from psychology, 'cultural' contagion from anthropology and 'financial' contagion from economics. In each of these cases, the linguistic coinage resonates with economic geographer André Siegfried's mid-twentieth-century observation in *Routes of Contagion* (his influential work on the geography of epidemics) that 'there is a striking parallel between the spreading of germs and the spreading of ideas' (1965 [1960], p. 85). In the humanities and social sciences, uses of the contagion metaphor inevitably highlight the affective or mental aspects of contagion rather than its physical ones. Social psychology, economics and 'meme' theory (or 'memetics'), for instance, all employ the metaphor of contagion to represent, at base, the transmission of ideas, emotions or impulses. In the discourse of memetics, in particular, the more negative connotations of disease that surround the contagion metaphor are largely thrown off. Instead, contagion – 'thought contagion' – becomes a byword for creativity and forms the fundamental process by which knowledge and ideas (both good and bad) are communicated and taken up.

Siegfried's analogy between physical contagion and the epidemic-like spreading of ideas or emotions was certainly not a novel one. Indeed, as I explain in Chapter 2 of this study, this correlation or correspondence between the physical and the mental or affective lies at the core of the earliest medical theories of contagious disease transmission and is detectable even in the etymology of the word *contagion* itself. This, quite obviously, renders problematic the idea that a clear line can be drawn between 'literal' (microbiological, medical, physical) contagion and 'metaphorical' (sociocultural, affective, mental) contagion. Even so, the much more recent spate of disciplinary coinings that draw on the language of epidemiology seems to suggest that contagion remains both an elusive and richly allusive concept, one that continues to exceed the bounds of its literal/medical definition.

Contagious Metaphor is a book that explores these apparent metaphors or tropes of contagion as they have emerged and proliferated in sociological and humanistic discourse from classical antiquity to the present day. Although sections of the study foreground chronology, this is not primarily a work of history, and is not intended to be an exhaustive account of all occurrences of the contagion metaphor across time and space – such a task would be impossible or at the very least vertiginous. Rather, in *Contagious Metaphor*, I have attempted to trace the connections between and among certain key themes and critical moments in the history of the contagion metaphor. Further, although this study draws upon both cognitive and literary-critical approaches to metaphor, it does not, perhaps, sit easily within either tradition. Contagion is a limit case for metaphorical language, and for this reason it is intriguing. As I have said, analysing the emergence and spread of cultural forms of contagion cannot simply be a matter of drawing a line between 'literal' and 'figurative' uses of the term, and, as a concept, contagion proves impossible to quarantine in this way. Literary scholar Donald Beecher has compellingly argued that 'the alignment between contagious diseases and transmissive emotions has been so close in Western culture as to blur the line between material cause and figurative application' (2005, p. 243). This confusion of discourses, Beecher continues, leaves the concept of contagion 'ambiguously hovering between material and metaphorical analysis', creating 'an epistemological anxiety around our own sense of the word "contagion"' (2005, p. 248).

This anxiety is not simply confined to the more 'cultural' uses of the word *contagion*, but has also spread to its medical use. As medical historian Martin Pernick notes, medical use of the word *contagion* has declined since the early twentieth century. 'Ironically, though perhaps not surprisingly', he explains,

> as *contagion* became equated with modern microbiology in mass culture, the term was dropped from the lexicon of medical science. Ever since its creation in the late 1910s, the official US public health handbook of infectious diseases has used the term *communicable* instead of *contagious*, and its extensive glossary of technical terms completely omits *contagion*. (Pernick 2002, p. 860)

Medical dictionaries, Pernick adds, now tend to consider *contagion* to be 'outdated' as a term, and he illustrates this with the following quote from *Stedman's Medical Dictionary*: 'The term [*contagion*] originated before development of modern ideas . . . and has since lost much of its significance, being included under the more inclusive term "communicable disease" ' (2002, p. 860).

Tracing the history of the contagion metaphor thus presents a challenge to the very idea of metaphor. As Paul Ricoeur puts it in his *Rule of Metaphor*, 'everyone agrees in saying that figurative language exists only if one can contrast it with another language that is not figurative' (1986 [1975], p. 138). If what we would usually consider to be the literal, medical definition of contagion is anything but stable, where does this leave an analysis of contagion *metaphors*? Moreover, considering the late evolution of contagion's 'literal' meaning, does it make it anachronistic to speak of contagion metaphors prior to the emergence of microbial germ theory? And, finally, if, throughout history, the physical and affective, cultural and mental aspects of contagion have been inseparable, can we talk about a contagion metaphor at all? The history, the etymology of contagion unsettles clear distinctions between the physical, the medical, the cultural and the affective. Moreover, it unsettles clear distinctions between the literal and the metaphorical, for contagion's metaphoricity taints even its most literal definitions.

In *Contagious Metaphor*, I am attentive to the 'epistemological anxiety' that both inheres in the concept of contagion and is engendered in its use. Indeed, this book is intended as a detailed investigation – a teasing out – of contagion's complexities. Moreover, *Contagious Metaphor* is not simply a study of cultural forms of contagion; it is a study of language and of how concepts are expressed in and through language. As such, its title is deliberately ambiguous, for *Contagious Metaphor* is not only a book about metaphors *of* contagion, but also a book about metaphor *as* contagion.

The first chapter is framed around these two approaches to the contagion metaphor. I begin by providing an overview of the ever-growing field of cultural or interdisciplinary studies of contagion, focusing particularly on the ways in which this scholarship has discussed the relationship between contagion and metaphor. I then turn to the question of metaphor *as* contagion, proposing that since classical times the two concepts have been inextricably linked. Specifically, I examine the ways in which the concepts of contagion and metaphor coalesce in classical theories of mimesis and in the figure of Dionysus – the god of metaphor and metamorphosis. Finally, I argue that the efflorescence of the contagion metaphor in contemporary discourse is remarkable not only for its pervasiveness across disciplines and discourses, but also for its ability to self-reflexively articulate the nature of its own emergence and spread. In other words, the contagion metaphor seems itself to operate contagiously, and in its exemplarity, I will argue, the contagion metaphor may suggest a framework through which the emergence and often epidemic-like reproduction of metaphor in general can be better understood.

Literary scholar Arnold Weinstein has remarked that contagion now seems to be 'in the air', and to 'possess a kind of drama and immediacy that permeate everyday thinking' (2003, p. 113). 'In the air' might ordinarily seem a throwaway cliché, but, in the context of contagion, the phrase takes on a fascinating recursiveness. In Chapter 2, I examine how the relationships among contagion, the element of air and geography play out in a number of literary 'plague narratives', namely Thomas Mann's *Death in Venice* (1912), Albert Camus's *The Plague* (1947) and Janette Turner Hospital's *Due Preparations for the Plague* (2003), a novel whose title invokes Daniel Defoe's 1772 book of the same name. In foregrounding the element of air, I argue, these narratives appeal to earlier, miasmatic theories of contagious disease, theories that relied upon a continuum between moral or affective and physical aspects of contagion.

By the end of the nineteenth century, microbial germ theory had all but ousted miasmatic theories of contagion. Yet, at the same time, proto social psychologists were turning to the concept of contagion – often framed as 'moral contagion' – to explain certain social phenomena, such as riots, group violence, mass convulsions and spates of suicides. Taken together, Chapters 3 and 4 explore the emergence and pre-history of these 'moral' and 'social' forms of contagion. Chapter 3 focuses on the birth of social contagion theory in the French *fin de siècle*, tracing its development through the work of Gabriel Tarde, Scipio Sighele and Gustave Le Bon, among others. Common among these developing theories of social contagion is the idea that examples are infectious or contagious. Indeed, the phrase 'contagion of example' (or a close variant) is ubiquitous in the nineteenth-century literature on social contagion, but this omnipresent phrase has been rewarded with little or no scholarly attention to date. Chapter 4 takes up the phrase 'contagion of example', and tracks its use from classical and religious sources, through early modern discourse, and up to the late nineteenth century. By performing this genealogy, of sorts, I argue that the 'moral' or 'social' contagion theory that emerged in the late nineteenth century had strong and deep roots in classical theories of mimesis and in Judeo-Christian theories of sin as imitation.

With the more moralistic or moralizing aspects of social contagion having been hived off in the second half of the nineteenth century, a rhetorical shift away from 'moral' contagion to 'mental' contagion became apparent in the early twentieth century. Chapter 5 investigates this mental aspect of contagion and examines the ways in which the contagion metaphor foregrounds the slip-page between germ-as-microbe and germ-as-idea. Perhaps the most prominent example of this shift to 'mental' contagion is the concept of the meme, which Richard Dawkins first proposed in his 1976 book, *The Selfish Gene*. In this chapter, I examine the ways in which Dawkins's meme has itself demonstrated its infective power, having spawned the subdiscipline of memetics and having become a kind of touchstone for recent studies in social and cultural contagion. Moreover, the chapter is devoted to analysing the rhetoric of the discourse that surrounds meme theory. Specifically, it examines the debate over the meme as metaphor. The meme, which Dawkins proposed as an analog of the gene, has, since its inception, raised the hackles of numerous scientists and humanists alike. Notable among these is Stephen Jay Gould, who has called the meme a 'meaningless metaphor' (qtd. in Blackmore 1999, p. 17). Contra Gould, I argue that the meme is anything but a 'meaningless' metaphor, if only for the reason that it self-reflexively foregrounds the politics of metaphor in complex and pro-ductive ways.

Internet memes, viral media, computer viruses and even financial contagions testify to what new media theorist Jussi Parikka (2007a) has called the 'viral logic' of the network. The final chapter of this book is devoted to the 'network' turn in epidemiology and the corresponding 'viral' turn in network theory. As the most recent formations in the history of the contagion metaphor, these 'viral' network phenomena and the epidemiological modes of analysis that have developed in response provide a fitting conclusion to *Contagious Metaphor*. Like their predecessors, they reveal the ongoing relevance of the contagion metaphor, which continues to expose the dynamics of the contact zone.

1

Contagious Metaphor

Metaphoricity is the logic of contamination and the contamination of logic.
Jacques Derrida, Dissemination. 1981 [1972].[1]

Metaphor is a metaphor is a metaphor is a metaphor.
Dennis Sobolev, 'Metaphor Revisited'. 2008.[2]

Since the late 1990s, a strikingly interdisciplinary body of scholarship has grown up around the concept of 'contagion' and its relationship to society, culture and thought. The emergence of this body of scholarship, which, for the sake of brevity, I will term cultural studies of contagion, can in part be traced to developments in the field of medical history. Although medical history is as old as medicine itself, historian John C. Burnham points to the influence of the 'New History' movement in the 1960s and 1970s in opening the field to distinctly sociocultural and historical perspectives. According to Burnham, the 'cross-fertilisation' between medicine and medical history began a century ago, in the early twentieth century (1999, p. 273). This process, he continues, 'intensified' in the 1970s as 'medical practitioners and academics writing medical history . . . expanded into each other's disciplinary territory', so much so that, by the turn of the twenty-first century, 'intellectual, technical, social, and cultural questions enlivened all of medical history' (1999, p. 273).

In the development of this interdisciplinary field of medical history, the history of disease has played a prominent role. Henry E. Sigerist – a medical historian who, according to Elizabeth Fee, 'did more than any other individual to establish, promote, and popularize the history of medicine in America' (1989, p. 127) – mapped out this role for the history of disease in a seminal 1938 essay titled 'The History of Medical History'. In this essay, Sigerist maintains that the history of disease must be the 'starting point' of medical history, and the 'first set of problems [medical history must] attack' (1938, pp. 173, 171).

The reason for its importance is twofold. First, Sigerist argues, contemporary medicine can and does benefit from an understanding of the history of disease (1938, p. 173). Second, and significantly for this study, he stresses that the analysis of disease necessarily leads on to sociological analysis: 'Once we are familiar with the incidence of disease at a given period', Sigerist explains, 'we want to know how society reacted against disease, what was done to restore and protect health' (1938, p. 174). Further, he adds, '[w]hen we study the history of disease we will soon find that its incidence is determined primarily by the *economic and social conditions* of a society' (1938, p. 179; emph. in original). The history of disease, therefore, *requires* an interdisciplinary outlook and an understanding of economic, social and cultural history. 'It is not enough', Sigerist argues,

> to know how to prevent disease; we must be able to apply our knowledge, and whether we succeed or fail in this endeavor depends on endless *non-medical* factors such as the attitude of society toward the human body, its valuation of health and disease, its educational ideal, and many other philosophic, religious, social, and economic factors.... The history of preventive medicine is most intimately connected with the general history of civilization. (Sigerist 1938, p. 177; emph. added)

Burnham, like Sigerist, identifies the history of disease as one of medical history's earliest and most significant strands, and one that especially benefited from the interdisciplinarity produced by the incursion of social historians into medicine in the 1970s (1999, pp. 257, 271). Burnham cites Caroline Hannaway as one medical historian who, in the late 1980s, 'praised the ways in which historians, virtually none of whom were medically trained, construed disease to raise questions – ranging from biology and geography to the patients' subjective experience of disease and illness – about the relationship of medicine to the surrounding culture' (1999, p. 271). By the late 1990s, a number of major studies exemplified this approach to the history of disease, notable among them Charles E. Rosenberg's *Explaining Epidemics and Other Studies in the History of Medicine* (1992), Terence Ranger and Paul Slack's edited collection *Epidemics and Ideas: Essays on the Historical Perception of Pestilence* (1992), Sheldon Watts's *Epidemics and History: Disease, Power and Imperialism* (1997) and Rosenberg and Janet Golden's edited collection *Framing Disease: Studies in Cultural History* (1997). The influence of these studies extended beyond medicine and history and into literary and cultural studies, where socio-historical approaches to disease were making their presence felt in works of interdisciplinary criticism, such as Athena Vrettos's *Somatic Fictions: Imagining Illness in Victorian Culture* (1995), Linda and Michael Hutcheon's *Opera: Desire, Disease, Death* (1996) and Alan Bewell's *Romanticism and Colonial Disease* (1999).

As the above titles suggest, the focus of these studies was more broadly on the concepts of disease or epidemic than on contagion. 'Contagion' was certainly a key term in many if not all of these studies, but, unlike 'disease' and 'epidemic', it did not emerge as a focal point for social/medical history until the late 1990s, when it, too, began appearing in the titles of major studies.[3] The emergence of 'contagion' as a keyword at the turn of the twenty-first century was not, however, limited to the discipline of medical history. Indeed, the language of epidemiology was spreading through disciplines as diverse as psychology, economics and literary and cultural studies. The early 1990s saw psychologists Elaine Hatfield, John T. Cacioppo and Richard L. Rapson (1994) building upon a much earlier epidemiological tradition in psychology (which I explore in Chapters 3 and 4), by positing 'emotional contagion' as a basic human mechanism. Around the same time, academic discussion of Dawkins's meme theory (the focus of Chapter 5) was shifting from genetic analogies to epidemiological ones: 'memetics' became cast as a theory of 'thought contagion'. And in economic discourse, perhaps the most salient – in a political sense – of all contemporary uses of the contagion metaphor was beginning to appear. According to economist Sebastian Edwards, the term 'contagion' rarely appeared in the economic literature prior to 1990, and yet 'surged' in the latter part of the same decade (2000, p. 873). Since that time, the phrase 'financial contagion' has multiplied in both academic and public discourse about finance and economics at a seemingly exponential rate.

Literary and cultural studies were similarly already showing signs of having caught the 'contagion' infection in the 1990s,[4] but it was not until the early 2000s that a distinctive, interdisciplinary cultural studies of contagion appeared, which attempted to draw together these strands of cultural, historical, literary and sociological analyses. Exemplary of this shift was Alison Bashford and Claire Hooker's edited collection, *Contagion: Historical and Cultural Studies* (2001b), closely followed by two notable special journal issues: *American Literary History*'s 'Contagion and Culture' issue of 2002 and *Literature and Medicine*'s 'Contagion and Infection' issue of 2003. The year 2005 again saw a proliferation of essay collections contribute to this developing cultural studies of contagion, notably Claire L. Carlin's *Imagining Contagion in Early Modern Europe* (2005); Mirjam Schaub, Nicola Suthor and Erika Fischer-Lichte's *Ansteckung: Zur Körperlichkeit eines ästhetischen Prinzips* (2005); and *Fibreculture Journal*'s 'Contagion' issue, which provided a springboard for an incipient viral network theory.

Moreover, as Priscilla Wald has recently pointed out in *Contagious: Cultures, Carriers, and the Outbreak Narrative* (2008), popular culture was also not immune to the mid 1990s spread of contagion. Accounts of 'emerging infections', such as HIV in the 1980s, she argues, 'put the vocabulary of disease outbreaks into circulation', leading to a spate of mid 1990s films and popular novels that featured storylines about contagious disease outbreaks (2008, p. 2). A rich year for outbreak narratives, 1995 alone saw the release of Wolfgang Petersen's *Outbreak* and Terry Gilliam's *12 Monkeys*, along with the publication of Robin Cook's *Contagion* and Patrick Lynch's *Carriers*.

The very public 'noise' around emerging diseases, such as HIV in the 1980s and SARS in the early 2000s, can go some way to explaining the remarkable cross-disciplinary discursive flowering of contagion in the last two decades, but it cannot explain everything. As Wald puts it,

> Contagion is more than an epidemiological fact. It is also a foundational concept in the study of religion and of society, with a long history of explaining how beliefs circulate in social interactions. The concept of contagion evolved throughout the twentieth century through the commingling of theories about microbes and attitudes about social change. Communicable disease compels attention – for scientists and the lay public alike – not only because of the devastation it can cause but also because the circulation of microbes materializes the transmission of ideas. (Wald 2008, p. 2)

Medical historian Margaret Pelling suggests that contagion's irruption in contemporary discourse is due 'in part to the social, political and moral climate induced by the recrudescence, in the latter twentieth century, of significant infectious disease' (2001, p. 16). And yet, she adds, 'it is historically inadequate' to think of contagion as 'purely medical', for 'ideas of contagion' have always been 'inseparable from notions of individual morality, social responsibility, and collective action'. The ongoing significance of contagion, its 'wide currency in a range of areas of thought and practice', Pelling stresses, is particularly 'reflected in an accretion of metaphor and analogy' (2001, pp. 16–17).

Contagion as metaphor

We cannot, therefore, properly consider the contagion phenomenon without considering the mechanics and implications of metaphor. Taken as a whole, cultural studies of contagion have certainly been attentive to the question of figurative language. In their introduction to *Contagion: Historical and Cultural Studies*, for instance, Bashford and Hooker maintain they 'are deeply interested in the metaphoric reach of contagion', for what is fascinating about contagion is its 'capacity . . . to simultaneously function as deeply resonant metaphor for the circulation of social, moral or political dangers through a population, and as visceral, horrible infection' (2001a, p. 5).

Further, the aforementioned special issues of *American Literary History* and *Literature and Medicine* each devoted an article to the question of contagion and metaphor. In her essay titled 'Contagion as Metaphor' for *American Literary History*, Cynthia J. Davis draws attention to the 'seductive' nature of contagion. Contagion, Davis points out, has a peculiar ability to be both content and method, 'both disease *and* the process of its spread' (2002, p. 830). For this reason, she argues, contagion has offered itself as a compelling analogy or metaphorical shortcut for explaining processes of cultural as well as disease transmission. And yet, Davis asks, can the analogy hold? 'Is contagion', she asks, 'an appropriate metaphor for culture?' (2002, p. 830).

Davis's question is one that is often repeated, if not explicitly then implicitly, in the literature on cultural contagion. Here, however, Davis is posing the question as a direct engagement with an earlier, seminal work on metaphors of disease, namely Susan Sontag's *Illness as Metaphor*. In her influential polemic, first published in the late 1970s, Sontag warns against the potentially dehumanizing and deleterious effects of disease metaphors. In Sontag's reading, these metaphors tend to 'mythicize' disease by connecting the physical to the moral and by figuring illness as a mysterious and malevolent 'predator' (1983 [1978], pp. 10–11). 'Any disease', she argues, 'that is treated as a mystery and acutely enough feared will be felt to be morally, if not literally contagious', and, particularly in the case of cancer, the very real effects of these metaphors can be felt in the fact that 'a surprisingly large number of people with cancer find themselves being shunned by relatives and friends . . . as if cancer, like TB, were an infectious disease' (1983 [1978], p. 10). Ultimately, Sontag claims, using cancer as a metaphor is not currently 'morally permissible' (1983 [1978], p. 89). Sontag does, however, foresee a future in which cancer may be 'partly de-mythicized', at which point it may be possible to use cancer metaphors 'without implying either a fatalistic diagnosis or a rousing call to fight by any means whatever a lethal, insidious enemy' (1983 [1978], p. 89).

In her response to Sontag, Davis both heeds and reiterates her call for a critical and ethical approach to figurative language. Although Davis concedes that 'it may not be possible to think without metaphors', she asserts that we should not use them unconsciously. Roping in some disease metaphors for rhetorical effect, Davis writes, we should 'think about' the metaphors we use and 'where necessary, identify more benign replacements for the most malignant ones' (2002, p. 832). In his essay titled 'Afterword: Infection as Metaphor' for *Literature and Medicine*, Arnold Weinstein also engages with Sontag's critique of disease metaphors. Yet, unlike Davis and Sontag, he appears to relish metaphor's ambivalence. Weinstein acknowledges Sontag's caution, but argues that 'illness cannot, *pace* Sontag, be cleanly separated from its metaphors, desirable as that might be' (2003, p. 107). Rather, he suggests,

> from a literary or even a social perspective, it is wiser to acknowledge that such metaphors have proven irresistible to societies under stress. They are able to catalyze mass social responses that become nightmarishly purgative for the state, a kind of macrocosmic mockery of the desired "cleansing" effect that Aristotle designated by the notion, *catharsis*. (Weinstein 2003, p. 104)

To take Weinstein's point further, if contagion metaphors have historically irrupted at times of social tumult or stress, the question of the metaphors' moral 'appropriateness' becomes, perhaps, less interesting than others that emerge when we take seriously contagion's repeated intrusions in the social field.

Contagious Metaphor is certainly not the first or the only study devoted to cultural aspects of contagion, and neither is it the first to draw attention to metaphors of contagion. What this study does do, however, is begin the work of tracing the genealogy of contagion metaphor in order to explain its contemporary pervasiveness. To some degree, it has a similar aim to philosopher Hans Blumenberg's project of 'metaphorology', which considers certain so-called absolute metaphors to be '*foundational elements* of philosophical language, "translations" that resist being converted back into authenticity and logicality' (2010 [1960], p. 3). Anthony Reynolds describes Blumenberg's metaphorology as an approach to philosophy that 'presupposes a pragmatic model of intellectual history, according to which not only concepts but also philosophical systems emerge as effects of the on-going work of metaphor' (2000, p. 78). In other words, and as I have previously argued in my research on cartographic metaphor,[5] the history of a metaphor has much to tell us. What metaphorology offers, according to Robert Savage, is 'a new form of historiography' that examines 'the vicissitudes of metaphor – the replacement of one metaphor by another, or the accretions in meaning undergone by a single metaphor' (2010, p. 144). Metaphorology 'probes texts for evidence of the conceptually irrecoverable presuppositions on which they operate, the "cultural subconscious" to which they give involuntary expression' (2010, p. 144).

In a sense, then, this study aims to probe the 'cultural subconscious' of the contagion metaphor in order to demonstrate how conflated its premises are. That is, contagion is interesting not simply because it oscillates between the medical and the social and the material and the cultural, but also because it highlights the problem of language: the problem of communication and dissemination. Might examining the metaphor of contagion, for instance, begin to explain its own seemingly contagious spread?

Metaphor as contagion

In the second part of this chapter, I move from thinking about the contagion metaphor from the perspective of medical history and contagion studies to thinking about the contagion metaphor from the perspective of a history of metaphor. By tracing this history of metaphor (a history that must necessarily be selective and truncated), I wish, ultimately, to argue that the contagion metaphor is a complex and recursive one, and one that draws attention to the problem of metaphor itself. As a concept, metaphor has had a varied past in the history of ideas, and my overview of this history will sketch a number of its key moments and traditions: Aristotle's definition of metaphor; the casting of metaphor as 'lie' in the empirical tradition; metaphor reconsidered in the work of Vico, Rousseau and Nietzsche; the twentieth-century development of interactionist and cognitive models of metaphor; and the post-structuralist 'rediscovery' of Nietzsche. It is the last of these moments that, I will argue, provides us with important clues for understanding the *contagiousness* of the contagion metaphor in contemporary discourse, as well as the determined ambivalence that surrounds it.

Aristotle's theory of metaphor

Aristotle provided the first, and still enduring, theory of metaphor in his *Poetics*, defining it as a process that entails 'giving the thing a name that belongs to something else; the transference being either from genus to species, or from species to genus, or from species to species, or on grounds of analogy' (1984a, p. 2332; sec. 1457b1). Although metaphor abounds in everyday and poetic language, the ability to create effective metaphors, Aristotle argues, is the sign of a true poet.

Not only is the ability to create metaphor innate, but it is also a 'sign of genius' in that it requires an 'intuitive perception' of resemblance, or similarity in difference (1984a, p. 2332; sec. 1459a). Although metaphor cannot be taught or learnt,[6] metaphor itself teaches, allows its listener or reader to learn something new. As Aristotle writes in his *Rhetoric*, 'strange words simply puzzle us; ordinary words convey only what we know already; it is from metaphor that we can best get hold of something fresh' (1984b, p. 2250; sec. 1410b). Despite his clear regard for figurative language, Aristotle considered metaphor to be secondary to proper or literal language. Further, although a well-tuned metaphor might allow its hearer to grasp a novel idea more readily than pedestrian proper language, it also remained the province of the born wordsmiths – the poets and the rhetors.

Aristotle's theory, as all commentators on the history of metaphor point out, remains the yardstick by which any new theory of figurative language must be measured. Many more recent theories of metaphor have critiqued it, but none has dismissed it, and Aristotle's theory remained virtually unchallenged and unchanged until the latter half of the early modern period. As philosopher Mark Johnson puts it in his overview of the history of metaphor, 'after Aristotle there followed over twenty-three hundred years of elaboration on his remarks' (1981, p. 8).

Metaphor as 'lie' in the empirical tradition: Hobbes and Locke

From the mid-seventeenth century, however, metaphor underwent a series of radical revisions. According to George Lakoff and Mark Johnson, 'with the rise of empirical science as a model for truth, the suspicion of poetry and rhetoric became dominant in Western thought, with metaphor and other figurative devices becoming objects of scorn once again' (1980, p. 190). Two English empirical philosophers exemplify this repudiation of metaphor, namely Thomas Hobbes and John Locke.

In his *Leviathan* (1651), Hobbes makes a sustained argument that metaphor has no place in rational philosophy. Metaphors, along with all the other rhetorical tropes, are 'absurdities', he argues, that must be distinguished from 'words proper' and 'not to be admitted' in the 'seeking of truth' (1651, p. 20). Metaphor for Hobbes is both deceitful and deceptive in that it says something *is* what it *is not*, and, as a result, it 'can never be true grounds of any ratiocination' (1651, p. 17). Interestingly, although he equates truth with proper language and metaphor with deception, Hobbes grants that there exists a still more problematic use of language than metaphor, and one that falls into the category of proper language. Even more perilous than metaphor is the rhetorical use of proper words that both stir emotional or subjective responses in their reader and betray the bias of their speaker. The use of metaphor, he acknowledges, is in fact 'less dangerous' than the use of loaded proper words if only for the reason that metaphors are upfront in their deception: they 'profess their inconstancy, which the other do not' (1651, p. 17).

Despite Hobbes's concessions to the paradoxical honesty of metaphor's deception, the attitude of empirical philosophers towards metaphor was only to worsen in the following decades. Locke, for instance, famously railed against metaphor and other figurative devices in his 1690 *Essay Concerning Human Understanding*. 'I confess', Locke writes,

> in discourses where we seek rather pleasure and delight than information and improvement, such ornaments as are borrowed from [figurative speech] can scarce pass for faults. But yet if we would speak of things as they are, we must allow that all the art of rhetoric, besides order and clearness; all the artificial and figurative application of words eloquence hath invented, are for nothing else but to insinuate wrong ideas, move the passions, and thereby mislead the judgment; and so indeed are perfect cheats . . . . (Locke 1959 [1690], p. 146)

Although Locke reserves his strongest criticisms for metaphor and figurative language, his anxieties appear to spread to language more generally. As Paul de Man dryly notes in his reading of Locke's *Essay*, '[a]t times it seems as if Locke would have liked nothing better than to be allowed to forget about language altogether, difficult as this may be in an essay having to do with understanding' (1978, p. 14). Indeed, the blind spot in Locke's argument, as de Man points out, is his own liberal use of figurative language in advancing his case *against* metaphor: 'Locke speaks of language as a "conduit" that may "corrupt the fountains of knowledge which are in things themselves" and, even worse, "break or stop the pipes whereby it is distributed to public use"' (1978, p. 16). What Locke's *Essay* paradoxically offers, de Man argues, is a 'theory of tropes', a fact Locke would be 'the last man in the world to realize and to acknowledge' (1978, p. 16).

Despite the paralogy at the heart of Locke's argument, by the late seventeenth century this positivist view of metaphor as at best an ornament to proper language and at worst an outright lie was well entrenched within empirical philosophy. Further, as Ted Cohen has pointed out, Hobbes and Locke's distrust and rejection of metaphor's role in reasoning and philosophy strongly influenced positivist and empirical philosophy well into the twentieth century. Although the work of these seventeenth-century philosophers 'may seem remote', Cohen writes, 'their import has prevailed until quite recently' in much positivist philosophy, which tends to treat metaphors as 'frivolous and inessential, if not dangerous and logically perverse' (1978, p. 5). By the mid-eighteenth century, however, the positivist understanding of metaphor – as exemplified by Hobbes and Locke – was beginning to be countered in Continental philosophy, most notably by Giambattista Vico and Jean-Jacques Rousseau.

Metaphor reconsidered: Vico, Rousseau and Nietzsche

In his *New Science* (*Principi di Scienza Nuova*), first published in 1725, Vico turns the established hierarchy of literal and figurative language on its head, arguing that metaphor is in fact the 'original' language and came prior to literal language. 'All the tropes', Vico writes,

> which have hitherto been considered ingenious inventions of writers, were necessary modes of expression of all the first poetic nations, and had originally their full native propriety. But these expressions of the first nations later became figurative when, with the further development of the human mind, words were invented which signified abstract forms or genera comprising their species or relating parts with their wholes. And here begins the overthrow of two common errors of the grammarians: that prose speech is proper speech, and poetic speech improper; and that prose speech came first and afterward speech in verse. (Vico 1984 [1725], p. 131; bk 2, sec. 409)

Around 1755, Rousseau also turned his attention to the question of figurative language in his 'Essai sur l'origine des langues' ('Essay on the Origin of Languages'), an essay that remained unpublished until the posthumous publication of his collected works in 1781.[7] In this essay, Rousseau seems almost to ventriloquize Vico when he proclaims that 'As man's first motives for speaking were of the passions, his first expressions were tropes. Figurative language was the first to be born. Proper meaning was discovered last' (1966 [1781], p. 12).

A century later, the philosopher and philologist Friedrich Nietzsche turned his attention to the paradox of metaphor. In the spirit of Vico and Rousseau and contra Hobbes and Locke, Nietzsche argued that all language is, at base, metaphorical. In his now-famous essay 'Über Wahrheit und Lüge im aussermoralischen Sinne' ('On Truth and Lies in a Nonmoral Sense', written in 1873 but unpublished during his lifetime), Nietzsche provides one of history's most incisive critiques of literal language. The notion of a 'literal' or 'proper' language, for Nietzsche, always goes hand in hand with the concept of 'truth'. We believe, Nietzsche argues, that we have recourse to a transparent, literal language that allows us to get at the essence of things by giving them proper names, a language that expresses truth. And yet, he maintains, this unproblematic relationship between words and things does not and cannot exist. That is, because the process of naming is itself metaphorical, there can be no literal language prior to metaphor. As a result, Nietzsche writes, 'we possess nothing but metaphors for things – metaphors which correspond in no way to the original entities' (1979 [1873], p. 83). What we think of as 'truth', Nietzsche concludes, is therefore nothing more than

A movable host of metaphors, metonymies, and anthropomorphisms: in short, a sum of human relations which have been poetically and rhetorically intensified, transferred, and embellished, and which, after long usage, seem to a people to be fixed, canonical, and binding. Truths are illusions which we have forgotten are illusions; they are metaphors that have become worn out and have been drained of sensuous force, coins which have lost their embossing and are now considered as metal and no longer as coins. (Nietzsche 1979 [1873], p. 84)

In Nietzsche's analysis, metaphor is not a 'cheat' or a 'lie', a deviation from a transparently 'truthful' literal language. In an ironic reversal, Nietzsche makes literal language the language of deception. In turn, metaphor becomes the only 'true' language in that, unlike literal language, it does not conceal its deceptiveness.

Johnson, somewhat misleadingly, suggests that 'philosophers generally ignored Nietzsche's radical equation of metaphor and thought' (1981, p. 16).[8] Certainly Nietzsche's 'On Truth and Lies' did not have an immediate effect on philosophical thought; however, it should not be forgotten that Nietzsche's essay was unfinished and at first unpublished. He began it in 1873, the year after the publication of his first book, *Die Geburt der Tragödie* (*Birth of Tragedy*), and he considered it part of his (equally unfinished) *Philosophenbuch*, or 'Philosopher's Book'. These fragments from Nietzsche's notebooks – part of his *Nachlass*, or literary remains – were published only after his death and some three decades after they were first written.[9] It is true to say that Nietzsche's 'On Truth and Lies' lay largely dormant for the first half-century of its published life, attracting little attention beyond dedicated Nietzsche scholars, just as it is true to say that the essay has been broadly overlooked (or at best dealt with in only a cursory way) in twentieth-century Anglo-American analytic or cognitive studies of metaphor. And yet, from the early 1970s, Nietzsche's unfinished essay was to have a remarkable influence on Continental philosophy and literary theory and was to become, in effect, a touchstone for the 'linguistic turn'.

Interactional and cognitive approaches to metaphor: Richards and Black

In the early twentieth century, while Nietzsche's essay was in hiatus, so to speak, new approaches to metaphor were beginning to challenge the received Aristotelian tradition, with its emphasis on comparison and resemblance. From the early 1920s, literary critic I. A. Richards had begun arguing for a greater appreciation of the power of metaphor,[10] but it was not until the following decade that he developed his stance into a new model of metaphor. In his *Philosophy of Rhetoric* (1936), Richards critiques what he sees as three problematic assumptions in the Aristotelian theory of metaphor: first, that having an '"eye for resemblances" is a gift that some men have but others have not'; second, that metaphor cannot be taught; and, third, that 'metaphor is something special and exceptional in the use of language, a deviation from its normal mode of working' (1936, pp. 89–90).

These assumptions, he continues, have caused metaphor to be 'treated as a sort of happy extra trick with words, . . . a grace or ornament or *added* power of language' (Richards 1936, p. 90; emph. in original). Far from being an 'ornament' of, a 'deviation' from or an 'exception' to proper language, Richards argues, metaphor is, in fact, language's 'constitutive form' and 'omnipresent principle of all its free action' (1936, p. 90). Further, he claims, all humans have an innate command of metaphor and metaphor itself is intimately connected to thought. Where the traditional, Aristotelian theory, he argued, 'made metaphor seem to be a verbal matter, a shifting and displacement of words', in reality, metaphor is 'fundamentally . . . a borrowing between and intercourse of *thoughts*, a transaction between contexts. *Thought* is metaphoric, and proceeds by comparison, and the metaphors of language derive therefrom' (1936, p. 94; emph. in original). In Richards's formulation, then, metaphor becomes both *cognitive* and *semantic*, while at the same time both thought and language become metaphorical. 'The mind', Richards says, is fundamentally 'a connecting organ' (1936, p. 125).

In order to demonstrate the 'transactional' or 'interactional' workings of metaphor, Richards introduces three new analytical terms – 'tenor', 'vehicle' and 'ground'. At base, he explains, a metaphorical statement consists of two halves, one of which (the 'tenor') receives attributes from the other (the 'vehicle'). For a metaphor to 'work', however, the tenor and vehicle must have shared characteristics, and these common attributes Richards terms the 'ground'. For instance, in the metaphorical statement 'metaphor is contagious', the tenor ('metaphor') is able to receive certain attributes from the vehicle (the concept of 'contagion' or 'contagiousness') because of their shared ground. The ground of a metaphor is not always immediately apparent – in Richards's words, it is often 'recondite' (1936, p. 117) – and our working example is no exception. Metaphor and contagion share, as I have argued, a complex and shifting ground. If we can condense the ground of 'metaphor is contagious' to one word, that word might be 'communication', but, as this exercise shows, the ground itself (with its connotations of infection and language) cannot escape the metaphorical.

Further, although the direction of transferred meaning is primarily from vehicle to tenor (from contagion to metaphor in our example), Richards suggests that the relationship between the two is more intricate. Indeed, he argues, the meaning of a metaphor takes place in the 'interaction' between tenor and vehicle, neither of which alone can account for metaphorical meaning, and neither of which, he implies, is unchanged in the interaction (1936, p. 100). In other words, in the statement 'metaphor is contagious', metaphor not only picks up the attributes of contagion, but also sends some of its own in the other direction. Each half is somehow affected, or even infected, by the other.

Richards's interaction theory of metaphor was to influence analytic philosopher Max Black, who, in the 1950s, made another significant intervention in the history of metaphor. In a 1955 essay simply titled 'Metaphor' and published in the *Journal of the Aristotelian Society*, Black questions why philosophy has tended to treat metaphor as an 'offence' or as 'incompatible with serious thought' (1954–55, p. 273). In order to clear a space for metaphor within (analytic) philosophy, Black assesses and rejects two dominant and related views of metaphor: what he terms the 'substitution' and 'comparison' views. The substitution view holds that a metaphorical statement can always be translated into a literal one, so that 'understanding a metaphor is like deciphering a code or unravelling a riddle' (1954–55, p. 281). Put another way, the substitution view considers metaphor to be, at base, a literal statement that has been somehow 'transformed'. The comparison view, in turn, considers metaphor to be merely the *presentation of [an] underlying analogy or similarity* (1954–55, p. 283; emph. in original). Black notes that the comparison view is, essentially, a 'special case' of the substitution view, for both rely upon analogy or similarity: where the former considers analogy to be the function that transforms the literal into the metaphorical, the latter 'holds that the metaphorical statement might be replaced by an equivalent literal *comparison*' (1954–55, p. 283; emph. in original).

However, as Black argues, a metaphor cannot simply be paraphrased as a literal statement without losing meaning. 'The literal paraphrase', he writes, 'inevitably says too much – and with the wrong emphasis' (1954–55, p. 293). Something is lost in the translation, and that something is, according to Black,

> a loss in *cognitive* content; the relevant weakness of the literal paraphrase is not that it may be tiresomely prolix or boringly explicit – or deficient in qualities of style; it fails to be a translation because it fails to give the *insight* that the metaphor did. (Black 1954–55, p. 293)

Comparison alone, Black argues, cannot account for the workings of metaphor, for metaphor is more than an encoded literal statement.[11] Metaphor, he writes, 'is not a substitute for a formal comparison or any other kind of literal statement, but it has its own *distinctive* capacities and achievements' (1954–55, p. 284; emph. in original). To account for these distinctive capacities, Black proposes a general 'interaction' view of metaphor to supplant the comparison and substitution views. In this, Black draws substantially on Richards's earlier interaction theory of metaphor, but he also extends or makes more explicit some of the finer points of Richards's argument. Black, for instance, claims that in some instances 'it would be more illuminating . . . to say that the metaphor *creates* the similarity than to say that it formulates some similarity antecedently existing' (1954–55, pp. 284–5; emph. in original). Further, where Richards does little more than suggest that a two-way (though not necessarily symmetrical) transaction occurs in the interaction between the two halves of a metaphor, Black makes the point explicitly. Using the example 'man is a wolf', Black argues that the metaphorical statement leaves neither half untouched: 'If to call a man a wolf', Black explains, 'is to put him in a special light, we must not forget that the metaphor makes the wolf seem more human than he otherwise would' (1954–55, p. 291).

Two schools of thought exist on the relative importance of Richards's and Black's interaction theories in the history of metaphor. Black does acknowledge the influence of Richards (along with the work of classical scholar William Bedell Stanford) on the development of his 'interaction view' of metaphor. However, Black acknowledges these precedent theories only in a footnote, in which he promptly casts doubt on their philosophical import. Richards and Bedell Stanford, Black states in his footnote, are the 'best sources' on the interaction view of metaphor; however, he continues, '[u]nfortunately, both writers have great trouble in making clear the nature of the positions they are defending' (1954–55, p. 285). Where Johnson describes Black's essay as 'perhaps *the* landmark by which we may orient ourselves in attempting to understand recent work on the subject [of metaphor]' (Johnson 1981, p. 19; emph. in original), Paul Ricoeur argues instead that Black's essay 'does not eclipse Richards' work . . . For Richards made the breakthrough; after him, Max Black and others occupy and organize the terrain' (Ricoeur 1986 [1975], pp. 83–4).

Lakoff and Johnson's 'conceptual metaphor theory'

As Johnson points out, although Black's ideas were not immediately accepted in the Anglo-American tradition of analytic philosophy, they prompted 'a trickle of philosophical interest in metaphor' that has since 'swelled to flood proportions' (1981, p. 20). Black's work, for instance, was instrumental in the development of Johnson's and George Lakoff's 'conceptual metaphor theory' (or CMT) in the early 1980s. Even though, broadly speaking, CMT resiles from the strong 'bidirectionality' suggested by Black's interactionist theory of metaphor, Black's work undoubtedly cleared a path for CMT. In *Metaphors We Live By* – the book that provided the groundwork for CMT – Lakoff and Johnson argue for the centrality of metaphor to the way we navigate our daily lives. Metaphor, they argue, 'is not just a matter of language, that is, of mere words'; rather, metaphor is a matter of thought, of cognition, for the human conceptual system and human thought processes are 'fundamentally metaphorical in nature' (Lakoff and Johnson 1980, p. 3). As such, what we usually think of as a metaphor – that is, the 'linguistic expression' of a metaphor – is, in fact, a surface effect of the metaphors that already exist within the human conceptual system (Lakoff and Johnson 1980, p. 6). In other words, where the traditional, empirical theory of metaphor holds that metaphor is secondary to literal language, Lakoff and Johnson's cognitive theory of metaphor holds that metaphorical language is, in fact, secondary to metaphorical cognition (Lakoff and Johnson 2003, p. 272).

As rhetorician and literary critic Wayne C. Booth has argued (and as would be apparent from the literature review above), Lakoff and Johnson's insistence on the cognitive-semantic nature of metaphor is not so much a radical incursion in the history of metaphor as an extension of earlier theories.[12] Indeed, recent commentators have even credited Aristotle's theory of metaphor as having 'cognitive' and 'semiotic' aspects that have otherwise been overlooked.[13] Nevertheless, the influence of Lakoff and Johnson's theory of metaphor within cognitive linguistics cannot be overestimated, and, in the form of CMT, an entire school of metaphorical analysis has grown up around the work of Lakoff in particular.

Within CMT, conceptual metaphor is schematized (or metaphorized) as a mapping: the transfer of a more concrete 'source' domain onto a more abstract 'target' domain. These categories are roughly analogous to Richards's 'tenor' and 'vehicle', so that in our example 'metaphor is contagious', 'metaphor' is the tenor/ target domain, while 'contagion' is the vehicle/source domain. Unlike Black's interactionist theory, however, CMT traditionally tends to reject the idea that the target domain can be mapped back onto the source domain (as in Black's example of 'man is a wolf'). Instead, CMT rests upon an 'invariance principle',[14] which in turn relies on a unidirectional model of metaphorical meaning. As Lakoff and Johnson explain in *Philosophy in the Flesh*, a metaphorical mapping is both unidirectional (from source to target) and asymmetrical: 'we trace images from the source domain in discussing the target domain', they write, 'but not conversely' (1999, p. 127). In other words, in a metaphorical mapping, the 'abstract' target domain is transformed by the source domain, but the more stable and 'concrete' source domain remains unaffected by the target domain. Moreover, CMT's metaphors for metaphor – 'source', 'target', 'mapping' and 'projection' – only reinforce this asymmetrical and unidirectional model of metaphorical transfer. And yet, because a metaphorical mapping is always asymmetrical and partial – because not everything in the source domain is (or can be) mapped onto the target domain – some interaction must still occur between the two domains. As Lakoff explains, the target domain can 'override' the source domain in the sense that its 'structure automatically limits what can be mapped' from the source domain (1993, p. 216). In this sense, the target domain must interact or communicate to some degree with the source domain, but its interaction is circumscribed, within CMT, by a strict unidirectional framework.

Subsequent theories that build upon CMT have attempted to unsettle this rigid unidirectionality. Notably, in Gilles Fauconnier and Mark Turner's theory of 'conceptual blending' (Fauconnier and Turner 1996, 1998, 2002), the source and target domains (now termed 'input spaces') are thought to interact in order to create a new, blended space. In this schema, movement primarily still occurs from the source to the target domains, but movement can, in exceptional cases, also move 'backwards', as it were, from the target to the source domains. Because of its retained emphasis on source-to-target directionality, cognitive linguist Antonio Barcelona has described conceptual blending theory as effectively a 'refined version of the unidirectionality thesis' proposed by CMT (2003, p. 8).

In recent years, a number of researchers applying CMT have also suggested that its rigid structure does not adequately account for the 'feedback' from target to source that is apparent in more complex, context-bound or literary metaphors.[15] John Douthwaite, for instance, has argued that 'the mapping process as described in classic or early CMT appears at times to be as mechanistic as the positivist and structuralist views of encoding and decoding as consisting of one-to-one relationships between form and meaning' (2011, p. 151). This, Douthwaite continues, has the effect of 'limit[ing] metaphor explication to the "underlying experiential basis" conjured up by the source domain' (2011, p. 152). One of the most pointed critiques of CMT, however, is to be found in Bo Pettersson's assessment of what he considers the often uncritical application of CMT to literary texts and literary metaphor. Pettersson presents four main criticisms of CMT: first, that CMT often elides its own status as an 'interpretive' stance; second, that its application to literary texts 'often reduce[s] much of the literary work to surface manifestations of cognitive metaphors, at times questionably interpreted as such'; third, that 'cognitive readings do not seem to be able to deal with the complexity and specificity of literature or with how it is read'; and, fourth, that 'cognitive literary criticism at times displays a disregard of other literary theory and criticism, which may lead to thwarted results or false claims of critical novelty' (2011, p. 94).

Taken together, critiques of CMT suggest that its rigid structure – though useful in analysing everyday, commonplace metaphors – fails to take into account a number of complexities, including the 'history' of metaphors and the broader sociocultural factors that mediate metaphorical meaning, the potential for a more complex correspondence between source and target domains, the generative play of language and metaphorical recursivity,[16] and alternative (read post-structuralist) theories of metaphor.[17] If we look again at our metaphorical statement 'metaphor is contagious', we can see that traditional CMT cannot fully account for its workings. CMT's insistence that the source domain ('contagion') be stable and concrete is patently impossible in this case (as this book as a whole argues, 'contagion' is in no way more concrete and stable a concept than 'metaphor'). So too is its insistence that that the source domain be quarantined from the influence of the target domain. Certainly, the movement between contagion and metaphor is asymmetrical, but it is still bidirectional, and, in the case of the contagion metaphor, I would argue that this bidirectionality is built into its 'communicative' ground.

In a 1992 article for *Poetics Today*, Mark Turner turned his focus to a conceptual metaphor not unlike the one at the centre of this book: what he calls the 'strange' and 'unconventional' metaphor 'language is a virus' (1992, p. 725).[18] The 'strangeness' of the 'language is a virus' metaphor comes, Turner states, not just from its 'venturing into biochemistry' or its 'loony conjunction of incompatible registers', but also because the metaphor 'lies outside the stock of common conceptual metaphors that speakers of English are expected to know' (1992, p. 725). To account for the metaphor in CMT, Turner must relate it to an underlying, 'conventional' and 'basic' conceptual metaphor. Where he can quickly interpret the metaphor 'this job is a detour' as an expression of the underlying basic metaphor 'LIFE IS A JOURNEY', the metaphor 'language is a virus' is not so immediately compliant (Turner 1992, p. 726). Turner is forced to turn to 'other principles' in order to decode it, and so he suggests the 'GREAT CHAIN [of being]' metaphor (which he and Lakoff defined in their 1989 book *More than Cool Reason*)[19] might be the underlying metaphor. Yet, he continues, 'language is a virus' cannot directly map onto the 'GREAT CHAIN', for neither *language* nor *virus*, he explains, has a 'clear place on the Great Chain' because both the source and the target domains lie outside the basic conceptual metaphor (Turner 1992, p. 726). So that he can account for the 'language is a virus' within the GREAT CHAIN metaphor, Turner must resort to mapping only 'part of The Nature of the Source onto part of The Nature of the Target' (1992, p. 727), and to explain this, he writes,

> The Nature of the Virus is to move from organism to organism, in a "communicable" fashion, infecting each organism and causing similar symptoms as it moves along. Those who have been infected typically exhibit symptoms and typically transmit the virus to others, who consequently develop the same symptoms. To understand "language is a virus", we map the generic-level information in The Nature of the Virus onto *language*, to arrive at the interpretation that language is something transmitted from person to person and that those who show the symptoms of "having language" pass language on to others, who consequently develop the same symptoms. It is odd to think of language as a communicable disease, yet we have no difficulty doing so because we possess a conceptual instrument that provides us with the requisite imaginative capacity. (Turner 1992, p. 732)

Thus, Turner reconciles the strange 'language is a virus' metaphor with CMT's invariance principle; indeed, he sees it as proof that the invariance principle works absolutely in order to create stable and reliable communication (1992, p. 736). I would argue, however, that Turner is only able to do this – to *reduce* 'language is a virus' so readily to a preconceived pattern – because he dismisses any further social, historical or cultural contexts that might have shaped the metaphor and its possible interpretation.

In his analysis, Turner maintains that 'scientific conceptions are ... irrelevant, except to the extent that the scientific conception has influenced our commonplace conception or conversely' (1992, p. 735). Medical history has demonstrated just how connected to one another medical and sociocultural conceptions of epidemiology and contagious disease are, and how these conceptions have (and, in some respects, have not) changed over time. As such, 'scientific conceptions' would indeed seem to be highly relevant to an analysis of the 'language is a virus' metaphor. And yet, Turner takes this no further: he does not suggest the ways in which changing understandings of and attitudes towards infectious disease (and, indeed, language) might have historically shaped, or might continue to be shaping, the metaphor itself. Just, as I have argued, we cannot properly understand the contagion phenomenon without taking into account the history of metaphor, we also cannot understand the contagion metaphor without taking into account the medical, sociocultural and historical contexts of contagion.

This seems to be a significant oversight in Turner's analysis, for even Sontag, who is otherwise deeply critical of disease metaphors, allows for possible change in a metaphor's reception based on sociocultural (not deep, pre-structured and cognitive) factors. It also seems to be a conscious, if not a political, oversight in CMT more generally. In an interview with Lakoff, Roberta Pires de Oliveira suggests that CMT treats the 'GREAT CHAIN OF BEING' conceptual metaphor as being 'in nature itself' and having 'no history' or 'roots' in Western culture (Pires de Oliveira 2001, p. 30). Lakoff simply counters Pires de Oliveira by arguing '[t]he claim that the GREAT CHAIN is just a matter of Western history, that it is not widespread in unrelated cultures and does not arise spontaneously in very young children, seems just to be an empirically false claim' (Pires de Oliveira 2001, p. 31). CMT's emphasis on the cognitive and embodied nature of metaphor is, without doubt, a vitally important one to the study of metaphor, and its analytical methods have enabled new insights into its workings. Within analytic philosophy and cognitive science, Lakoff's theories, in particular, have led to a new and heightened appreciation for the real-world effects of metaphor. In his 2007 book *The Stuff of Thought*, for instance, cognitive scientist Steven Pinker describes Lakoff as 'the messiah of metaphor', and the 'strongest advocate' of what he calls the 'metaphor metaphor' (2007, p. 245). The 'metaphor metaphor' for Pinker is, in essence, a kind of meta metaphor, namely 'the idea that

TO THINK IS GRASP A METAPHOR' (2007, p. 238). In short, Pinker argues, CMT has demonstrated that 'metaphor really is a key to explaining thought and language' (2007, p. 276).

And yet, I would argue, in its quest to reduce all metaphorical statements to fixed, underlying conceptual metaphors, 'traditional' CMT cannot fully account for complex metaphors, such as the contagion metaphor. In order to take into account the 'extended context' (to bend Charles Forceville's term to my case) of the contagion metaphor, we must then return to an earlier thread in this history of metaphor – to Nietzsche and his 'rediscovery' in twentieth-century Continental philosophy.

Nietzsche 'rediscovered': Metaphor, mimetic contagion and the linguistic turn in Continental philosophy

In the introduction to *Nietzsche and Metaphor*, his 1993 translation of Sarah Kofman's *Nietzsche et la métaphore* (1972), Duncan Large remarks on the 'extraordinary intensification of interest in Nietzsche which gripped the French intellectual scene' in the 1960s and early 1970s (1993, p. x). Large traces the origins of this newfound interest in Nietzsche to the publication of two key texts – Martin Heidegger's two-volume *Nietzsche* in 1961 and Deleuze's *Nietzsche et la philosophie* (*Nietzsche and Philosophy*) in 1962. Deleuze's study, in particular, spurred strong interest in Nietzsche, whose work was seen to anticipate the 'linguistic turn' of post-war French philosophy. As Large explains:

> In his 1966 *The Order of Things*, Foucault himself highlights the importance of "Nietzsche the philologist" as "the first to connect the philosophical task with a radical reflection upon language". However, the "linguistic turn" in French Nietzsche reception had already been inaugurated at least as early as *Nietzsche and Philosophy*, in which . . . Deleuze portrays a Nietzsche who argues that "[t] he whole of philosophy is a symptomatology, and a semiology". (Large 1993, p. xiv)

Interestingly, although Deleuze's *Nietzsche and Philosophy* was instrumental in linking Nietzsche's name to the linguistic or rhetorical turn in philosophy, Deleuze makes no mention of Nietzsche's 'On Truth and Lies' or his reworking of the problem of metaphor. In a practical sense, the reason for this neglect of metaphor in Deleuze's *Nietzsche and Philosophy* might be twofold. First, Heidegger's influential study of Nietzsche similarly did not consider Nietzsche's essay on metaphor. Second, at the time Deleuze's study was published, there was no extant French translation of Nietzsche's 'On Truth and Lies'. By the end of the decade, however, philosopher Angèle Kremer-Marietti had remedied this situation with her 1969 translation of Nietzsche's *Philosophenbuch*, included in which was her translation of 'On Truth and Lies' (translated as 'Introduction théorétique sur la vérité et le mensonge au sens extra-moral'). Within five years, Kremer-Marietti's translation of 'On Truth and Lies' would become a standard reference in a grow-ing body of post-structuralist French philosophy that addressed Nietzsche and the question of metaphor more broadly – a body of work that included Kofman's *Nietzsche et la métaphore* (*Nietzsche and Metaphor*) (1972), Derrida's *Marges de la philosophie* (*Margins of Philosophy*) (1972) and Ricoeur's *La métaphore vive* (*Rule of Metaphor*) (1975).

In short, in the 1970s and 1980s, a 'New Nietzsche' emerged, developing out of the work of Deleuze, Pierre Klossowski, Kremer-Marietti, Kofman, Derrida, Ricoeur, de Man, Jean Granier, Paul Valadier and Eric Blondel, among others. This Nietzschean turn in post-structuralist theory both tapped into and extended Continental philosophy's renewed appreciation of figurative language, with 'metaphor' increasingly standing in (synecdochically, perhaps) for tropological language in general. Although Genette was strongly critical of this reduction of the figural to metaphor alone,[20] post-structuralist theory tends to treat metaphor not only as the analogon of figurative language, but also as epitomizing the prob-lem of language itself.[21] With the notable exception of Deleuze and Guattari – who reject that their writing is figural and who, like Baudrillard, declare the end of metaphor[22] – the vast majority of twentieth-century post-structuralist theo-rists ascribe an unprecedented critical and creative power to metaphor, a power that has tangible and practical effects. Foucault, for instance, saw metaphor as a powerful critical technique or tool (1984, p. 254); de Man explored its 'prolifer-ating and disruptive power' (1978, p. 30); and Ricoeur argued that metaphor has a 'metamorphic' power to transform language and reality (1973, p. 82).[23]

Along with this return to Nietzsche came two corollary emphases, both of which are critical to an analysis of metaphors of contagion and metaphor as contagion: the 'Dionysian' nature of metaphorical language and the complex relationship between metaphor and mimesis. In the Nietzschean tradition, Dionysus is the god of metaphor and of metamorphosis.[24] In classical schol-arship, moreover, he is a contagious god. According to Carl (Károly) Kerényi, Dionysus is the god of *epiphaneia* and *epidemia* (1976, p. 139): he is a god who brings both the productive contagion of epiphanic rapture and the destructive contagion of epidemic madness. As Kerényi explains, '[i]n certain cult forms,

Dionysos is represented as the god who arrives', and this arrival or 'epiphany'
was 'known in Greece not only as *epiphaneia*, but also as *epidemia*, "arrival in the
land"' (1976, p. 139). This 'divine "epidemic"' of the Dionysian arrival, Kerényi
continues, is implicitly linked with the notion of contagious disease, for, he
argues, its 'kinship with "visitation by a disease" is undeniable at least insofar as
it was always the incursion of something overpowering' (1976, p. 139). In Euripides's *Bacchae*, Dionysus/Bacchus is described as an 'effeminate stranger who
corrupts our women with a new disease [νόσον]²⁵ and thus infects [λυμαίνεται]
our beds' (1828, p. 21, lines 353–5). In his reading of Euripides's play, René Girard has drawn attention to the 'contagion' that Dionysus's arrival invokes:

> Having implanted his cult in Asia, Dionysus returns to his native city of Thebes
> disguised as a young disciple who exerts on everyone he meets a strange seduc-
> tive power. The god is confronted with the disbelief of his own family. To punish
> them, he causes his aunt Agave, his cousin Ino, and other Thebans, to become
> possessed by the Bacchic spirit. Guided by the god, the women flee their homes
> to lead on the slopes of neighboring Cithaeron a vagabond existence. Even the
> aged succumb to the Dionysiac contagion. (Girard 1977 [1970], p. 488)

In the violent and universal contagion that he spreads, Dionysus is, according to
Girard, 'the god of crowds and of their uncontrollable reactions, the god of collective terrors which strike unexpectedly' (1977 [1970], p. 499). The 'outbreak' of
Dionysian contagion, Girard maintains, 'spells the disintegration of social institutions and the collapse of the cultural order' (2005 [1972], p. 135).

At base, the Dionysian contagion is a *mimetic* one. As William Storm argues,
the notion of the Dionysian is 'connected specifically and fundamentally to the
act of mimetic impersonation' (1998, p. 17). Moreover, in his theatricality, Dionysus incites concatenating, cascading imitation. In Euripides's *Bacchae*, Dionysus
represents contagion, mimesis and metamorphosis, such that, Storm explains,
'the represented character of Dionysus has the power to change the look, attitude, and behaviour of those who come under his influence – and, of course, he
can also transform himself' (1998, p. 17). In Socratic thought, too, according to
Mihai Spariosu, the 'Dionysian ecstatic experience' is considered a pre-rational
and 'highly contagious' one:

> Socrates points out the infectious, mimetic nature of the feeling of power, which
> mysteriously propagates itself from the Muse to the poet to the crowd. Once it is
> let loose, in accordance with a familiar snow-balling effect, this feeling of power
> will reach ecstatic peaks and then, unless it is carefully guided, will erupt into
> volcanic, devastating violence. (Spariosu 1984, p. 19)

This strong and often tacit connection between Dionysus and mimetic contagion led Hermann Koller, in his 1954 study of mimesis, *Die Mimesis in der Antike*, to speculate that the origin of the term *mimesis* lay in the imitative tradition of the Dionysian cult drama. While Koller's speculation has been discredited on a number of grounds[26] – not least of which a lack of historical evidence – Spariosu suggests it may not be entirely without merit:

> Although Koller's hypothesis may be hard to verify historically because of the scant evidence available, theoretically it is justifiable: He attempts to find evidence for a mimetic theory of music and dancing in the archaic period, based on the archaic performative function of *mimesis*. Even though it remains debatable whether such a theory was ever fully developed, its usefulness would have been obvious: music, poetry, and dancing were originally part of the holistic, mythopoeic complex, and as they became increasingly separated, the Greek thinkers must certainly have felt the need to reflect upon them. (Spariosu 1989, p. 18)

Whether or not mimesis begins with Dionysus, imitation remains strongly connected to the notion of the Dionysian and the dramatic. This connection is, moreover, starkly registered in Nietzsche's reading and reinterpretation of Dionysus in *The Birth of Tragedy*, his first major work, published the year before he wrote his essay on metaphor. According to Nidesh Lawtoo, in its emphasis on mimetic contagion, *The Birth of Tragedy* evokes a 'Dionysian patho(-)logy', in which 'the question of affective mimesis underscores the process of artistic creation, the actor's impersonation and the public contagion that ensues' (2009, p. 676). In his essay 'Nietzsche and Mimesis', Mark P. Drost has also argued that Nietzsche's concept of Dionysian mimesis is at base both a theory of art and a theory of life: 'In the throes of the Dionysian impulse', Drost explains, 'the artist begins with an ecstatic insight and transforms himself as an imitation of that state of ecstasy' (1986, p. 314). In Nietzsche's *Birth of Tragedy*, he concludes, tragedy as an art form

> reveals itself as a necessary mimetic condition that justifies existence through artistic principles. The limits of imitation are the limits of the complementary power that art yields to nature. From these strands of consideration Nietzsche's vision of art can be called a theory of mimetic complement. (Drost 1986, p. 317)

In his unpublished *Philosophenbuch*, Nietzsche provides further insight into his thinking about imitation or mimesis and its relationship to metaphor and analogical thinking. Imitation, he begins, is common to all cultures and is the means by which 'instinct is gradually produced' (1979 [1872], p. 49). He continues, stating that '[a]ll comparison (primal thinking) is imitation', and via this comparative and imitative process 'arise *types*, which strictly imitate the first, merely similar, specimens, i.e. what are copied are the greatest and most powerful specimens' (1979 [1872], pp. 49–50; emph. in original). This process of imitation, Nietzsche maintains, is implicitly linked with the process of metaphorization:

> Imitation presupposes first the reception of an image and then a continuous translation of the received image into a thousand metaphors, all of which are efficacious. Analog. What power forces us to engage in imitation? The appropriation of an unfamiliar impression by means of metaphors. Stimulus and recollected image bound together by means of metaphor (analogical inference). Result: similarities are discovered and reanimated. A stimulus which has been *repeated* occurs once again in a recollected image. (Nietzsche 1979 [1872], p. 50; emph. in original)

Mimetic contagion and metaphorization are thus part of the very same, fundamentally human, process of meaning-making. Imitation is, Nietzsche stresses, the exact 'opposite of knowing', for 'knowing certainly does not want to admit any transference, but wishes instead to cling to the impression without metaphor and apart from the consequences' (1979 [1872], p. 50). Even so, he continues, 'there is no "real" expression and *no real knowing apart from metaphor....* *Knowing* is nothing but working with the favorite metaphors, an imitating which is no longer felt to be an imitation' (1979 [1872], pp. 50–1; emph. in original). Thus, read alongside *The Birth of Tragedy*, Nietzsche's unfinished *Philosophenbuch* renders clear the implicit links between metaphor, mimesis, metamorphosis and contagion, links that Kofman, Derrida, Ricoeur and de Man, and others were to harness in their 'New-Nietzschean' rethinkings of language and epistemology. Moreover, what Nietzsche's metaphorology revealed is the ambivalence at the core of the very earliest theories of mimesis, which are themselves intimately linked to metaphor and to contagion.

Numerous scholars have pointed out the relationship between metaphor and imitation in Plato's and Aristotle's definitions of mimesis.[27] As Derrida points out in *Margins of Philosophy*, both mimesis and metaphor rely on the '*theoretical* perception of resemblance or similarity' (1982 [1972], pp. 237–8; emph. in original). In the Aristotelian tradition, in particular, Derrida argues, metaphor can be regarded as 'an effect of *mimēsis* and *homoiosis*, the manifestation of analogy', and as becoming 'a means of knowledge, a means that is subordinate, but certain' (1982 [1972], p. 238). Similarly, Ricoeur argues that metaphor, when '[r]elocated on the foundations provided by *mimêsis*, ... ceases to be arbitrary and trivial' (1986 [1975], p. 40). Instead, metaphor becomes not only 'a deviation in relation to ordinary usage, but also, by means of this deviation, the privileged instrument in that upward motion of meaning promoted by *mimêsis*' (1986 [1975], p. 41).

In both the Platonic and Aristotelian traditions, mimesis is also linked with contagion, but to somewhat different ends. In Book Three of the *Republic*, Plato describes imitation as a function of poetry, and a problematic one at that. Plato, speaking through the figure of Socrates,[28] proceeds to question whether imitation should be prohibited in the ideal republic. He cautions that society's guardians – if they are to imitate anything at all – should imitate only good examples. They should never 'depict or be skilful at imitating any kind of illiberality or baseness, lest from imitation they should come to be what they imitate' (Plato 1973, p. 83; sec. 395c).

This capacity for imitations to 'grow into habits and become second nature' (Plato 1973, p. 83; sec. 395d) lies at the heart of Plato's concerns about mimesis, and has led numerous scholars to argue that Plato's theory is predicated on a (strongly negative) notion of mimetic contagion.[29] This negativity towards mimetic contagion is recast in the Aristotelian theory in much more positive terms. According to Gebauer and Wulf, where Plato 'responded to the ambivalent character of mimesis with the demand that it be controlled, . . . Aristotle sees precisely in one's mimetic interaction with passions and desires a defense mechanism against the power of affect' (Gebauer and Wulf 1995, p. 57). Nevertheless, in both accounts, mimesis is intimately related to the contagion of example – a concept I examine in greater detail in Chapter 4.

Moreover, in Plato's theory, mimesis is never an imitation of reality, but always-already an imitation of a prior imitation. Platonic mimesis is, Gebauer and Wulf explain, directed neither 'at the production of a real thing' nor 'at the production of an appearance of the Idea'; instead, '[i]t aims at the representation of appearance, at the production of phenomena, which have a relation to the world of the real' (1995, p. 39). The poet, according to Plato, is not a creator but a mere 'imitator', one who is unaware that their works are 'but imitations thrice removed from the truth, and could easily be made without any knowledge of the truth, because they are appearances only and not realities' (1973, p. 292; sec. 602b–c). Plato's distinction between mimetic representation and 'reality' is, by extension, a distinction between words and things, a distinction then put to service in Plato's critique of writing in the *Phaedrus*. As Ronald Bogue explains, in the *Cratylus*, Plato

> takes up the question of the relation between names and objects and argues that
> "the name is an imitation (*mimema*) of the thing", that "names rightly given are

the likenesses and images (*eikonas*) of the things which they name" (430b, 439a). Such images are only partial imitations of things and not their doubles (432a–d), and hence knowledge of names must be subordinated to knowledge of things (439a–c), yet a natural relation still exists between them. Writing, by contrast, is unnatural, says Socrates in the *Phaedrus*, a dead simulation of living speech which bears the same relationship to words as painting does to actual things (275d–e). . . . Writing, like painting and tragedy, is a form of bad mimesis, a simulation that creates false resemblances, whereas speech exemplifies good mimesis, a true resemblance that is properly subordinate to the model it copies. (Bogue 1984, pp. 1–2)

In the *Phaedrus*, Plato portrays writing not only as a 'bad' mimesis, but also as a dangerous, seductive drug (*pharmakon*) that leads to forgetfulness, a loss of understanding and a wild and indiscriminate profusion of discourse (1995, pp. 80–1; secs. 275A, 275B, 275E). Derrida famously responds to Plato's speech/writing dichotomy in his 1972 *La dissémination* (*Dissemination*). The *Phaedrus* is, in Derrida's words, 'Plato's Pharmacy' – a text that belies its own indebtedness to the *pharmakon* of writing and its own mimetic and metaphoric processes. In positing speech as 'good' mimesis, Derrida argues, Plato cannot help but resort to 'scriptural' metaphors to describe how speech is 'written' (*graphetai*) in 'the soul of the learner' (1981 [1972], p. 149). As such, speech is figured in the *Phaedrus* as, paradoxically, '*another sort of writing*' (1981 [1972], p. 149; emph. in original).

As Derrida's analysis reveals, metaphor (resolutely on the side of 'bad' mimesis) is put to work in Plato's *Phaedrus* against itself, while, at the same time, it undermines what it is intended to support. ' "Good" repetition', Derrida explains, is 'always haunted or contaminated by "bad" repetition' (1993 [1989], p. 7) so that 'metaphoricity' becomes both 'the logic of contamination and the contamination of logic' (1981 [1972], p. 149). 'Contamination', with its connotations of 'pollution' and 'infection', is an apt metaphor for metaphor. But 'contamination' has a specific philological meaning, too, that is germane to this analysis. In philology, the term 'contamination' signifies '[t]he blending of forms, words, or phrases of similar meaning or use so as to produce a form, word, or phrase of a new type' ('Contamination' 1989). Like writing, metaphor is the irrepressible *pharmakon* of Western philosophy, a supposedly 'supplementary' form of language that continually rejects its supplementarity and 'opens the wandering of the semantic' (Derrida 1982 [1972], p. 241). Metaphor is, as Derrida so eloquently puts it in *Margins of Philosophy*, 'the chance and risk of *mimēsis*', the 'moment of the detour in which the truth might still be lost' (1982 [1972], p. 241).

In a 1989 interview published as 'Rhetorique de la drogue' ('Rhetoric of Drugs'), Derrida goes even further, arguing that the *pharmakon* is explicitly linked to concepts of contamination, contagion, infection, virality and parasitism. Anything, Derrida argues, that affects 'the proper' has 'the form of a virus (neither alive nor dead, neither human nor "reappropriable by the proper of man", nor generally subjectivable)' (1993 [1989], p. 23). As such, rhetoric itself is 'a parasitic or viral structure: in its origins and in general' (Derrida 1993 [1989], p. 23). In a later interview with Peter Brunette and David Wills, Derrida makes the point yet more forcefully, drawing attention to the 'virology' that is threaded through his entire body of work:

> All I have done, to summarize it very reductively, is dominated by the thought of a virus, what could be called a parasitology, a virology, the virus being many things. . . . The virus is in part a parasite that destroys, that introduces disorder into communication. Even from the biological standpoint, this is what happens with a virus; it derails a mechanism of the communicational type, its coding and decoding. On the other hand, it is something that is neither living nor nonliving; the virus is not a microbe. And if you follow these two threads, that of a parasite which disrupts destination from the communicative point of view – disrupting writing, inscription, and the coding and decoding of inscription – and which on the other hand is neither alive nor dead, you have the matrix of all that I have done since I began writing. (Derrida 1994, p. 12)

What the Derridean and 'New Nietzschean' theories of metaphor and rhetoric offer is an awareness of the 'Dionysian' nature of language, of its fundamental, infectious and irreducible metaphoricity. Metaphor becomes the problem of language, of representation, of mimesis and of influence. Moreover, through a Nietzschean lens, our metaphorical statement – 'metaphor is contagious' – becomes paradoxically literal, suggesting that the contagion metaphor itself might offer a framework for understanding *why* certain metaphors, at certain times, emerge and proliferate unpredictably and, seemingly, epidemically.

2

Pestilence and Poison Winds:
Literary Contagions and the Endurance
of Miasma Theory

Recent interdisciplinary studies of contagion have stressed the vital importance of geography in understanding the spread and containment of epidemics,[1] and contagious disease has been of particular interest to the geographical subdisciplines of historical and medical geography.[2] As Sigerist has noted, '[t]he history and the geography of diseases are most intimately connected and cannot be investigated separately' (1938, p. 173), and, certainly, even the earliest historical accounts of epidemics reveal that the question of contagion is always a question of geography. In his famous account of the plague of Athens, for example, Thucydides (c. 460–395 BC) begins by tracing the geographical movements of the plague northward from its supposed origins in Ethiopia, through Egypt, Libya and the Persian Empire, to its arrival in Athens (2006, pp. 82–5). The Athenian plague was thought to have entered the city state in 430 BC by way of Piraeus, its port city and principal site of trade, returning twice in the following three years. A more recent example of this attention to the relationship between geography and contagion is the work of French economic geographer André Siegfried. In the mid 1950s, Siegfried began research into the geographies of contagion – research that would be published posthumously in 1960 and translated into English as *Routes of Contagion* in 1965. In this slim volume, Siegfried blends geography and epidemiology, mapping out the land, sea and air routes of a number of historical epidemics.

When we encounter contagion, then, we also necessarily encounter geography. In this chapter, I wish to extend this geographical thinking about contagion to ask what it might mean to think of an *aerography* of contagion. Geography, contagion and the element of air have historically overlapped in interesting ways, but I argue that they also continue to do so, and particularly in cultural expression. Rethinking the element of air in relation to contagion from an interdisciplinary perspective enables us to see the ways in which air has come to signify a more ambiguous, affective form of contagion that is also bound up with the spread of ideas and information.

The forgetting of air

For Luce Irigaray, air is the element forgotten by philosophy; it has been forgotten by those such as Martin Heidegger, whose masculine philosophical gaze, she argues, has been too firmly focused upon the materiality of the *ground* to see that air is, in fact, 'the mediation of all reflection', the 'mediation and medium of life' (1999 [1983], pp. 13–14). But that is not to say that air is absent from philosophy. For Irigaray, Heidegger's downward-looking focus on the ground belies the fact that his philosophy is predicated on the very condition of air. As Ann Murphy explains, Irigaray 'insists that [Heidegger's] understanding of technology remains indebted to a metaphysics that forgets the materiality of air, a materiality that unknowably subtends his understanding of nature' (2007, p. 85). Remembering air means we need to recognize its materiality and its mediating power.[3] And yet, Irigaray maintains, by existing in a state of flux between presence and absence, and by not showing itself, air has 'allow[ed] itself to be forgotten' (1999 [1983], p. 14). Yet, despite – or perhaps because of – its ontological ambiguity, air has been at the very core of theories of contagious disease for the majority of the past two millennia.

Although geography was an important element in describing outbreaks such as the plague of Athens, neither the sea nor the land provide the key to early theories of contagion and disease. Rather, in theories of contagion from the Classical period, extending through the Middle Ages, the Renaissance and even through the eighteenth and nineteenth centuries, it is the element of air that is accorded a primary role. According to Robert Parker, Diodorus Siculus attributed the cause of the plague of Athens to a moral 'pollution' or contamination: a burial on the sacred island of Delos that required a later purification. This causal link between moral pollution and physical contagion, Parker continues, finds 'a rationalization . . . in the Hippocratic doctrine that plagues are caused by *miasmata* in the air' (1983, p. 218), in other words, that infectious diseases such as plague, malaria (literally, 'bad air') and cholera are caused by foul or polluted air. As I shall explain further, this classical 'miasmatic' theory of contagion proved remarkably resilient, and it was only with the advent of microbial germ theory in the mid- to late nineteenth century that it was, for the most part, abandoned as a superseded and disproven medical science.

Given this, it is unsurprising that the word 'miasma' does not appear at all in Siegfried's *Routes of Contagion*, and yet the element of air seems to remain an important concern to him. Siegfried's work is interesting to a possible aerography of contagion because of two speculations he makes. First, he notes that, in the past, certain aspects of physical geography might be considered to have contained contagion or inhibited its spread. However, he states, in 'the era of ultra-rapid communications born of air travel', contagion may no longer be quarantined by geography (1965 [1960], p. 29). Second, Siegfried concludes *Routes of Contagion* by suggesting that marked similarities exist between the spread of disease and the spread of ideas: 'there is a striking parallel', he argues, 'between the spreading of germs and the spreading of ideas or propaganda' (1965 [1960], p. 85). The spread of religions or doctrines are a particular case in point for Siegfried, for they 'spread like epidemics, following the same lines of least resistance, coming up against the same obstacles, first striking out, depending on the transport available – towards the main centres of communication and distribution, from which they then spread in all directions' (1965 [1960], p. 95).

Siegfried uses, variously, metaphors of seeds, germs and even pollen to characterize infectious ideas, and he uses mainly geographical and medical tropes to describe their spread and diffusion. He avoids atmospheric tropes, including as I have said miasmatic ones, and stresses the necessity of a 'human intermediary' or 'human reservoir' for infection to take place. And yet, he says, direct human contact is not necessary for ideas to spread: 'infection may take place through the reading or the hearing of something from a distant source, or through the sight of some image' (1965 [1960], p. 87). Without the requirement of physical human contact, the paradoxically ever-present but unseen element of air must come into play, if only indirectly and in a largely unacknowledged way. In Siegfried's model of idea diffusion, it is the human mind itself that becomes airborne: the mind becomes a 'winged germ, often invisible' (1965 [1960], p. 93). And herein lies the paradox: where contagion in the medical sense has the material reality of the microbe to fall back on as the base unit of viral transmission, the sort of contagion of ideas Siegfried is talking about has no such materially identifiable base unit. Although contagious ideas spread only by way of contact, this contact, for Siegfried, does not require physical touch and, as such, it relies upon the unspoken interposition of air or the atmosphere.

In this chapter, I wish to suggest that there exists a continuing connection between contagion, geography and air that links aerographies of contagion to moral geographies. This deep but often elided connection can, I argue, be drawn out by examining fictional 'plague narratives' in which contagion, both physical and moral, is figured as spreading from specific, negatively cast geographic or sociogeographic regions. In particular, I will examine four main texts that span almost three centuries: Daniel Defoe's political writings about contagion in the early eighteenth century, Thomas Mann's 1912 novella *Death in Venice*, Albert Camus's 1947 novel *The Plague* and Janette Turner Hospital's 2003 novel *Due Preparations for the Plague*. Aside from Hospital's more recent novel, these are 'canonical' plague narratives that have become requisite primary texts for the study of the plague, or disease more broadly, as it is represented in literature.[4] I am interested in these texts not only because each has a strong geographical element (in each narrative, for instance, the plague – figurative or otherwise – is depicted as having its source in the torrid zone south of Europe), but also because the figurative contagions these narratives present are almost inevitably themselves figured in terms of air or wind, and particularly in terms of a southern wind that drives the pestilence northward from Africa and the Middle East to Europe.[5]

This emphasis on air in the novels of Mann, Camus and Hospital might, on the one hand, be read as an attentiveness to this element overlooked by philosophy; on the other hand, however, it could be read as a retrograde step. Almost paradoxically, the focus on air in these novels hearkens back to those early miasmatic theories of disease and contagion that were dispelled by the development of microbial germ theory in the second half of the nineteenth century. Before I turn to analysing these plague narratives, and in order to set them in the context of the medical paradigms that they engage with, I will provide a brief outline of the history of miasmatic theories of contagion.

Miasma and contagion from the Hippocratic scholars to germ theory

In the work of the Hippocratic scholars, we see the earliest expressions of miasma theory, or, rather, a specific application of the concept of miasma to the problem of disease.[6] The Greek *mia-* (μία-) denotes 'defilement, the impairment of a thing's form or integrity' (Parker 1983, p. 3), so that the term *miasma* (μίασμα), in its general sense,

> encompassed both the notions of staining or tainting and also of physical or moral defilement. In the Hippocratic writings, miasma acquired further shades of reference. In the attempt to explain epidemics naturalistically, and not as punishments for sin and defilement, the air became significant as the cause of disease outbreaks and its tainting by miasmas the reason why a disease affected a number of people at the same time. . . . The exact nature or character of these miasmas remained undefined, but general sources of the putrefaction of the air included stagnant marshes and pools, vapours from a variety of sources including corpses of humans and animals, sick persons, excreta, spoiled foodstuffs, decaying vegetable matter, and exhalations that came from the ground through ruptures or clefts. (Hannaway 1994, p. 295)

The Hippocratic texts also connected miasma and contagion to atmospheric conditions and climate as well as to the bodily humours. The 'atmospheric-miasmatic' Hippocratic theory of disease, writes Lois N. Magner, analysed disease 'in terms of the relationship and interactions between individuals and their environment – including weather conditions and other local circumstances' (2009, p. 20). Indeed, this conflation of climatic and meteorological (particularly wind) conditions with miasma and contagion continued well into nineteenth-century medical discourse. As Pamela K. Gilbert explains, in the nineteenth century many epidemic diseases were 'often believed to be caused by bad air and wind conditions, and it was conventional to include meteorological information in sanitary reports' (2008, p. 193, note 11).

Moreover, just as the cause of miasmatic disease could be moral, so too could the disease itself. That is, the disease produced and spread by miasma did not have to be physical in nature; rather, it could take the form of what we would now consider to be a mental or psychological disorder. In his *Moralia*, Plutarch tells the story of a suicide epidemic that spread among the women of Miletus. In his account (which, as we will see in Chapter 3, would become a touchstone for eighteenth- and nineteenth-century theories of moral and social contagion), Plutarch states that, although the cause of the outbreak was unknown, the 'most popular conjecture' was that it was miasmatic in origin: 'the air had acquired a distracting and infectious constitution' that caused in the women 'an alteration and derangement of mind' (1960, p. 509). Although Frank Cole Babbitt's translation of the Women of Miletus story, cited above, stresses the infectious nature of the air, the Greek text offers us neither 'infectious' (λοιμώδης) nor

the word 'miasma' (μίασμα); it gives, simply, 'air' (ἀήρ). And yet 'air' is a word
that, in Greek, itself strongly connotes miasma. As William Smith explains in his
Dictionary of the Bible, the Greek ἀήρ was used 'to denote the lower portion of
the atmosphere, the region of vapors, clouds and mist, in opposition to αἰθήρ,
the pure upper air or ether' (1868, p. 56).

To add to these complexities, early theories of contagion also pose the problem of definition, for classical texts provide no clear-cut distinction between the
two terms 'miasma' and 'contagion'. Dominik Wujastyk and Lawrence I. Conrad
caution that we cannot simply map our current understanding of the word *contagion* onto classical Greek or Latin conceptions of disease. The word *contagio*
(meaning, literally, to 'touch together') might appear frequently in Latin texts,
they grant, 'but nowhere in ancient Latin literature does an author discuss the
process he has in mind when using this word, and in many cases it comprises a
synonym for "disease" and refers to the progression within the body – rather like
putrefaction or "colouring" – of some illness that had originated there' (2000,
p. xi). Likewise, Vivian Nutton advises that the term '*contagio* cannot always be
translated as "contagion", and even when it can, there is never the implication
that what is being transmitted from person to person is a disease entity. What
passes is an emanation, an effluxion . . ., a miasma' (2000, p. 151).

This confusion between the terms 'contagion' and 'miasma' also continued
into the nineteenth century, along with the emphasis on meteorological
explanations for disease. As Christopher Hamlin notes, in the early to mid-
nineteenth century, unambiguous definitions of 'miasma' and 'contagion'
remained elusive, for the terms were, he argues, 'variously and vaguely defined
and used' (1998, p. 60). Many scientists, Hamlin argues, considered the terms
to be synonymous, and even for those who considered contagion and miasma
to refer to 'alternative forms of disease-specific poison', the concepts 'were still
often not fully distinct, for both reached their victim through the air, though at
greater or lesser distance from their source' (1998, pp. 60–1). Indeed, although
the terms 'miasma' and 'contagion' had, by the middle of the nineteenth
century, come to refer to two competing philosophies of disease prevention –
contagionism and miasmatism (or anti-contagionism) – the boundaries
between the two scientific camps were similarly not rigidly demarcated, despite
their apparent opposition.[7]

Over the course of two millennia, then, the Hippocratic theory that disease was, at base, miasmatic in origin remained largely undisputed, although
the understanding of what miasma might comprise certainly did change over
time. In the second century AD, the Roman physician Galen confirmed and

expanded upon the Hippocratic theory of miasma,[8] as did the Persian physician Avicenna in the tenth century AD.[9] Even Girolamo Fracastoro's sixteenth-century theory of 'fomites'[10] or contagious 'seeds', which has often been viewed, however simplistically, as a forerunner of germ theory, did little to displace miasma. As Nutton explains, Fracastoro's theory of contagious seeds was less a radical scientific shift away from miasma theory than a gradual expansion and a new metaphor for existing theories of disease. For Fracastoro's contemporaries, Nutton concludes, it was '[b]etter to treat the patient visible before the doctor and to avoid malodorous miasmata than to chase unprofitably after invisible and hypothetical seeds' (1983, p. 34).[11] In the late seventeenth century, Antonie van Leeuwenhoek's pioneering work with microscopes enabled him to be the first to observe 'animalcules' or microorganisms, yet the following century also saw a return to Hippocratic ideas regarding disease. Moreover, in this eighteenth-century 'revival', miasmas and the atmosphere more generally 'gained a prominent place' (Hannaway 1994, pp. 304–5).

Miasma theory was only seriously challenged in the nineteenth century, as Agostino Bassi, John Snow, Louis Pasteur and Robert Koch contributed to a developing microbial germ theory. In the case of cholera, for instance, John Snow's discovery around 1854 of a link between contaminated water and the cholera bacterium presented a significant challenge to the prevailing miasmatic theory of cholera's spread. Snow's theory that cholera was waterborne and not airborne certainly did not effect an immediate and decisive overturning of miasmatic theories of contagion;[12] however, Snow has retrospectively been considered to be the 'father' of modern epidemiology.[13] As the evidence for microbial germ theory accumulated and gained wider acceptance, air began to be displaced from its position as the principal medium for the transmission of disease, and ever-clearer distinctions between miasma and contagion – defined as 'disease transmission by direct or indirect contact' ('Contagion' 2007) – began to be drawn.

Plague narratives, the troping of air and wind, and Daniel Defoe's *Due Preparations for the Plague*

Despite the decline of miasma theory and the correlative de-privileging of air in contagion theory, I wish to argue that air seems to remain an important link between physical and affective contagion in twentieth-century cultural discourse. Mann's *Death in Venice*, Camus's *The Plague* and Hospital's *Due*

Preparations for the Plague are all cultural products of an age in which germ theory had effectively trumped miasma theory, yet all three works depict contagions or plagues that have physical/medical and mental/affective aspects, and in all three, as I have said, the element of air or the trope of wind figure strongly.

This link between the physical and the affective in contagious disease is, of course, not in itself remarkable. Except in the most rarefied scientific discourse, any public discourse about contagion throughout history has implicitly or explicitly linked the physical aspects of contagion (symptoms, disease, death and so forth) with its mental, spiritual or affective ones (such as other forms of panic that accompany plagues – the burning down of houses, stockpiling of foods, rampaging, looting and so forth). This inevitable and inescapable entanglement of the physical and affective aspects of contagion is what Arnold Weinstein would call 'plague logic', a logic that, he argues, is at work as much in contemporary concerns around bioterrorism as it is in Sophocles's *Oedipus the King*, a play whose action is instigated by the outbreak of a plague, itself caused by a religious pollution. 'We are worried', Weinstein writes, 'about literal bioterrorism, but we are also obsessed with the "plague logic", the suspicion that particular groups are secretly boring their way into our society, jeopardizing our security, poised to strike us in our collective vital organs' (2003, p. 103).

This blending of the physical, the affective, the moral and the cultural so apparent in plague narratives (and discourse on contagion, more generally) is, furthermore, built into the very *term* 'contagion'. As Vivian Nutton argues, the 'Latin *contagio* contain[s] both an element of touching and of sharing'. *Synanachrosis* (συνανάχρωσις), the closest Greek equivalent to the Latin *contagio*, shares this emphasis on touch, and furthermore contains 'a main root frequently associated with moral as well as physical illness' (Nutton 2000, p. 141). Fourteenth-century uses of the word *contagion* also, according to Priscilla Wald, 'referred to the circulation of ideas and attitudes'. Moreover, the term, Wald continues,

> frequently connoted danger or corruption. Revolutionary ideas were contagious, as were heretical beliefs and practices. Folly and immorality were more often labelled contagious than were wisdom or virtue. The medical usage of the term was no more and no less metaphorical than its ideational counterpart. The circulation of disease and the circulation of ideas were material and experiential, even if not visible. Both displayed the power and danger of bodies in contact and demonstrated the simultaneous fragility and tenacity of social bonds. (Wald 2008, p. 13)

Daniel Defoe's early eighteenth-century political writings on the plague provide
a telling example of this continued tendency for contagion to present, simultaneously, physical, mental and moral aspects. Defoe was about five years old when
the Great Plague arrived in London in 1665, killing an estimated 100,000 people,
or a third of London's population. Defoe was so affected by the plague and convinced that it would return to an unsuspecting and unprepared populace that
in 1722 he published two books about the plague of 1665, namely *Journal of the
Plague Year* and *Due Preparations for the Plague*. I am most interested here in the
latter work, because it is the one that provides direct inspiration for Hospital's
2003 novel of the same name. In *Due Preparations*, Defoe warns that the plague
is on England's doorstep, with outbreaks being reported on the Continent. In
particular, he is exercised by the recent 1720 outbreak at Marseille, brought by
the merchant ship the *Grand-Saint-Antoine* on its return journey from Syria.
Defoe argues that England is not prepared for a new outbreak of plague, but not
just in a physical sense. He is concerned that England is not mentally or spiritually prepared.

At the outset of *Due Preparations*, Defoe makes clear he is dividing his subject into two sections: preparations against the plague and preparations for the
plague, the first of which he calls 'preparations for the body', and the latter he
calls 'preparations for the soul' (1974 [1722], p. 9). Before going on to tell stories that illustrate these two principles, Defoe outlines his current thinking on
the transmission of contagious diseases, which is a tempered version of miasma
theory. 'The effluvia of infected bodies', Defoe says, 'may, and must be indeed,
conveyed from one to another by air; so words are conveyed from the mouth of
the speaker to the ear of the hearer by the interposition and vibration of the air'
(p. 16). Again, we can see here the analogy between the communication of disease and the communication of ideas via the element of air. Defoe grants there is
a limit to airborne contagion because 'those effluvias cannot extend themselves
a great way' and dissipate like bad smells over a distance, yet he also cautions his
readers to 'observe the blowing of the winds' if they might happen to live near,
or in the outskirts of, an infected town (pp. 16–17).

Defoe's warnings about preparing the soul for the plague are, on the whole,
moral ones. He says that the vices of the English have developed into a 'dread-
ful kind of fuel for a contagion, and miserably prepare us for a plague upon our
bodies' (p. 43). Dependent as it is on matters of geography, trade and transport, the plague is peculiar in that it gives its potential victims time to prepare.
Unlike the 'ordinary distemper', the plague 'generally approaches a country by

slow degrees, and you have many months' warning of it before it comes; so that if it swept all away in a day, there is no room to call it severity, for every one had warning of it beforehand' (p. 97). To prepare for the plague, Defoe advises by way of a fictionalized story about a family who survived the Great Plague of 1665, a person needs to 'prepare for death as seriously and with as much application as if they were already infected and had the distemper upon them' (p. 104). In this story, a young woman works to convince her merchant brothers that physical preparedness for the plague is not enough. Only by being spiritually prepared can English people be properly ready for the plague in both its physical and spiritual guises. As Defoe has one of his characters say, 'I know of no preparation for the plague but a preparation for death. He that is ready to die is ready to have the plague' (pp. 136–7).

For Weinstein, Defoe's plague narratives exemplify 'what literature brings to the table' in considering contagious disease. Defoe, Weinstein writes, explores 'all the explanations that were put forward to explain London's plague: God's anger, contagion, and miasma. He may favor one over the others, but he is curious about all of them; above all, he is concerned to *represent*, not to explain' (2003, p. 109). By drawing out and articulating the social and emotional aspects of contagious disease, Defoe's work speaks to the way in which 'literary texts about disease are revelatory and can tell us something about the repressed fears and the emerging fault lines of a culture in ways that the epidemiologist as such cannot chart' (Weinstein 2003, p. 109).

Pestilence and poison winds: Thomas Mann's *Death in Venice*

This complex interaction between physical and moral contagion and the element of air evident in Defoe takes on a slightly different, but equally powerful, inflection in Thomas Mann's 1912 novella *Death in Venice* (*Der Tod in Venedig*). Mann's protagonist, the writer Aschenbach, travels to Venice on a whim and there becomes obsessed with a Polish boy named Tadzio, who is staying with his family at the same hotel. Aschenbach's obsession is like an infection that takes him over – he follows the boy and his family around Venice and cannot take his eyes or mind off him. Yet, in the background, another, more literal, contagion is brewing. Aschenbach gradually becomes aware that Venice is stricken by a pestilence and that the authorities are trying to keep the fact quiet. Aschenbach is ambivalent about this shadowy contagion: although he wants to get to the bottom of it, he does not necessarily want word to get out in case the object of his fascination, the boy Tadzio, were to leave because of it. Indeed, in his analysis of *Death in Venice*, René Girard argues that, by 'sid[ing] with the epidemic when he chooses not to inform the Polish family of its presence in Venice', Aschenbach 'has become the very embodiment of the plague' (1974, p. 848).

In Mann's novella, it is air and wind that herald contagion. Soon after his arrival, Aschenbach opens his window, and catches the scent of the stagnant lagoons at the Lido. Immediately, he begins to consider leaving Venice: 'Once, years before, after weeks of bright spring weather, this wind had found him out; it had been so bad as to force him to flee from the city like a fugitive. And now it seemed beginning again – the same feverish distaste, the pressure on his temples, the heavy eyelids. It would be a nuisance to change again; but if the wind did not turn, this was no place for him' (1990 [1912], pp. 25–6). This wind that has sought him out is the sirocco (*scirocco* in the German text), a southerly wind that, according to the narrator 'excites and enervates at once' (p. 32). When Aschenbach asks locals about the smell of carbolic in the city, they are quick to deny a plague outbreak, instead blaming the unwholesome air brought by the sirocco (pp. 47–8).

The sirocco has long been linked with disease. Variously known as *scirocco, siroc, jugo, ghibli* or *auster*,[14] the sirocco is a southerly wind that blows into Europe from the north coast of Africa across the Mediterranean Sea, bringing with it the hot air of the Sahara. The Hippocratic view of the south wind (*νότος*) as a harbinger of disease, the opposite of the 'healthy' north wind (Hippocrates 1923b, pp. 171–2), found full and dramatic expression in Ovid's *Metamorphoses*,[15] and was well entrenched by the seventeenth century. In his 1622 'History of the Winds', for example, Francis Bacon maintains that '[i]n a south wind the breath of men is more offensive, the appetite of animals is more depressed, pestilential diseases are more frequent, catarrhs common, and men are more dull and heavy' (1858 [1622], p. 156). Writing in the late eighteenth century, and in calling for a greater understanding of the effects of climate on human society, Johann Gottfried Herder explicitly links miasma with the sirocco and other pestilential winds that transfer the 'secret poison' of contagious disease (1968 [1784–1791], p. 16). Increasingly, the sirocco offered itself as an apt metaphor for contagious, revolutionary ideas: in 1799, US Congressman Fisher Ames railed against mob-government, or 'mobocracy', likening it to the 'winged curse' of the sirocco, whose vapours leave men to 'die in the open air for want of respiration' (1809 [1799], p. 97).

This view of the sirocco as a corrupting and a 'poison' wind continued well into the nineteenth century in both medical and popular discourse.[16] For instance, in his research into atmospheric influences on the spread of contagion, Scottish physician Somerville Scott Alison describes the sirocco as a particularly noxious southern wind: 'The Sirocco blows off the deserts of Africa, passing over the Mediterranean sea, there imbibing a large quantity of water, converted into vapour, and rushes up the fair shores and degenerate population of Italy. Its immediate effect is to relax the system, and to open up all the pores on the surface of the body. These effects are very hurtful to health, and become particularly so when they are long continued, as sometimes happens' (1839, pp. 162–3). Interestingly, Alison appears to imply that the 'degenerate population' of Italy is more susceptible to the sirocco's unhealthy vapours.

Towards the end of *Death in Venice*, and shortly before he himself succumbs to the disease, Aschenbach discovers that the pestilence plaguing Venice is, in fact, cholera. Writing in the early twentieth century – more than 50 years after Snow's discoveries and nearly 30 years after Koch isolated and identified the cholera bacterium in 1884[17] – Mann is aware that cholera is a waterborne disease and is not, in fact, transmitted in the air or via miasma. Moreover, Mann alludes to his knowledge of germ theory by directly mentioning the cholera *vibrio* or bacterium within the text, as well as providing an extended description of the disease's spread northwest from India to Italy:

> For the past several years Asiatic cholera had shown a strong tendency to spread. Its source was the hot, moist swamps of the delta of the Ganges, where it bred in the mephitic air of that primeval island-jungle, among whose bamboo thickets the tiger crouches, where life of every sort flourishes in the rankest abundance, and only man avoids the spot. Thence the pestilence had spread throughout Hindustan, ranging with great violence; moved eastwards to China, westward to Afghanistan and Persia; following the great caravan routes, it brought terror to Astrakhan, terror to Moscow. Even while Europe trembled lest the spectre be seen striding westward across country, it was carried by sea from Syrian ports and appeared simultaneously at several points on the Mediterranean littoral; raised its head in Toulon and Malaga, Palermo and Naples, and soon got a firm hold in Calabria and Apulia. Northern Italy had been spared – so far. But in May the horrible vibrios [*die furchtbaren Vibrionen*] were found on the same day in two bodies: the emaciated, blackened corpses of a bargee and a woman who kept a greengrocer's shop. (Mann 1990 [1912], p. 58)

Mann also deliberately situates his novella in Venice – a waterborne city – a city where the elements of water and air meet. As Linda and Michael Hutcheon argue in their compelling reading of Mann's novella and Benjamin Britten's operatic adaptation, Venice is a particularly 'appropriate setting for a cholera epidemic' (1996, p. 137). Venice is geographically and medically apt because, '[a]s a port city at the heart of a busy mercantile society, it was badly hit by the bubonic plague in the sixteenth and seventeenth centuries'. Moreover, Venice is metaphorically apt because the 'mercantile history of the city continues in debased form in the Venetians' denial of the cholera epidemic for commercial reasons. The fabled beauty of the city cannot be separated, in the imagination of non-Italian writers in particular, from associations with decadence and moral corruption' (Hutcheon and Hutcheon 1996, p. 137) – an attitude we can see reflected in Alison's account of the Italian sirocco.

Further, the sirocco carries with it the pestilence historically associated with the south, a contagion that, in Mann's novella, finds a further correlate in the figure of Dionysus. The very night Aschenbach discovers the true nature of the pestilence plaguing Venice, he has a visceral dream of a Bacchanale in which he ultimately rejects his Christian self-control and gives himself over to Dionysus, the 'stranger-god'. The contagious cult of Dionysus, like the plague of Athens and the sirocco, has its origin south of Greece (Kerényi 1976, pp. 75, 138), and scholars have variously placed Dionysus's birthplace of Nysa in Ethiopia, Arabia, Egypt, Syria and even India (Otto 1965 [1933], pp. 62–3). The scene of Aschenbach's dream-orgy, moreover, is befitting to Dionysus, the god of contagion: it is miasmatic and malodorous with the 'the steam of panting bodies, the acrid stench from the goats, the odour as of stagnant waters – and another, too familiar smell – of wounds, uncleanness, and disease' (Mann 1990, p. 62).

In these ways, *Death in Venice* presents a complex interplay between miasma theory and germ theory – between two otherwise opposed medical paradigms. Hutcheon and Hutcheon note that in Mann's novella, '[e]choes of consumption combine with both modern scientific information about cholera's etiology and earlier miasma theories to offer a complex and historically rich ground for the representation of a disease and of the person suffering from it' (1996, p. 136). I would add to this that Mann strategically draws attention to the element of air precisely because it expresses more strongly the etymology of the Latin *contagio*, which, as I argued earlier, links physical with moral or affective contagion. When word of the contagion finally breaks out in Venice, panic spreads despite all efforts to keep it in check. Panic is in the air, but it is precisely a lack of air that kills Aschenbach, for the type of cholera afflicting Venice is the 'dry' (*die trockene*) variety, whereby the victim suffocates due to extreme dehydration.

Communicative contagion: Albert Camus's *The Plague*

Wind, air and airlessness are also predominant themes in Albert Camus's novel of 1947, *The Plague* (*La Peste*), which narrates an outbreak of the bubonic plague in the Algerian coastal city of Oran, roughly contemporaneous with the novel's publication. Camus does not provide a specific year for his plague, simply stating that the events occurred in '194–'. Although the plague of the novel's title is of the bubonic and pneumonic types, it is thought that Camus based his plague on the cholera epidemic that struck Oran in 1849, and critics such as Lulu M. Haroutunian (1964) have also argued that Camus's novel is influenced by his own battle with tuberculosis.

From the outset, Camus asks us to read his plague metaphorically, if not symbolically, by quoting as an epigraph Defoe's reflections upon his *Robinson Crusoe*: 'It is as reasonable to represent one kind of imprisonment by another, as it is to represent any thing that really exists, by that which exists not' (Defoe 1790, p. vi).[18] Camus's 'island' or place of imprisonment – the enclosed setting for his plague – is Oran, a city he describes as being 'grafted onto a unique landscape, in the centre of a bare plateau, ringed with luminous hills and above a perfectly shaped bay' (1960 [1947], p. 3). And yet, despite Oran's position overlooking the south-western coast of the Mediterranean, Camus notes the regrettable fact that the city 'turns its back' on the sea.[19] Cut off from the sea by town planning and, later, by quarantine, Oran is cut off from its refreshing northerly breezes. Instead, opening itself up to the southerly winds that bear into it from the Algerian Sahara, Oran is bound to the desert – indeed is itself a kind of desert (Camus 1970 [1954], p. 111).

According to Laurent Mailhot, there are two types of 'Camusian' wind: the wind of carefree liberty and the 'pure', fiery wind of the desert and the plague (1973, p. 208). It is, of course, this latter wind that blows through Camus's *The Plague* and propels its narrative. The past-tense narrator, whom the reader discovers at the close of the novel is the doctor Rieux, describes the almost year-long period of quarantine in a reserved, almost detached, way. Rieux provides an eyewitness account of the plague, but he also relies on the written account of Tarrou, a visitor to Oran, whose notebooks provide a 'discursive diary' of the plague (Camus 1960 [1947], p. 22). The narration is also continually attended by a description of the city's climate and its relative windiness or windlessness. In early summer, the plague shifts form – from bubonic to pneumonic – slowly at first, but gaining momentum as the months progress. As the contagion becomes airborne, the desert winds also begin to make themselves felt in Oran. At the

outset of the novel, Oran is described as a city in which 'you never hear ...
the rustle of leaves' (p. 1), and, at the beginning of summer, the city is described
as deathly still, making it impossible to tell 'if the air was heavy with menace
or merely with heat and dust' (p. 136). However, by mid August, when 'the
plague had swallowed up everything and everyone', Oran is overtaken by a high
wind, which its citizens fearfully accuse of 'carrying the infection, "broadcasting
germs"' (pp. 162–3).

The opening of a crematorium to burn the dead only worsens this fear.
Despite doctors' protestations that the effluvia (*exhalasions*) emitted from the
crematorium are completely harmless, the residents in the affected district
become 'convinced germs were raining down on them from the sky', causing the
authorities to build a device to divert the miasmatic vapours. As the high wind
rages, it comes to signify more than the city's climatic conditions. Fanning the
existing social unrest in a city that had been quarantined for months, the high
wind that takes over Oran at the close of summer has 'an incendiary effect on
certain minds', inciting 'frequent attacks on the gates of the town' (p. 164). By
November, Rieux notes that the plague's mutation from bubonic to pneumonic
was well advanced: '[t]he pneumonic type of infection ... was now spreading
all over the town; one could almost believe that the high winds were kindling
and fanning its flames in people's chests' (p. 226).

This high wind that appears with the onset of the pneumonic plague not
only instils fear in the city's inhabitants about its miasmatic potential, but it also
becomes a metaphor for the plague itself. In two of the novel's most moving
scenes – the deaths of the magistrate Othon's young son and of Tarrou – the
plague is metaphorized as a wind that attacks and invades the sufferers' bodies.
Rieux describes the plague as a 'storm-wind', whose 'fierce breath' blows 'gusts
of fever' that leave its victims 'gasping for breath' (p. 204). By early February, the
plague wind is almost held at bay, no longer 'thresh[ing] the air above the houses
with its flail'. Yet, only a few days before the end of the city's period of quarantine,
it has sought out Tarrou and is 'launching its last offensive ... whistling softly in
the stagnant air of the sickroom' (pp. 274–5). It is this sound that Rieux recog-
nizes he 'had been hearing since the long vigil began. And now it was for him
to wait and watch until that strange sound ceased here too, and here as well the
plague confessed defeat' (p. 274).

Wind might signify the plague, but what does the plague signify? Camus's
hope, expressed in his notebooks, was that his plague would demonstrate
that his theory of the absurd 'teaches nothing'; the moral of his novel is that
the plague 'has served nothing and nobody. Only those whom death has

touched personally or through their family have learned anything' (Camus 1966, pp. 15, 32). And yet, Camus also states quite explicitly that he wishes to express 'by means of the plague the suffocation from which we all suffered and the atmosphere of threat and exile in which we lived. At the same time, I want to extend this interpretation to the notion of existence in general. The plague will give the image of those whose share in this war has been that of reflection, silence – and moral suffering' (1966, p. 35). Camus's *The Plague* is a revolt against fascism and against institutionalized religion, but the novel's plague cannot be reduced to either one; its meaning is unclear and resists definition.

However, Camus clearly was influenced by Antonin Artaud's 1934 essay 'The Theater and the Plague',[20] in which Artaud argues that the plague is a 'psychic entity' (1958 [1934], p. 18) that has a 'spiritual freedom' beyond rats, microbes and physical contact (1958 [1934], p. 21). At the beginning of his essay, Artaud relates an anecdote about the viceroy of Sardinia, Saint-Rémy, who woke one night in 1720 following bad dreams. Saint-Rémy has been affected by 'rumors about the plague, these miasmas of a virus from the Orient' (Artaud 1958 [1934], p. 17). His nightmare is that he has been infected by the plague, and yet he has had no contact with the plague or with the plague-boat he sees in his dream. The dream, however, is enough for him to drive away, with the threat of cannon, a boat that seeks to dock at Cagliari. That boat is the *Grand-Saint-Antoine* on its way to Marseille, where it will initiate the plague of 1720 that would, in turn, prompt Defoe to write his *Due Preparations for the Plague* and *Journal of the Plague Year* two years later.[21]

Although there is no physical contact between the virus and Saint-Rémy, Artaud argues there is still a 'palpable communication, however subtle' established between the two: these relations, which are 'strong enough to liberate themselves as images in his dream, are all the same not strong enough to infect him with the disease' (1958 [1934], p. 17). By extension, the theatre, he argues 'like the plague, is a delirium and is communicative' (1958 [1934], p. 27); like the plague, the theatre 'is the revelation, the bringing forth, the exteriorization of a depth of latent cruelty by means of which all the perverse possibilities of the mind, whether of an individual or a people, are localized' (1958 [1934], p. 30).

Camus's plague is certainly less liberatory than Artaud's, but it is nonetheless just as communicative. The plague is that which defines, necessitates and compels the idea of humanity. Shortly before his death, Tarrou tells Rieux: 'each of us has the plague within him; no one, no one on earth, is free from it. And I know, too, that we must keep endless watch on ourselves lest in a careless moment we breathe in somebody's face and fasten the infection on him. What's natural is the microbe. All the rest – health, integrity, purity (if you like) – is a product of the human will, of a vigilance that must never falter' (Camus 1960, p. 242). The plague can never be ignored, and it requires its due preparations. It is the humanists, Camus argues, who are claimed first, for they are the ones who 'fancied themselves free', who 'disbelieved in pestilences' and who did not take 'their precautions' (1960, pp. 35–6).

An aerography of contagion: Janette Turner Hospital's *Due Preparations for the Plague*

Turning finally to Hospital's 2003 novel *Due Preparations for the Plague*, we can see some of Defoe, Mann and Camus's ideas about contagion converging. But where the tension in Defoe and Mann is predominantly between physical and moral contagion, in Camus and Hospital we see not so much a preoccupation with moral contagion, but with a contagion of affect and of information. Hospital's novel directly references Defoe's *Due Preparations* and Camus's *The Plague*, along with Boccaccio's fourteenth-century plague narrative *The Decameron*, and she skilfully melds and reworks these influences. As in Defoe's book, at the centre of Hospital's novel is a young woman trying to convince those around her that a kind of contagion is spreading among them. In this case, however, it is not a contagion in the narrow, medical sense of the word. Hospital's *Due Preparations* is set in the year 2000, 13 years after the hijacking of Air France Flight 64. The reader discovers, as the novel progresses, that Flight 64 was hijacked by Islamic terrorists of unclear nationality; that the plane lands in a number of places, including Morocco, Frankfurt, Toulouse and, finally, Tikrit; that children and nursing mothers are released when the plane lands in Germany; that the remaining captives are given protective suits and gas masks before the plane is filled with toxic gas; and that the plane is blown up in Iraq with, apparently at first, no further survivors.

Sam, the young woman at the centre of the novel, is one of the child survivors of Flight 64 and has formed a club – the Phoenix club – with other surviving children. Sam is certain that there remain unanswered questions about the hijacking, questions the US authorities do not want answered. However, or perhaps because of this, members of the Phoenix club are, one by one, disappearing in what appear to be suicides. Sam tracks down Lowell Hawthorne – whose mother died on the flight – and convinces him that there is some kind of conspiracy underlying the hijacking. But the reader, and Lowell, soon realizes that his connection to Flight 64 and to Sam goes deeper than he had imagined. At the outset of the novel, we learn that Lowell's father, Mather Hawthorne, who worked for US intelligence and seemed to have had some connection to the hijacking, has recently died in a car accident. His father's jittery psychiatrist passes on to Lowell his father's bequest – a collection of notebooks and a set of videos, including one titled the Decameron tape, all of which document the unfolding of the hijacking.

Networks of people, of communication, of conspiracy begin to spread as if by contagion. Too many people on the plane seem to have tenuous, but nevertheless resonant, ties to one another. Events begin to seem more than coincidental, as though Mather Hawthorne's death has released a virus that begins once more to infect and connect lives 13 years after the event. Characters are described as contagious: Lowell is 'highly infectious with doom' (Hospital 2003, p. 15), while Sam's aunt is described as 'mov[ing] away from Sam as though Sam might be infectious' (p. 58). Another character, Génie, 'think[s] of herself as carrying a virus of bereavement . . . like malaria: lurking about in the blood, dormant sometimes, flaring up without warning' (pp. 123–4).

For Sam and Lowell, their contagion has its source in the element of air – in the hijacked plane and in the toxic gas. Furthermore, there is another sirocco in this novel, another sirocco that both reveals and conceals the conspiracy of silence surrounding the hijacking. 'Sirocco' is the code name of a triple agent – he might be Algerian, Egyptian or Saudi – hired by the US government to uncover a French Islamic terrorist cell by convincing its members to engineer a controlled hijacking. This is Operation Black Death: a deadly plague sent to infect and kill off the Paris-based cell. And Sirocco is the wind sent to deliver the pestilence. Yet, Sirocco, who describes himself as '[t]he wind off the Sahara. Sandstorms. The hot wind that burns where it blows' (p. 151), proves as fickle as his code name. Sirocco turns the tables on his US contacts (one of whom is Mather Hawthorne, code name 'Salamander'), stages a real hijacking, contrives to assemble on the plane a group of people who form a complex network of partially hidden connections, and initiates his own, biochemical, Operation Black Death.

Salamander's Decameron tape documents the last 24 hours of this operation, in which Sirocco removes ten hostages from Flight 64 following its final landing in Tikrit and seals them in an underground bunker filled with sarin and mustard gas. Sirocco demands the release of one prisoner for each of the hostages, but Salamander's superiors do not wish to bargain. The tape, which Salamander has edited from Sirocco's live transmissions of the hostages' deaths, is his 'act of propitiation', his act of memorializing murders his government sought to cover up and to erase from the record (p. 281). The tape is also Salamander's 'indictment', for, he tells his psychiatrist, 'Sirocco is not the worst of it. The worst is *seeing* and not intervening to *stop*. The worst is that this happened under hi-tech surveillance. The worst is those who watched and monitored and voted: *accepted collateral damage*' (p. 273).

In a simple reading, Hospital's Sirocco is the contagious wind of terrorism blowing from the southern rim of the Mediterranean – from Algeria, Libya, Saudi Arabia. It is certainly no accident that Hospital names her bioterrorist 'Sirocco', and in doing so, she invokes the long history of linking pestilence with southerly winds and the ongoing tendency, as Philipp Sarasin puts it, for political language to 'equate political enemies or ethnic and "racial" aliens metaphorically with the threat of infection, or directly with infectious germs' (2008, p. 268). According to Sarasin, this historical use has expanded to encompass terrorism, which in turn has been equated with 'bioterrorism' since the end of the Clinton administration (2008, p. 268). So, is Hospital merely repeating highly problematic if not deeply injurious stereotypes of the West's 'enemies'? I would argue no, for Sirocco is a more complex and ambivalent figure. In masterminding the hijacking, Hospital's Sirocco not only releases an affective contagion that will lie almost dormant for 13 years, he also sets in train the unravelling of the conspiracy surrounding the hijacking. He sets in place a viral network of information, and where his is a contagion that reveals, the US government's cover up is one that conceals.

Moreover, Sirocco's biochemical weapons are precisely the ones the USA has supplied him with and trained him to use. As Salamander tells his students in his intelligence course, Camus 'might not have specifically foreseen hijackings, sarin, and mustard gas, but he knew the rodents and their toxins would reappear' (Hospital 2003, p. 270). Hospital's plague is a plague for the twenty-first century, and *Due Preparations* is an aerography of contagion, a novel that 'mak[es] the air conditions explicit' (Sloterdijk 2009 [2002], p. 84). Indeed, *Due Preparations* resonates with Peter Sloterdijk's recent work *Terror from the Air*, in which he links terrorism to an 'assault on the air'. Terrorism in the age of gas warfare exploits its victim's need to breathe, thereby making the victim complicit in the act of terror – 'an unwilling accomplice in his own annihilation' (2009 [2002], pp. 22–3).

Hospital's novel not only foregrounds the role of air in bioterrorism, but also the complex topologies of disease diffusion in an age of air travel. As the case of the 2002 SARS outbreak exemplifies, Siegfried's concerns about the potential for air travel to radically increase the diffusion of contagious disease (and, by his own extension, contagious ideas) were well founded. According to Tatem et al., although comparatively few deaths resulted from the SARS pandemic, SARS highlighted the links between air travel, the spread of infectious disease and the globalized economy, for the disjunct between the perceived risk of the poorly understood virus and its actual risk had harmful consequences for economic and social stability (2007, p. 302). In effect, concerns about SARS were equally, if not more, virulent than the virus itself. As Wald argues, germs and ideas are inseparable; 'communicable disease', she writes, 'is a function of social interactions', and air travel has only emphasized this:

> The unprecedented mobile carrier makes especially apparent the intricate networks of human existence and human interdependence. . . . The networks of daily existence have transformed the herd into an amorphous entity constituted through the airwaves as well as air travel. Communicable disease marks the increasing connections of the inhabitants of the global village as both biological and social, the communicability of germs and ideas "broadcast" together in an ever more elaborate network of human existence. (Wald 2008, p. 22)

In an essay about SARS and the urban environment, Bruce Braun also stresses the importance of a networked or topological understanding of contagious disease diffusion in the twenty-first century. According to Braun, epidemics such as SARS have once more brought to the fore a 'topological understanding of the body', not unlike that of the nineteenth century, which, he says, quoting Nikolas Rose (2007), located the clinical body 'within a series of extra-corporeal systems – flows of air, water, sewage, germs, contagion, familial influences, moral climates, and the like' (Braun 2008, p. 263). Paraphrasing Eugene Thacker (2005), Braun notes that ' "health security" is today increasingly about networks fighting networks' (Braun 2008, p. 261). And yet, Braun argues, we should avoid 'apocalyptic warnings of global pandemics' resulting from the speed-up effect of modern air travel. The question is not so black and white: 'To be sure', Braun writes, 'networks are "dangerous" . . . but the networks that compose urban lives also include elements that *mitigate* against a global pandemic' (2008, p. 261). Indeed, Thacker himself suggests that the 'best network counter-offensive' would be a benign virus, one that would 'inhabit the very air we breathe, vaccinating us against a potential threat that we did not know existed' (2005, p. n. pag.). This 'benign' airborne virus would in turn, he argues, require 'an increased emphasis on the "vital" properties of the network in itself', one that would blur the line between contagion and transmission (n. pag.).

Rethinking air in the context of contagion, then, requires that we consider ourselves to be part of a broader network that links the natural world with the social, the economic, the geographical and the cultural. In an Irigarayan sense, remembering air requires that we remember our place in the world, for as Kelly Oliver writes, Irigaray considers air to occupy a 'unique place among the elements in that it *is* place' and is 'constitutive of the whole of the world' (2001, p. 214; emph. added).

Despite the demise of miasma theory, air has remained as a vital, perhaps even vitalist, current in discourse about contagion. This current is particularly visible as it runs – though not unchanged – through Defoe, Mann, Camus and Hospital, all of whom overtly stage their remembrance of air. Both literally and metaphorically, the element of air has continued to form a bridge between physical and affective contagion. What has changed, however, is the moral judgement attached to contagion: in Hospital, Thacker and Braun, for instance, we see the emergence of a more ambivalent, topological contagion that is yet bound up with the element of air. In Hospital's *Due Preparations*, air becomes the invisible medium that expresses the impossibility of containing or quarantining information and that paradoxically makes visible hidden networks of meaning and distribution.

Air brings to the fore these connections, and it also requires that we remember the inseparability of germs and ideas. By tracking tropes of air and contagion through literary works that span some 300 years, and reading them in relation to theories of contagious disease, I have endeavoured to illustrate how air has continued, in cultural expression, to signify a more ambiguous, a more affective form of contagion. This form of contagion, which is increasingly being recognized in topological or networked understandings of contagious disease transmission, is one that is fundamentally bound up with information, with the spread of ideas and with viral networks.

The French *fin de siècle* and the Birth of Social Contagion Theory

As René Girard has noted, 'between the plague and social disorder there is a reciprocal affinity' (1974, p. 834), one that is starkly rendered both in classical myth and in contemporary plague narratives. When transposed into the social realm, the plague, Girard continues, becomes a 'transparent metaphor for a certain reciprocal violence' – that is, a metaphor whose efficacy is based on its underlying 'contagious character' and a form of violence predicated on *mimesis* and the contagiousness of mimetic desire, on processes of imitation and exemplification:

> The idea of contagiousness implies the presence of something harmful, which loses none of its virulence as it is rapidly transmitted from individual to individual. Such, of course, are bacteria in an epidemic; so is violence when it is *imitated*, either positively, whenever bad example makes the usual restraints inoperative, or negatively, when the efforts to stifle violence with violence achieve no more, ultimately, than an increase in the level of violence. Counterviolence turns out to be the same as violence. (Girard 1974, p. 837; emph. in original)

Researchers in the fields of social theory and social psychology have long been concerned with the question of how ideas and emotions – particularly negative ones – are transmitted among groups of people. Inevitably, this question has been framed in terms of contagion, imitation and example, just as it is by Girard. We need look no further than the 1980s and 1990s to see the most recent flourishing of the contagion metaphor in the social sciences. These two decades, for instance, witnessed the emergence and consolidation of phrases such as social contagion[1] and affective or emotional contagion[2] in psychology, and cultural contagion[3] in sociology and anthropology. Along with these terms came a clear emphasis on developing socio-psychological models for understanding social influence and so-called contagious behaviours.

If there is something of a *fin-de-siècle* anxiety evident in the disciplinary flurry around these apparently metaphorical uses of contagion at the close of the twentieth century, it was not for the first time. Indeed, this discursive formation contains clear echoes of a similar turn-of-the-century flowering of the contagion metaphor in the social sciences exactly a century before. In France, at the close of the nineteenth century, social theorists contributing to the nascent disciplines of sociology and psychology were turning to the concept of contagion – framed as 'moral' or 'imitative' contagion – to explain newly emergent social phenomena resulting from broader processes of modernization, urbanization and the development of mass media. As Daniel Beer explains, in the second half of the nineteenth century

> the very experience of modernization was generating population concentrations in the urban centers, which were bound together by the structures of a mass society and mass politics that only facilitated the spread of emotions and states of mind across large expanses of territory, often mediated by the printed word. Seen in these terms, both the creation of a modern unified society itself and the rise of mass politics were unavoidably beholden to dark and irrational human instincts. (Beer 2007, pp. 535–56)

For social scientists and psychologists in the mid- to late nineteenth century, connecting 'contagion' to the social provided a connotatively rich, even visceral, conceptual handle for explaining and modelling emerging and seemingly chaotic forms of crowd behaviour and social influence. By the late nineteenth century, those miasmatic theories that, as we saw in the previous chapter, drew causal links between the moral and the physical had largely been overturned by microbial germ theory. Conceptions of the human body, too, had been refashioned. As Christopher E. Forth writes,

> Against the relatively porous body posited by Enlightenment physicians, the biomedical body of the nineteenth century was conceived in rather different terms: the skin was no longer viewed as a passively permeable boundary, but was considered more or less sealed. After the discoveries of Pasteur many physicians conceded that while microbes could penetrate the body's surfaces, these minute bodies carried diseases rather than the moral qualities of others. Such conclusions, however, failed to explain how an idea could pass from person to person, animating entire groups as if their individual wills had been nullified by some external suggestion. . . . Despite the metaphorical nature of moral contagion, many physicians employed the language of microbiology to explain the dynamics of this special form of contamination. (Forth 2001, p. 63)

The nineteenth-century construction of 'moral' or 'imitative' contagion as a particular kind of malady was rhetorically persuasive on two competing levels. First, it tapped into the age-old Hippocratic theories of contagion predicated on moral pollution, whose vestiges – even though largely erased from medical discourse – were still circulating in contemporary cultural, religious and philosophical discourses. Second, and almost paradoxically, employing the rhetoric of contagion allowed the social sciences to partake of the scientific cachet enjoyed by the biomedical sciences and to posit social or moral contagion as a malady equal in significance, if not severity, to physical contagion.[4] For instance, in 1869, Paul Jolly, a medical doctor and member of the Paris Academy of Medicine, made one such case for the effective equivalency of moral contagion to physical contagion. In an article published in the medical journal *L'Union Médicale*, Jolly contends that imitation is a 'true contagion' and a conceptual counterpart to physical contagion (1869, p. 369). Where physical contagions, such as smallpox, have their origin in the viruses that transmit them, imitative contagion has its origin in example. Just as diseases remain dormant within the body until they develop at the slightest cause, so too are passions kept in check by reason until awakened by the effect of imitation. Moral contagion, Jolly is at pains to point out, is not simply an empty image, a hollow expression, a mere metaphor; moral contagion is, rather, the 'representation of a physiological fact of the utmost importance in the aetiology of certain [moral] diseases' (1869, p. 369).[5]

The London riots of 2011 provide a telling example of how little the discourse surrounding moral contagion has changed in nearly 150 years. Newspaper reports stressed the 'contagious' nature of the rioting, *The Economist* claimed that 'Britain has a history of contagious rioting' ('The Fire This Time' 2011), and the *Australian* ran an article with the headline 'Mob Mentality Turns Contagious' (O'Neill and Hamilton 2011, p. 13). In an article on the riots for the *Guardian* newspaper, epidemiologist Gary Slutkin makes an argument not far removed from Jolly's. Violence, Slutkin argues, 'is an epidemic – one that behaves with the characteristics of an infectious disease' (2011, p. 18). Where Girard claims contagion (characterized as the plague) is a *transparent* metaphor for violence, both Jolly and Slutkin deny social contagion any figural status. Slutkin states, even more forcefully than Jolly, that saying 'that violence is an epidemic is not a metaphor; it is a scientific fact' (2011, p. 18). 'To review the events of the past week in London through this lens', he continues,

> we see a grievance (citizens upset that a civilian has been shot by law enforcement officials) that occurs within in the context of frustration and general

dissatisfaction (poverty, unemployment) serving as the precipitating cause for an outbreak of violence. These conditions set the stage for an outbreak in the same way that poor sanitation, overcrowding, and contaminated water set the stage for cholera. Once the event is triggered, it moves from person to person, block to block, town to town. This pattern is not unique to London: it is evident in past riots throughout the US, from Cincinnati to Crown Heights in New York to the Los Angeles riots ignited by the Rodney King beating. (Slutkin 2011, p. 18)

Slutkin's argument in many respects replays those made by nineteenth-century physicians and psychologists who were increasingly interested in the seemingly contagious workings of crowd psychology. As Beer argues, in the late nineteenth century, an 'epidemiological construction of mass psychology developed in parallel with the model of bacteriological epidemiology' (2007, p. 541), and this socio- or psycho-epidemiological model, as Jolly's article exemplifies, was evident both in medical and social-psychological discourse surrounding what was, at the close of the nineteenth century, variously termed moral, imitative and mental contagion.[6] Alexandre Métreaux argues that this 'epidemiological approach is historically interesting because it sheds light upon the role and the limitation of metaphors in an emergent discipline such as crowd psychology' (1982, p. 285). What I wish to focus on in examining this epidemiological model are its rhetorical supports, which, I will argue, invoke and hold in tension both miasmatic/affective and microbial/physical theories of contagion.

Social contagion at the *fin de siècle*: Le Bon, Tarde and Sighele

The social contagion theory that emerged in Europe at the nineteenth-century *fin de siècle* is inextricably tied to the emergence of a distinctive mass psychology based on 'a model of hypnotic suggestion' (Jonsson 2006, p. 73) and is virtually synonymous with the names Gabriel Tarde and Gustave Le Bon. Although the idea of the crowd is avowedly central to the development of social contagion theory, this chapter will not provide a systematic history of crowd psychology in late nineteenth-century France – for this, readers are directed to the work of Robert A. Nye (1975), Susanna Barrows (1981) and Jaap van Ginneken (1985, 1992). Rather, this and the following chapter will provide a genealogy, of sorts, of social contagion as it is reflected in and develops out of two interlinked formations of the contagion metaphor.

One of these formations is the term 'moral contagion', which becomes prevalent in nineteenth-century sociological discourse, gradually making way for less value-laden formations, such as 'mental', 'affective' and 'social' contagion in the twentieth century. The other is the concept of the 'contagion of example' (the focus of Chapter 4), which in nineteenth-century sociology predictably accompanies invocations of 'moral' or 'imitative' contagion, but which also has a history traceable to the sixteenth century at least. The ubiquity, long history and ultimate significance of the phrase 'contagion of example' has been overlooked in the literature on social contagion theory, and I argue the phrase is one that, in foregrounding the dual processes of imitation and exemplification, provides a link between 'moral' and 'social' contagion. In the following chapter, I will also argue that the endurance of the 'contagion of example' phrase provides a connection with those classical theories of mimesis and metaphor outlined in Chapter 1, as well as with early modern theological debates over the nature of sin. In this genealogy, then, I again wish to draw out the shift from moral to affective or thought contagion, this time as it appears in nineteenth- and twentieth-century social theory. Moreover, in this and the following chapter, I want to articulate the unexamined lines of influence that connect nineteenth- and twentieth-century social contagion theory to a line of philosophical thought about the nature of imitation that runs through such thinkers as Cicero, Lucius Annaeus Seneca, Plutarch, Tacitus, St Augustine, Erasmus, Jean-Jacques Rousseau, Edward Gibbon and Edmund Burke.

Where to begin, then? No genealogy can escape the arbitrary in selecting its starting point, and this one will be no exception to the rule. It will also fit the standard mould of studies of social contagion theory and crowd psychology in two ways. First, it will follow convention by singling out the 1890s as a decisive moment in their interwoven histories. Second, it will focus on a particular triumvirate of social researchers and proto social psychologists – Gustave Le Bon (1841–1931), Gabriel Tarde (1843–1904) and Scipio Sighele (1868–1913) – whose combined work is generally considered to introduce a form of social contagion theory (though not one used the exact phrase 'social contagion') as the basis for a psychology of crowd behaviour.

Of the three writers I will also, quite conventionally, begin with Le Bon – the great scientific 'popularizer'[7] – and his 1895 work *Psychologie des foules* (translated into English as *The Crowd: A Study of the Popular Mind* in 1896). Following

Le Bon, I will turn to Tarde and the young Italian criminologist Sighele, whose influence has regularly been overlooked in favour of (and, arguably, by) both Tarde and Le Bon, his older, more established French counterparts.

Le Bon, the contagious crowd and the popularization of crowd psychology

As van Ginneken points out, the medically trained amateur sociologist Gustave Le Bon is often erroneously represented within histories of social psychology as the lone founding father of crowd psychology (1985, p. 375). For instance, in their review of the social-psychology literature on contagion, David A. Levy and Paul R. Nail credit Le Bon with first using the term 'contagion' in regard to psychology and social influence (1993, p. 237). As we shall see, this is at once both incorrect and entirely in keeping with Le Bon's own self-aggrandizing propaganda on the matter. Le Bon was, in Métreaux's words, 'undoubtedly the most outspoken, dogmatic and colorful representative of crowd psychology' and one who 'succeeded at building up an effective network of communication outside that of the official social sciences' (1982, p. 280).

In keeping with this portrait of Le Bon as a 'colourful' figure, in *Psychologie des foules*, Le Bon has furnished us with some of the most dramatic and portentous statements about social contagion. According to Le Bon, '[i]deas, sentiments, emotions, and beliefs possess in crowds a contagious power as intense as that of microbes' (2002 [1895], p. 78).[8] Moreover, in a crowd, he claims, 'every sentiment and act is contagious, and contagious to such a degree that an individual readily sacrifices his personal interest to the collective interest' (Le Bon 2002 [1895], p. 7).[9] This tendency, he argues, goes against basic human nature and is apparent only in the social susceptibility generated by the crowd. Crowds can be stirred up to do virtually anything – 'to pillage a palace, or to die in defence of a stronghold or a barricade' – through the act of 'rapid suggestion', and specifically by way of 'example [which is] the most powerful in its effect' (2002 [1895], p. 77).[10] Crowds, Le Bon maintains, are guided 'by examples not by arguments' (2002 [1895], p. 79),[11] so much so that individual reason makes way for mass contagious imitation. Indeed, according to Le Bon, imitation is 'in reality a mere effect of contagion' and this 'mechanism' of contagion is, in turn, 'so powerful a force that even the sentiment of personal interest disappears under its action' (2002 [1895], pp. 79, 80).[12] Just one example may suffice to give a sense of Le Bon's self-promoting claims to be the originator of these concepts. Following his statement that imitation is 'a mere effect of contagion', he continues, 'Having shown its influence elsewhere, I shall confine myself to reproducing what I said on the subject fifteen years ago. My remarks have since been developed by other writers in recent publications' (2002 [1895], p. 79).

Historians of crowd psychology now tend to agree that Le Bon was at best a popularizer and synthesizer of existing work and at worst a scientific 'vulgarizer' and plagiarist. When *Psychologie des foules* appeared in 1895, it became an immediate bestseller, and, as van Ginneken notes, it has been described as 'one of the best-selling scientific books in history' (1985, p. 375). Jan Goldstein has, more bluntly, called *Psychologie des foules* a 'best-selling work of scientific vulgarization', in which Le Bon 'pronounced his era "the era of crowds" and provided a rambling description of the crowd mentality, which included among its components the eradication of the individuality and sense of moral responsibility of the crowd's members and the establishment of a psychological homogeneity through "contagion"' (1984, p. 182).

Although, as Nye points out, Le Bon's 'distrust of democratic politics' and excoriating critique of the French Republic was a point of commonality among the *fin-de-siècle* crowd psychologists (1975, p. 62), Susanna Barrows calls Le Bon 'a precocious and enduring pessimist' in his portrayal of the crowd as an irrational mass completely under sway of social or moral contagion (1981, p. 162). J. S. McClelland goes even further, arguing that Le Bon was not only a 'publicist' and a pessimist but also, effectively, a plagiarist:

> It did not worry Le Bon that the psychology of the crowd existed in at least two separate and competing versions in the works of Scipio Sighele and Gabriel Tarde. Le Bon simply took the most pessimistic things that others had to say about the crowd and out of them built a theory which was his own only in the sense that most of the nuances had been lost in the editing. (McClelland 1989, pp. 197–8)

Le Bon's 'borrowings' from his contemporaries certainly did not go unnoticed even in the 1890s, and, as van Ginneken points out, 'most histories of social psychology fail to mention that Le Bon's primacy was immediately contested' (1985, p. 375). Le Bon's most direct challenger was Scipio Sighele, who claimed that in *Psychologie des foules* Le Bon had 'pirated' his own work of criminal psychology *La folla delinquente*, published in 1891, and had used the same examples as the late French historian and literary critic Hippolyte Taine (1828–93) (van Ginneken 1985, p. 375).[13] Tarde, to whom I shall now turn, was apparently less inclined to publicly contest Le Bon, but there is no doubt that Le Bon also 'borrowed' greatly from Tarde's works.[14]

Tarde, imitation and the contagion of example

When we consider that the 1890s debate over the origins of crowd psychology partly hinged on who came up with the idea that contagious imitation is a fundamental and inescapable social reality, the debate itself does tend to take on an ironic hue. Tarde himself, as Terry N. Clark writes, emphasized that knowledge 'advances in small increments, and even the most creative discoveries are heavily dependent on antecedent ideas. The most outstanding inventions are those which recombine already acquired bits of knowledge into highly original syntheses' (1969, p. 25). Le Bon's shortcomings, critical studies seem to suggest, stem from the fact that his synthesis was simply not original enough and that he was too willing to take full credit where very little indeed was due. Tarde, too, was not one to copiously and meticulously cite sources and influences,[15] but his synthesis of existing work and his contribution to crowd psychology, those same critical studies suggest, were highly original.

By the time he published *Les lois de l'imitation* in 1890, Tarde had already established a reputation within France both as a criminologist and a sociologist, and he had cultivated this reputation while fulfilling his professional duties as *juge d'instruction* or examining magistrate of Sarlat, the French town in which he was born. By 1890, Tarde had held the position of magistrate for two decades, and soon after the publication of *Les lois de l'imitation* he moved to Paris to become director of the legal statistics bureau in the French Ministry of Justice. It was not until 1900 – only four years before his death – that Tarde would take up his first full-time academic position, as Chair of Modern Philosophy in the Collège de France.

As numerous scholars have noted, Tarde's developing social theory was strongly tied to and influenced by his professional legal practice, and his anti-deterministic sociology exhibited a strong and assertive independence from the dominant positivist and biologistic theories of his day. What Auguste Comte and Herbert Spencer had failed to detect, in Tarde's view, was that all social action relies upon a fundamental phenomenon: the innate human urge to imitate. In his *Les lois de l'imitation*, Tarde describes imitation as an 'elementary fact' (*fait élémentaire*) and an 'elementary social act' (*acte social élémentaire*) operating alongside invention (1903 [1890], pp. 185, 144). Tarde bluntly states

> man is wrong in thinking that he imitates because he wishes to. For this very will to imitate has been handed down through imitation. Before imitating the act of another we begin by feeling the need from which this act proceeds, and we feel it precisely as we do only because it has been suggested to us. (Tarde 1903 [1890], p. 193)

Imitation, for Tarde, underpins social action; indeed, he argues, society *began* 'on the day when one man first copied another' (1903 [1890], p. 28). These imitations propagate by way of a process of *contagion*, and those examples or acts that more readily elicit imitation, Tarde describes as *contagious*. 'We see', he writes, that 'individual initiatives and their contagious imitations, have accomplished everything, socially' (1903 [1890], pp. 122–3).

Tarde offers little or no commentary on his use of the term 'contagion' in *Les lois de l'imitation*.[16] Unlike Jolly, he makes no explicit argument for the equivalency of his imitative contagion to physical contagion and makes no comment on its figural (or otherwise) status. Tarde also makes no reference to the established literature on moral contagion; indeed, the only reference he provides for his use of the term 'contagion' is an oblique and a curiously positioned one. In the table of contents, the reader is informed that the final section of chapter three is devoted to 'An idea of Taine's. The contagion of example and suggestion. Analogies between the social and the hypnotic state. Great men. Intimidation is a nascent social state' (1903 [1890], p. xxvi). The 'Taine' Tarde refers to here is the same Taine Sighele accused Le Bon of plagiarizing. His idea, which Tarde draws from Taine's 1870 book *De l'intelligence*, is that the 'brain is a *repeating* organ' (Tarde 1903 [1890], p. 74; emph. in original).[17]

Tarde's reference to Taine is, on the surface, part of his developing argument that in understanding how society works, sociology must 'yield' to psychology and take an interest in physiology (1903 [1890], p. 74). That is, if sociology can accept that imitation underpins social action, then we also need to understand *how* the brain imitates. However, there is also a strange elision here between this 'idea of Taine's' and what the table of contents indicates will follow: a discussion of 'the contagion of example and suggestion'. For, more recently than *De l'intelligence*, Taine had famously characterized the revolutionary impulse as dangerously 'contagious' in volume two (*La révolution*) of his still-in-progress magnum opus, *Les origines de la France contemporaine* (1876–94). In book one of *La révolution* – a diatribe against revolutionary fervour and popular uprising – Taine describes the birth of the French Revolution as a kind of 'spontaneous anarchy'. The unfortunate origins of this anarchy could be traced to the food shortages caused by the terrible winter of 1788–1789, but its ultimate causes, Taine writes, lay in the contagious workings of the 'violent and overexcited crowd' (1878b, p. 1).

In crowds, according to Taine, 'the passions . . . become intensified through their mutual interaction', leading to 'a state of frenzy, from which nothing can issue but dizzy madness and rage' (1878b, p. 101). These revolutionary crowds, he contends, are particularly susceptible to example, and within them, unscrupulous leaders come to the fore to 'march ahead and set the example in destruction' (Taine 1878b, p. 14). In this, Taine continues, 'the example is contagious: the beginning was the craving for bread, the end is murder and incendiarism' (1878b, p. 14).[18] Indeed, Taine sarcastically points out, the advent of the new Constitution calls for a new kind of leader, one who is characterized by a 'contagious' enthusiasm, a lack of scruples and an abundance of presumption. Ideally suited for this role of infecting the populace, he continues, are 'the village attorney, the unfrocked monk, the "intruding" and excommunicated curé, and above all, the journalist and the local orator, who, for the first time in his life, finds that he has an audience, applause, influence and a future before him' (Taine 1878b, p. 210).

In book two of *La révolution*, published three years later in 1881, Taine makes an even stronger connection between revolution, moral and physical contagion, when he argues that revolution is a 'disease' (*maladie*) with an 'epidemic and contagious character' (*caractère épidémique et contagieux*), which in the case of the French Revolution was spread, in part, by the Jacobin political clubs (Taine 1881b, p. 234). 'The body', he continues

> has its epidemic, its contagious diseases; the mind has the same; the revolutionary malady is one of them. It appears throughout the country at the same time; each infected point infects others. In each city, in each borough, the club is a centre of inflammation which disorganises the sound parts; and the *example* of each disorganised centre spreads afar like a miasm. Everywhere the same fever, delirium, and convulsions mark the presence of the same virus. That virus is the Jacobin dogma. (Taine 1881b, p. 234; emph. added)[19]

At the time of writing *Les lois de l'imitation*, Tarde had certainly read Taine's history of the French Revolution; indeed, Tarde directly cites *La révolution* in both his earliest book-length study, *La criminalité comparée* (1886), and in his second book, *La philosophie pénale* (1890), which was published the same year as *Les lois de l'imitation*. At base, in *Les lois de l'imitation* we can see Taine's version of contagious and imitative crowd behaviour stripped of its overtly negative revolutionary overtones, generalized, and blended with the sociological theories of Alfred Espinas and Herbert Spencer to become Tarde's essential 'social fact'.

In Tarde's formulation, some acts and behaviours are certainly more contagious – in the sense of inviting or even demanding replication – than others. Thirst, Tarde posits, is more contagious in an imitative sense than hunger (but perhaps less contagious than sexual desire), while yawning is more contagious than sneezing or coughing (1903 [1890], pp. 194–5). Following the logic through, he adds,

> All passions and needs for luxury are more contagious than simple appetites and primitive needs. But shall we say, as to passions, that admiration, confidence, love, and resignation are superior in this respect to contempt, distrust, hatred, and envy? In general, yes, otherwise society would not endure. For the same reason, and in spite of frequent epidemics of panic, hope is certainly more catching than terror. Indolence is likewise more so than ambition and avarice, the spirit of saving than avidity. And this is very fortunate for the peace of society. Is courage more catching than cowardice? I am much less certain of this. (Tarde 1903 [1890], p. 196)

Yet, the contagiousness of an example not only inheres in the act, but is also affected by the relative *prestige* of the person – the exemplary figure – who performs the act. Imitation proceeds, according to Tarde, '*from the inner to the outer man*' (1903 [1890], p. 199; emph. in original), but is also subject to external, top-down forces. In feudal or monarchical systems, the aristocrat's prestige made their example (whether good or bad) ever more contagious, ever more liable to be imitated. In the post-Revolutionary, increasingly urbanized France of the late nineteenth century, however, the focus must move away from the top-down authority exerted by the aristocrat to the dispersed network of relations formed by the crowd. As Tarde writes,

> The march of imitation from top to bottom still goes on, but the inequality which it implies has changed in character. Instead of an aristocratic, intrinsically organic inequality, we have a democratic inequality, of an entirely social origin, which we may call inequality if we wish, but which is really a reciprocity of invariably impersonal prestiges, alternating from individual to individual and from profession to profession. In this way, the field of imitation has been constantly growing and freeing itself from heredity. (Tarde 1903 [1890], pp. 367–8)

But, Tarde cautions, this does not mean 'modern man' is freer than his feudal or pre-revolutionary counterpart. At base, Tarde maintains, betraying his allegiance to the hypnotic method, '*society is imitation and imitation is a kind of somnambulism*' (1903 [1890], p. 87; emph. in original), and modernity and urbanization have done little to change this fundamental reality. Modernization has, Tarde grants, brought about a revolution in human volition, but one that is less revolutionary than we might think: the 'passive obedience to ancestral orders, customs, and influence' characteristic of the previous regime has at the end of the nineteenth century, he argues, not so much been 'replaced' as 'neutralised' by the individual subject's 'submission to the pressure, advice, and suggestions of contemporaries' (1903 [1890], p. 246). 'The modern man', Tarde explains, merely 'flatters himself that he is making a free choice of the propositions that are made to him, whereas, in reality, the one that he welcomes and follows is the one that meets his pre-existent wants and desires, wants and desires which are the outcome of his habits and customs, of his whole past of obedience' (1903 [1890], p. 246).

Nevertheless, in Tarde's account, urbanization does offer the possibility for further invention and innovation, because 'the nervous plasticity and openness to impressions of adults in cities' allows them to look outward and to 'model themselves upon new types brought in from outside' (1903 [1890], p. 248). As Jussi Kinnunen puts it, in Tarde's diffusionist model, the 'penetration' of novel inventions is what enables 'major social change' (1996, p. 433). Even though their imitation is bound to their 'whole past of obedience', the urbanized subject is both more open to imitating novel ideas or examples and more able to become, in turn, a contagious example, communicating their idea to their contemporaries via a concatenating and exponential process of contagious imitation.

Tarde's theory of social influence as the imitation of contagious examples had an immediate and significant but relatively short-lived impact on European sociology at the turn of the century. As we shall soon see, the publication of *Les lois de l'imitation* in 1890 influenced both Sighele's *La folla delinquente*, published in Italy the following year, and Le Bon's *Psychologie des foules*, published five years later. In 1903, the year before Tarde's death, the first English translation of *Les lois de l'imitation* appeared. Yet, following his death, Tarde's influence weakened and, as Kinnunen explains, there was a 'scientific discontinuity in the field of sociological diffusion research for nearly forty years' (1996, p. 436). Kinnunen points to three notable factors that gave rise to this 'discontinuity': a shift in sociology's focus to the field of communication; a lack of methodological tools to support analysis of social diffusion; and the rise to prominence of Émile Durkheim, who 'became *the* authority in the field of sociology in France' and who treated Tarde as his 'whipping boy' (Kinnunen 1996, pp. 436, 431; emph. in original).[20]

Close to a century after his death, however, Tarde's work – particularly his 1890 *Les lois de l'imitation* and his 1893 essay 'Monadologie et sociologie'[21] – began to receive renewed interest, this time from cultural theorists interested in Tarde's seemingly prescient micro-level network analysis of social and cultural influence. In the later twentieth century, a 'New Tarde' (Toews 2003) emerged, as his epidemiological approach to 'microsociology' was taken up by, among others, Gilles Deleuze and Félix Guattari, Bruno Latour and Nigel Thrift. Latour and Thrift turn to Tarde in framing their respective 'actor-network' and 'non-representational' theories, and Tarde is also considered a forefather of Richard Dawkins's meme theory,[22] which I will deal with in greater detail in Chapter 5.

As early as 1969, Deleuze began the work of reclaiming Tarde from Durkheim's shadow. In *Difference and Repetition*, Deleuze argues that Tarde's greatest contribution is that he introduces a 'microsociology' (2004 [1968], p. 158), and, by 1980, Deleuze and Guattari were claiming that Tarde's

> long-forgotton [sic] work has assumed new relevance with the influence of American sociology, in particular microsociology. It had been quashed by Durkheim and his school (in polemics similar to and as harsh as Cuvier's against Geoffroy Saint-Hilaire). Durkheim's preferred objects of study were the great collective representations, which are generally binary, resonant, and overcoded. Tarde countered that collective representations presuppose exactly what needs explaining, namely, "the similarity of millions of people". That is why Tarde was interested instead in the world of detail, or of the infinitesimal: the little imitations, oppositions, and inventions constituting an entire realm of subrepresentative matter. Tarde's best work was his analyses of a minuscule bureaucratic innovation, or a linguistic innovation, etc. The Durkheimians answered that what Tarde did was psychology or inter-psychology, not sociology. But that is true only in appearance, as a first approximation: a microimitation does seem to occur between two individuals. (Deleuze and Guattari 1987 [1980], pp. 218–19)

More recently, Latour has argued that sociology 'could have been an even more relevant discipline' had it 'inherited more from Tarde' (2005, p. 14). Tarde's radical challenge to sociology (with its inherited Durkheimian legacy), according to Latour, is that where Durkheim maintains 'we "should treat social facts as a thing"', Tarde instead 'says that "all things are society", and any phenomenon is a social fact' (2002, p. 120). Further, Latour claims that Tarde's microsociology can essentially be considered an 'early ancestor' of Latour's own actor-network theory (or ANT) (2005, p. 15). Tarde's formula of '[a]gency plus influence and imitation', Latour argues, 'is exactly what has been called, albeit with different words, an actor-network' (2002, p. 119).

More recently again, Nigel Thrift explains in great detail why Tarde's work has offered itself so readily to theorists such as Deleuze and Guattari and to network-based, material-semiotic theories such as Latour's ANT and his own non-representational theory. In particular, Thrift explains,

> Tarde's work suggests the possibility of resurrecting an epidemiological model which is based on processes of imitative contagion, not least because the spread of feelings (through gesticulation, bodily movements, motor co-ordinations and repetitions, as well as all the technologies of the body that now exist) is such fertile ground for thinking about mental contagion. (Thrift 2008, p. 231)

Tarde's epidemiological model was certainly innovative and influential, and Tarde himself was, as Thrift puts it, 'an original in his emphasis on understanding imitation as a process of snowballing mimetic desire, as reverberating circles of influence, rather than as simple mechanical copying' (2008, p. 232). Indeed, Matthew Potolsky describes Tarde as being 'among the most important psychological theorists of mimesis in the later nineteenth century' (2006, p. 117). However, Tarde was not the first to connect contagion to social influence; furthermore, in the early 1890s he was also not the only social scientist positing an epidemiological model of crowd behaviour.

Sighele and the nineteenth-century pre-history of social contagion theory

In 1891, at the age of 23, the Italian criminologist Scipio Sighele published his first and major book, a study of the criminal tendencies of crowds titled *La folla delinquente*. Sighele is a name not often cited beyond dedicated historical studies of crowd psychology and, unlike the work of Tarde and Le Bon, Sighele's *La folla delinquente* has never been translated into English.[23] Yet, within a year of its original publication, *La folla* would be published in French as *La foule criminelle*[24] by Félix Alcan, who had published Tarde's *Les lois de l'imitation* in 1890 and who would publish Le Bon's *Psychologie des foules* only three years later in 1895. Sighele was certainly familiar with Tarde's work, and in *La folla* he cites Tarde's two major studies published the previous year: *Les lois de l'imitation* and *La philosophie penale*.

Where Tarde provides virtually no historical context for his epidemiological model of imitation, in *La folla* Sighele takes care to plot out the history of 'moral contagion' in socio-psychological research. He remarks that many writers have observed how, at times, imitation takes on 'acute' forms, both in its intensity and the extent of its spread. Moreover, Sighele adds, the apparently voluntary nature of these acute forms of imitation has led these writers to attempt to explain the phenomenon using what he calls the 'hypothesis of moral contagion' (*l'hypothèse de la contagion morale*) (1892, p. 39). In an extended footnote, Sighele introduces his reader to a roll call of writers who have framed contemporary discussion of moral contagion, including François de La Rochefoucauld (1664), Prosper Lucas (1833), Louis Florentin Calmeil (1845), Alexandre Brierre de Boismont (1856), Paul Jolly (1869), N. Ebrard (1870), Prosper Despine (1870), Paul Moreau de Tours (1875) and Paul Aubry (1887), all of whom affirmed a parity between moral and physical contagion.[25]

Leaving aside for the moment Sighele's passing mention of the seventeenth-century writer of maxims, La Rochefoucauld,[26] the earliest cited work is Lucas's 1833 doctoral dissertation presented to the Paris Faculty of Medicine, a pamphlet titled *De l'imitation contagieuse ou de la propagation sympathique des névroses et des monomanies*. Lucas, whose later work on heredity would influence Charles Darwin's *Origin of Species* (1859), argued in his thesis for the recognition of a form of 'imitative contagion'.

Medicine, Lucas argues, has come late to the question of human imitation, and he notes that the ancients, poets, historians and philosophers had all attempted to explain the mysterious phenomenon before doctors turned their attention to it (1833, p. 3). Imitation, Lucas continues, is a natural, inherently human, phenomenon that can be divided into two general categories: mimicry and sympathetic imitation. Where mimicry (*phénomènes d'imitation mimique*) is voluntary, physiological or natural, sympathetic imitation (*phénomènes d'imitation sympathique*) is involuntary and potentially pathological and morbid (1833, p. 4). Underlying both forms of imitation – but with particularly harmful effects in the latter – is the power of example. In the case of a suicide epidemic, for instance, Lucas maintains, contagious imitation can always be traced to an originating example, though he is careful to explain that the contagiousness of the example depends on the susceptibility or predisposition of the person who copies it (1833, 30, 55). At base, as Goldstein explains, Lucas's theory of moral contagion relied on

> the "communication" of the "example": a pattern of heightened nervous vibra-
> tion in one individual would set up a corresponding pattern in other individuals
> in proximity. But such a gross formulation required qualification. Just as some
> individuals had a natural immunity to epidemic physical illnesses (again the
> analogy between moral and physical contagion), so some resisted the ravages of
> contagious mental and nervous diseases and did not succumb to the "example"
> even when exposed to it. The decisive factor, or so Lucas asserted, was the degree
> of "similitude" between the "example" and the potential sympathetic imitators.
> (Goldstein 1984, p. 204)

We might add to Sighele's list of influences Étienne Esquirol's *Maladies mentales* (1838), a work that Sighele cites in *La folla*, but that is not included in his foot-note overview. Here, Esquirol maintains that all nervous illnesses are spread 'by a form of moral contagion and by force of imitation' (1838, p. 247).[27] Influenced by Esquirol, Calmeil – to return to Sighele's literature review – also employs the phrase 'contagion morale' to describe particular forms of mental illness in his 1845 book *De la folie* (1845, p. 151). A decade later, the noted psychiatrist Brierre de Boismont published a major work on suicide, namely *Du suicide et de la folie suicide*, in which he maintained that suicide was propagated by way of imitation, itself a 'sort of moral contagion' (1856, p. 610). Further, Brierre de Boismont argued that, along with poverty and laziness, the contagion of exam-ple (*la contagion de l'exemple*) was one of the most powerful causes of this moral contagion (1856, p. 105).

In 1870, in a pamphlet titled *De la contagion morale*, Despine proposed a general 'law' of moral contagion based on the contagion of example (*contagion des . . . exemples*) (1870, pp. 4–5). Also in 1870, and following Brierre's lead, Ebrard claimed that suicide – propagated by imitation and the 'epidemic' power of example – was the gravest of all the age's moral illnesses (1870, pp. 208–13, 217). Suicide was, Ebrard claimed, a 'social evil' that had reached epidemic pro-portions: 'in a word, it was a *malaria*, a new kind of moral disease of our century' (1870, pp. 83–4; emph. in original).[28]

Ebrard's claim was soon followed and echoed by Moreau de Tours in his thesis titled *De la contagion du suicide – à propos de l'épidemie actuelle* (1875), and both works clearly influenced Émile Durkheim's later and more famous study of suicide, namely *Le suicide: étude de sociology* (1897), in which Durkheim attempts to distinguish between 'moral epidemics' and 'moral contagions' (Durkheim 1962 [1897], p. 132). The most recent author cited in Sighele's literature review of this nascent social contagion theory is Moreau de Tours's student[29] Aubry, who in 1887 published a treatise on the 'contagion of murder,' a phenomenon that, he maintained, 'exists without contest' (Aubry 1887, p. 13). Aubry's *La contagion du meurtre* is also notable in that it provides an overview of the literature on contagion, one that likely formed the basis of Sighele's own genealogy of moral contagion.[30]

An eighteenth-century precursor: Philippe Hecquet and the concept of 'moral contagion'

Most twentieth-century histories of crowd psychology if they look beyond Le Bon do not then look beyond Prosper Lucas in tracing the emergence of 'moral contagion' as a concept and as a phrase.[31] In this, they appear to follow early commentators, such as Aubry (1887), Sighele (1891) and Durkheim (1962 [1897]), who tend to treat Lucas as a point of origin. In most accounts, then, the phrase 'moral contagion' is a nineteenth-century coinage, traceable to the early 1830s and becoming a 'vogue' term by the 1890s. Goldstein, however, argues that moral contagion in medical discourse has its roots in the eighteenth rather than the nineteenth century, developing 'not through systematic investigation or abstract speculation but in the course of the contemporary interpretation and subsequent reinterpretation of a series of events which came to be regarded as salient and exemplary instances of the phenomenon' (1984, p. 185). These 'prototypal events', Goldstein continues

> are the affair of the Jansenist convulsionaries in Paris in the 1720s and 1730s; an outbreak of convulsions in a Haarlem orphanage, treated and reported by the great eighteenth-century Dutch physician Hermann Boerhaave; the vogue of the mesmerist *baquets* in Paris in the 1780s; and an event from ancient history which became a justificatory touchstone for eighteenth- and early nineteenth-century medical men – a wave of suicides among the women of Miletus, as described in Plutarch's *Moralia*. (Goldstein 1984, p. 185)

The continued repetition of and allusion to these instances of moral contagion in the medical literature, Goldstein argues, meant that they 'became a medical tradition, a formulaic rehearsal of verities' (1984, p. 185). By connecting contemporary outbreaks of moral contagion to similar ones documented in ancient texts, moral contagion could thus be seen to be an age-old problem rather than a completely novel one. Plutarch's account of the inexplicable mass suicide of the Milesian women could be placed on an historical continuum of moral contagion and, to some degree, medicalized, its 'miasmatic' underpinnings brought up to date. And yet, on the other hand, classical themes could just as easily be read into accounts of these more contemporary moral contagions, and, writing in the late nineteenth century, Erwin Rohde did not fail to notice their 'Dionysian' nature:

> Bacchic dance-worship and its exaltation reminds us of the phenomena which have attended similar religious epidemics such as have in more recent times occasionally burst out and overflowed whole countries. We may in particular recall to mind the accounts which we have of the violent and widespread dance-madness which, soon after the severe mental and physical shock suffered by Europe in the Black Death of the fourteenth century, broke out on the Rhine and for centuries could not be entirely stamped out. Those who were attacked by the fever were driven by an irresistible impulse to dance. The bystanders, in convulsions of sympathetic and imitative fury joined in the whirling dance themselves. Thus the malady was spread by contagion [*breitete sich das Leiden epidemisch*], and soon whole companies of men, women, and girls, wandered dancing through the country. (Rohde 2001 [1890–94], p. 284)

To return to Goldstein's argument, in looking beyond Lucas and in tracing moral contagion into the eighteenth century, Goldstein introduces a new contender for the claim to inventing or, perhaps more correctly, medicalizing the concept of moral contagion. This contender is Philippe Hecquet, a notable French physician who in 1722 was dean of the Faculty of Medicine of Paris. In 1733, Hecquet published a brochure, titled *Naturalisme des convulsions dans les maladies de l'épidémie convulsionnaire*, on the recent outbreak of Jansenist convulsions at the Saint-Médard cemetery. By 'invok[ing] the model of the "epidemic" and of "contagion"', Goldstein contends, Hecquet 'became the first formulator of the theory of moral contagion' (1984, p. 187).

Christopher E. Forth somewhat misreads Goldstein's thesis when he paraphrases it in his 2001 essay on moral contagion. 'The term "moral contagion"', Forth writes, citing Goldstein, 'was first coined in 1733 by Philippe Hecquet, a French physician who used the analogy of an epidemic to explain an incident of collective religious convulsions' (2001, p. 62). In fairness, Goldstein does not state that Hecquet 'coined' the term 'moral contagion'. And certainly, Hecquet did not coin it (or, for that matter, use it in his 1733 pamphlet).[32] As we will see in the following chapter, the phrase has at least one precedent, appearing as it does (as '*contagio morum*') more than two centuries earlier in Desiderius Erasmus's sixteenth-century *Adages*.

Further, Goldstein takes care not to claim that the phenomenon of moral contagion is an eighteenth-century discovery without precedent. Indeed, as Goldstein points out, Lucas himself 'stressed that observation of the phenomenon of moral contagion was ancient; what was recent was the explanation of that phenomenon by science' (1984, p. 203). Where commentators on social contagion theory or the history of crowd psychology tend to be content with treating moral contagion as a nineteenth- or, at the outset, eighteenth-century invention, Goldstein does acknowledge there is a pre-history to the concept, and one that Lucas also affirms, however casually. Yet, Goldstein too is content to leave it there, summing up this pre-history in a passing comment.

Certainly for the purposes of providing a contained and coherent history of moral contagion in medical/psychological discourse, focusing almost exclusively on the French *fin de siècle* and treating Hecquet or even Lucas as a natural starting point is perfectly defensible, and my intent is not to propose an earlier 'originator' who has been overlooked in the literature to date. I do, however, want to begin the work of tracing the pre-eighteenth-century history of moral contagion, work that also necessitates expanding the discussion of moral contagion beyond the relatively neat confines of the French and Italian collective psychologists and criminologists.

From moral contagion to the 'contagion of example'

What we see emerging from the time of Hecquet on is a plethora of references in the medical/psychological literature to, variously, 'moral contagion' (Despine, Sighele, Durkheim), 'imitative contagion' (Lucas, Brierre de Boismont, Jolly, Tarde, Durkheim) and 'contagious' ideas and emotions (Le Bon). Evident in this array of terms, which I have arranged in a loosely chronological way, is a shift from the moral to the mental, from contagious acts (generally socially unacceptable ones, such as drunkenness, suicide or murder) to contagious ideas and emotions, and by the early 1900s, as I will explain further in the following chapter, Le Bon's 'emotional' contagion and Taine's 'mental' contagion largely take over from the other nineteenth-century forms.

This shift from the moral to the affective and mental is a point I will return to in the following chapter; for the moment, though, I want to focus on the simple fact that the nineteenth century spawned not one dominant social contagion metaphor but a conglomerate of metaphors. Subsequent researchers have tended to subsume these disparate terms under the broader heading of 'moral contagion',[33] despite the fact that 'moral contagion' is itself by no means a constant within the literature. If one phrase *does* indeed connect nineteenth-century studies of social contagion and acts as a thread running through them, it is the phrase 'contagion of example', a phrase that, unlike 'moral contagion', has apparently had no study, large or small, devoted to it.

Studies of the emergence of social contagion theory not only overlook the pervasiveness of the phrase 'contagion of example' and its variants in favour of 'moral contagion', but they also largely overlook formations of the metaphor occurring beyond France and Italy.[34] Without a doubt, the socio-psychological concept of contagion was predominantly a French invention, but it was not *exclusively* so. In 1827, Scottish philosopher Dugald Stewart published the third volume of his *Elements of the Philosophy of the Human Mind*. In this volume, Stewart proposes 'a principle or law of sympathetic imitation', based on 'the contagious power of example' (1827, p. 106) and influenced by Bacon and Burke's accounts of the human faculty for imitation. Among his conclusions regarding the nature of imitation, Stewart writes,

> one of the most interesting is, the contagious nature of certain bodily affections, even when unaccompanied with any mental passion or emotion. This appears from the rapidity with which convulsive and hysterical disorders are propagated among a crowd. It is of importance, however, to recollect, (although, perhaps, to some the caution may appear superfluous and trifling,) that this contagion is not, like that of a fever, the immediate consequence of unconscious vicinity, or even of contact. It operates, some how or other, through the medium of the *mind*; inasmuch as it necessarily implies a knowledge or perception (received either by the eye or by the ear) of the agitated condition of the person from whom the affection is caught. (Stewart 1827, p. 137; emph. in original)

Stewart's description of sympathetic imitation, of contagious examples and of crowd behaviour must by now seem strikingly familiar if not derivative, and yet it was published five years before Lucas's *De l'imitation contagieuse* and more than 60 years before Tarde's *Les lois de l'imitation*. Considering this, it seems surprising that Stewart's work does not appear to have been recognized in any of the extant studies of nineteenth-century crowd psychology or moral contagion, which have, as I have suggested, focused almost exclusively on French and Italian texts and influences. Stewart's work may not have any direct or even indirect influence on the nineteenth-century French crowd psychologists, but it does suggest the existence of prior influences that led, in the nineteenth century, to the expression of multiple, even discrete theories of social or moral contagion. An example such as Stewart's 'law of sympathetic imitation', I would argue, not only suggests a broader geographical and philosophical basis for the emergence of social contagion metaphors in the nineteenth century, but also reinforces the significance, if not self-referential contagiousness, of the phrase 'contagion of example' to a study of social contagion. In the following chapter, then, my aim is to begin the work of taking this concept – the contagiousness of example – into account and tracking it through classical, biblical and early modern discourse to demonstrate how it becomes a commonplace phrase, one that permeates and infects even nineteenth-century social-scientific formulations of social contagion theory.

The Contagion of Example

From the air . . . we say, The raging tempests of sedition, the whirlwinds of trouble, the infection of ill examples.
> Henry Peacham, 'Metaphor'. The Garden of Eloquence. 1593.

Rien n'est si contagieux que l'exemple.
> La Rochefoucauld, Maximes. 1665.

La contagion de l'exemple et la suggestion.
> Gabriel Tarde, Les lois de l'imitation. 1890.

From where or from what tradition, then, does this phrase 'contagion of example' come? Just as early modern theories of infectious disease drew heavily on classical and religious notions of contagion, early modern metaphors of disease and contagion, as Margaret Healy explains, invariably 'have biblical and/ or classical roots' (1993, p. 22). Both 'contagion of example' and 'moral contagion' are potent examples of this phenomenon, containing as they do traces of classical theories of mimesis and influence as well as biblical theories of sin. Plato's conception of mimesis as infectious or contagious (as outlined in Chapter 1) is certainly relevant here, and a foundational text in thinking about the relationships between imitation, the social and metaphors of contagion and infection.[1] In addition, early modern writers tend to invoke a suite of classical writers whose work develops Plato's ideas, notably Lucius Annaeus Seneca (c. 4 BCE–65 CE), Cicero (106–43 BCE), Tacitus (56–177 CE) and Plutarch (46–120 CE).

Even Sighele's literature review, outlined in the previous chapter, provides a hint of these substrate lines of classical influence when among his references to psychologists and medical practitioners he mentions that 'before them, La Rochefoucauld (*Maxims*) had already alluded to the phenomenon of moral contagion' (1892, p. 38). The particular seventeenth-century maxim to which Sighele is referring is the one cited as an epigraph to this chapter: La Rochefoucauld's famous 'rien n'est si contagieux que l'exemple' or 'nothing is contagious as an example'. In the first standardized edition of La Rochefoucauld's maxims, the editor D. L. Gilbert stresses the relationship between this particular maxim and the work of the first-century Stoic philosopher Seneca. Gilbert notes, in particular, the influence of Seneca's moral essays 'De tranquillitate animi' ('On Tranquility of Mind') and 'Vita beata' ('On the Happy Life'), as well as Seneca's moral letters to Lucilius, the Roman governor of Sicily (*Epistulae morales ad Lucilium*) (Gilbert 1868, p. 122). Specifically, Gilbert draws attention to epistle 123, 'On Luxury', in which Seneca writes '[i]t must be reckoned among the causes of our evils that we live by example. Neither are we governed by reason, but led away by custom' (Seneca 1786, p. 359).

Indeed, a number of maxims that are inflected through the literature on social influence and moral contagion are drawn from Seneca's moral letters and essays. Seneca's sixth letter to Lucilius, for instance, contains his famous maxim 'quia longum iter est per praecepta, breve et efficax per exempla' or 'the way of precepts is long, whereas the way of example is short and effective' (Seneca 1825, p. 4). In his influential *L'académie Françoise* of 1577,[2] Pierre de la Primaudaye quotes this maxim, linking it directly with the contagion of example. Primaudaye warns that the Magistrate, as head of the Republic, must take seriously their role and must guard against corrupting the public body by way of the contagion of bad example (*garde bien par mauvais exemple d'apporter contagion à tout le corps public*) (1577, pp. 284–5). Michel de Montaigne also quotes another, the seventh, of Seneca's letters to Lucilius when in his essay on solitude he writes, 'Contagion is very dangerous in the crowd. A man must either imitate the vicious or hate them. Both are dangerous, either to resemble them, because they are many, or to hate many, because they are unresembling' (1842 [1580], p. 102).[3]

Another key classical source in the development of this rhetoric of contagious example is the Ciceronian notion of the 'infectious' power of example wielded by powerful leaders. In his *Treatise on the Laws* (*De legibus*) (51 BC), Cicero puts forward the notion that by the power of their example a nation's leader can infect (*infici solet tota civitas*) or infuse into a city (*infundunt in civitatem*) their vices or their virtues, thereby inciting the multitudes who imitate them (*permulti imitatores principum existunt*). As such, Cicero maintains, corrupt leaders 'do more harm by their example than by the crimes they commit' (1841, p. 158).[4]

Yet, perhaps the most influential source is Plutarch's *Moralia* (c. 120 AD). Plutarch's account of the women of Miletus, as Goldstein notes, was central to the development of the medico-psychological concept of moral contagion during the eighteenth and nineteenth centuries, but his essay titled 'How to Tell a Flatterer from a Friend' (or 'Adulator')[5] is also a key touchstone for early modern writers concerned with social influence. For Plutarch, as for Plato, there is something infectious or contagious about mimesis, and flattery, he warns, is its most 'pestilential' instantiation. In 'Adulator', Plutarch cautions that a person should imitate only the best attributes of their peers. Imitating or even being in close contact or association (ὁμιλίαν, συνήθειαν) with a base person or evildoer can have a contaminating or tainting (ἀνάχρωσις) effect (1888, p. 129; sec. 9). The term ἀνάχρωσις (or *anachrosis*) has a primary meaning of 'discolouring', but also carries with it overtones of 'taint' or 'infection'. It is also virtually identical to the term *synanachrosis* (συνανάχρωσις), meaning 'infecting contact'. In his essay on the existence of a Greek verbal equivalent for the word 'contagion', Vivian Nutton argues that *synanachrosis* is perhaps the closest we can find. Etymologically speaking, he argues, *synanachrosis* is the Greek equivalent for the Latin *contagio*, and it appears, he suggests, most often in the writing of Plutarch (Nutton 2000, p. 141).[6]

Among the many translators of Plutarch's 'Adulator' was Desiderius Erasmus. In Erasmus's early sixteenth-century Latin translation of the essay, Plutarch's *anachrosis* predictably becomes a 'contagion' (*contagio*), and one that 'infects' those nearby (*inficit vicinum*) (Erasmus 1518, p. 270). English-language translations from the seventeenth century on follow a similar pattern, repeating and reinforcing the translation of *anachrosis* as 'contagion'. In his 1603 translation, Philemon Holland draws out the connotations of 'discolouring' and 'taint' inherent in the term *anachrosis*, but he also retains the term 'contagion'. Imitation of vice, in Holland's translation, can lead to a person being 'tainted with infection of some ill quality . . . much like as they who by contagion catch rheumatic and bleared eyes' (1911 [1603], p. 48). In their translations, both Erasmus and Holland expand Plutarch's *anachrosis*, separating out its connotations of 'tainting' and 'infection', so that their use of the term 'contagion' becomes analogical. In other words, they employ the term 'contagion' effectively as a simile to indicate that imitation of bad examples can have a tainting effect like that of contagious disease. However, in George Tullie's late seventeenth-century translation of the same passage of 'Adulator', social contact itself becomes contagious: by imitating 'base and dishonourable actions', in Tullie's translation, a person may 'chance insensibly to contract some ill habit or other by the very contagion of familiarity and conversation' (1684, p. 17).

These early modern translations of Plutarch's essay on flattery highlight, I would argue, the role translation plays in drawing out, making explicit, and even reinforcing the trope of contagious imitation or contagious example already so prevalent in moral literature of the sixteenth and seventeenth centuries. Further, this function of translation in circulating and consolidating the trope of contagious example is perhaps even more apparent in translations of Tacitus's *Histories* (100–10 AD). In book two of the *Histories*, Tacitus describes a certain disaffection spreading through the troops of the would-be Roman Emperor Vitellius. The term Tacitus uses to explain the spread of this affective contagion is not the Latin *contagio*, but *contactus*: 'Simul ceterae legiones contactu, et adversus Germanicos milites invidia, bellum meditabantur' (1850, p. 102; bk 2, sec. 50). The Latin *contactus* (derived from *contingo*) is strongly suggestive of the English 'contact', and indeed its primary meaning is physical contact or 'touch'. However, like *contagio* and *synanachrosis*, *contactus* also connects the concept of touch to that of infection, and in many cases refers to 'a touching of something unclean, a contagion, infection' (Lewis and Short 1879; 'Contactus'). As such, English-language translations of Tacitus's *Histories* tend also to translate *contactu* as *contagion*, thereby emphasizing the contagiousness of social influence. For instance, Henry Savile in his late sixteenth-century translation of the *Histories* translates the same passage thus: 'and with all the rest of the Legions, partly by contagion, and partly upon envy to the German soldiers, projected war in their minds' (1598, p. 81). More pithily, in their 1864 English translation of the *Histories*, Alfred John Church and William Jackson Brodribb simply translate *contactu* as the 'contagion of example' (Church and Brodribb 1864, p. 103).

Erasmus, the *Adages* and 'contagio morum'

Erasmus's influence on consolidating and extending the classical insistence on the continuity of physical and moral contagion went far beyond translating Plutarch's essay on flattery. In 1500, Erasmus published the first edition of his *Adages*, a collection of about 800 Greek and Latin sayings, which he continued to expand and republish until his death in 1536. In its final version, the *Adages* (*Adagiorum chiliades*) amounted to more than 4500 proverbs, but within this massive work there is one group of adages that draws attention to Erasmus's interest in questions surrounding sin, imitation and social influence. Tellingly, Erasmus grouped this handful of adages under the heading 'contagio morum', or moral contagion. Clearly, then, not only was Erasmus familiar with the concept of 'moral contagion', but he also considered it to be an important theme in classical thought.

By the time the 1536 edition of the *Adagiorum chiliades* was published, Erasmus had collated some seven adages under the 'contagio morum' index heading. These included the proverbs 'Oscitante uno deinde oscitat et alter' ('When one yawns, immediately another yawns too'), 'A bonis bona disce' ('Learn goodness from the good'), 'Ne gustaris quibus nigra est cauda' ('Taste not of anything with a black tail'), 'Si juxta claudum habites, subclaudicare disces' ('If you live next to a cripple you will learn to limp') and 'Corrumpunt bonos mores colloquia prava' ('Evil communications corrupt good manners'). For each adage, Erasmus provides a detailed explanation and interpretation. In his commentary on 'Oscitante', Erasmus invokes Aristotle's *Problemata*, the book of 'problems', in which Aristotle asks, 'Why is it that when men yawn others usually yawn in sympathy?' (Aristotle 1961, p. 171) – an age-old question that is similarly posed in much of the nineteenth-century sociological literature on moral contagion.[7] Erasmus adds to this a moral aspect, stating that the adage is 'applicable whenever, by an example of sin, someone is provoked to a similar deed. This happens by some obscure power of nature, so that anyone who sees someone yawning is forced to yawn himself' (2005, p. 56). Further, he adds, even 'some emotions are communicated in a similar way' (2005, p. 56).

'A bonis bona disce' is alone among the 'contagio morum' adages in its emphasis on the potential *good* that might be achieved by way of moral contagion. Erasmus attributes this saying to the sixth-century BCE poet Theognis of Megara, whom Aristotle quotes in his *Nichomachean Ethics*. In quoting Theognis's maxim 'learn goodness from the good', Aristotle, Erasmus writes, 'is demonstrating that virtue is best learnt from the company of good men, since friends correct each other if any error is committed and find themselves spurred on to virtuous action by the presence of others' (2006, pp. 379–80). The remaining adages all stress the negative effects of moral contagion. In explaining the curious proverb 'Ne gustaris', Erasmus points to the interpretation Plutarch provides in his essay 'On the Education of Children'. Plutarch, Erasmus says, interprets the phrase to mean 'Do not have anything to do with wicked people and those whose character is black and disreputable' (Erasmus 1982, p. 32). Of a similar vein and provenance is the 'si juxta' adage. Erasmus notes the proverb's appearance in Plutarch's 'On the Education of Children', and states that the 'point of the proverb' – admittedly a politically incorrect if not offensive one by contemporary standards – 'is that association with wicked men is very dangerous, because faults of the body and still more faults of the mind pass like an infection from one man to another' (1989, p. 266). Here, Erasmus again remarks on the 'underlying natural sympathy' that 'makes a man yawn when he sees someone else yawning' and he quotes from Plutarch's essay on flattery, stating that 'we imitate unconsciously even the faults of those with whom we live' (1989, p. 267).

The last of Erasmus's 'contagio morum' adages that I will comment on here is 'corrumpunt bonos', which is variously translated as 'Evil communications corrupt good manners' or 'Bad company corrupts good morals'. Erasmus attributes the line to fourth-century BCE comic dramatist Menander,[8] yet he also notes that 'the Apostle St Paul did not disdain to quote [the adage] in his first epistle to the Corinthians' (Erasmus 1989, p. 267). The biblical passage Erasmus is making specific reference to is 1 Cor. 15.33, where Paul admonishes: 'Be not deceived: evil communications corrupt good manners'.

Paul's strategic use of the 'corrumpunt bonos' maxim in his first letter to the Corinthians (c. 53–7 CE) is a notable example of the transference of the classical notion of contagious example into biblical discourse. Biblical scholar Michael F. Hull points out that Paul's quotation of Menander in this passage is 'strange', especially given that it represents 'the only quotation from a non-biblical source in [Paul's] letters'. However, Hull continues, 'the oddity is somewhat mitigated by the popularity of Menander, whose plays were very influential in the Greco-Roman world' (2005, p. 93). This is not, of course, to say that Paul was consciously aware of his source. Indeed, biblical scholars tend to agree that 'corrumpunt bonos mores colloquia prava' was likely a commonplace phrase, perhaps even a cliché, at the time Paul was writing his first letter to the Corinthians (Heil 2005, p. 226; M. Hull 2005, p. 93; Pascuzzi 2005, p. 87). Rather than a conscious reference to Menander, Paul's quotation was more likely a rhetorical appeal, a calling into play of a well-worn maxim.

The effect, though, is noteworthy. Not only was Paul's quotation of Menander out of character, it also bestowed on the maxim a kind of 'holiness'. As Erasmus points out in his commentary on the phrase, Tertullian (160–220 CE) claims that Paul did nothing less than 'sanctify' Menander's line of verse (Erasmus 1989, p. 267). Erasmus's discussion of 'corrumpunt bonos' thus provides, I would argue, a key point of contact between classical and biblical sources. Yet, it is not the only or even the most dramatic example of the connection between classical and biblical notions of contagious example. Indeed, one of the most heated and long-lived debates in the history of Christian thought is underwritten by this very question.

By generation or imitation: Pelagius, Augustine and the fifth-century debate over 'contagious sin'

Early in the fifth century, Pelagius, a British monk living in Rome, took exception to the doctrine of original sin being espoused by St Augustine, the bishop of Hippo. The debate itself centred on a passage from another of St Paul's letters, this time to the Romans: 'Wherefore as by one man sin entered into the world, and death by sin; and so death passed upon all men, for that all have sinned' (Rom. 5:12, KJV). According to biblical scholar Alexander Souter, Pelagius was drawn to Paul's Epistles, and by 410 he had written and published a commentary on them – the *Commentarii in espistolas S. Pauli* – based on Jerome's late fourth-century Vulgate text. Spreading out from Rome, Souter notes, Pelagius's commentary 'circulated over the Western world', and, even though it was apparently published anonymously, Pelagius was widely recognized as its author (c. 1906, p. 2).

Pelagius's commentary on Rom. 5:12 was to be the most controversial aspect of his text. As Brinley Roderick Rees explains, this 'crucial passage' in Paul's Epistle to the Romans 'is notoriously difficult to follow, let alone to interpret' (1991, p. 56). Unlike his first letter to the Corinthians, in which Paul 'is concerned solely with the origin of physical death in Adam's sin', in Rom. 5:12-21, Paul 'sees Adam's sin not only as the origin of physical death but also as the origin of sin, and Adam's descendants as *infected* with sinfulness by some mysterious means which he does not attempt to explain' (B. R. Rees 1991, p. 56; emph. added). In order to resolve this problem and to provide an explanation for the transmission of sin from Adam to all humans, Pelagius states in his commentary that it occurred

> By example or by pattern [*exemplo vel forma*]. Just as through Adam sin came at a time when it did not yet exist, so in the same way through Christ righteousness was recovered at a time when it survived in almost no one. (Pelagius 2002, p. 92)

At base, Pelagius was arguing against the dominant Traducianist notion of original sin. Traducianism, as Theodore S. De Bruyn explains, 'refers to the notion that the human soul is transmitted by parents to their children' and, by extension, that 'the sin of Adam is transmitted from generation to generation along with the soul' (1988, pp. 30–1). In the Traducian view, sin is inescapable in that it is transmitted through propagation or generation (the term itself is derived from the Latin *tradux*, meaning a vine shoot prepared for propagation). For

Pelagius, however, this was 'tantamount to a denial of human responsibility, since for [him] freedom consists in the ability to choose between good and evil, and human responsibility is predicated upon human freedom' (De Bruyn 1988, p. 37). Rather than being traduced, or transmitted via *propagation*, Pelagius argued that sin is instead transmitted through *imitation*. That is, humans sin because they choose to imitate the sin of Adam, and they can overcome this sin by choosing to imitate Christ's beneficent example.

For Augustine, Pelagius's argument was heresy, for it placed too much emphasis on free will and denied the doctrine of original sin to which he sub-scribed. Augustine was driven to respond to the heresy of Pelagius and his followers in a treatise titled 'De peccatorum meritis et remissione', which he published around 411. In this treatise, Augustine takes Pelagius to task over his interpretation of Rom. 5:12. He explains first the Pelagians' stance, stating that they believe

> The death mentioned in that passage is not the death of the body which they deny Adam merited by sinning; it is, rather the death of the soul which occurs in the sin itself, and this sin passed from the first man to other human beings not by propagation, but by imitation. Hence they refuse to believe that in the case of little children original sin is removed by baptism, since they maintain that there is no sin at all in newborns. (Augustine 1997, p. 38)

Augustine does grant that sin is related to imitation: 'Of course', he acknowl-edges, 'all those who through disobedience transgress God's commandment imitate Adam'. However, he adds, 'it is one thing for [Adam] to be an example for those who sin by their will; it is something else for him to be the origin of those born with sin' (1997, pp. 38–9). Rather, Augustine holds, Adam not only provides an example of sin for willing sinners to imitate, he also 'infects in himself with the hidden corruption of his carnal concupiscence all those who are to come from his lineage' (1997, p. 39). In the Latin text, Augustine does not directly speak of 'infection'; rather, he uses the word *tabes*, meaning 'wasting' or a 'wasting disease', to describe the sin transmitted by propaga-tion. Later in the same treatise, however, he speaks of the 'contagion of sin' (*peccati contagione*) to refer to original sin (Augustine 1913, pp. 11, 144). Adam's example infects both outwardly and inwardly: his example provokes the sin of imitation, but, more importantly, his sin has *engendered* an inescap-able original sin that is contagious by the simple fact of its being genetic or 'generative'.

Contagiosa res: Augustine and the pears

Augustine certainly did not deny the contagion of example,[9] as a famous anecdote from his *Confessions* (397–398 CE) beautifully illustrates. In book two of the *Confessions*, Augustine relates a story from his adolescence:

> There was a pear tree near our vineyard laden with fruit, though attractive in neither colour nor taste. To shake the fruit off the tree and carry off the pears, I and a gang of naughty adolescents set off late at night after (in our usual pestilential way) we had continued our game in the streets. We carried off a huge load of the pears. But they were not for our feasts but merely to throw to the pigs. Even if we ate a few, nevertheless our pleasure lay in doing what was not allowed. . . . I had no motive for my wickedness except wickedness itself. It was foul, and I loved it. I loved the self-destruction, I loved my fall, not the object for which I had fallen but my fall itself. (Augustine 1991, p. 29; bk 2, sec. 4)

This anecdote, of course, makes some fairly heavy-handed allusions to Genesis 3 and the primordial scene of deception and sin in the Garden of Eden – another superficially trivial theft of fruit that has significant moral consequences. As such, Augustine's analysis of his motivation for the theft is predominantly an analysis of individual sin. His theft, Augustine writes, was like Adam's an act of 'vicious' and 'perverse' imitation of God, a way of 'making an assertion of possessing a dim resemblance to omnipotence' (1991, p. 32; bk 2, sec. 6).

And yet, Augustine is at pains to point out, he was not alone in his act of theft. Indeed, he says, not only was he not alone in committing the theft, had he been alone he 'would never have done it' (1991, p. 33; bk 2, sec. 8). He might, he grants, have acted on his own in stealing the fruit had he actually desired the pears themselves, but he did not (evidenced by the fact the adolescents immediately discarded the fruit they had plundered). Instead, Augustine says, his 'pleasure . . . was in the crime itself, done in association with a sinful group' (1991, p. 33; bk 2, sec. 8).

Adam, too, was not alone in his theft; moreover, as we know, he was not the first to commit the theft that, in the Christian worldview, condemned humankind to mortality. In this case, why then is Adam considered the sinful 'example' rather than Eve, who first tasted the fruit of the tree of knowledge? In an essay on the anecdote of the pears, Garry Wills explains that, for Augustine, Adam's original sin was caused by 'a false ideal of companionship' with Eve (2002, p. 61). Further, in Augustine's view, Adam's sin, unlike Eve's, was a conscious one; that is, although Eve was deceived by the lie of the serpent, Adam was not, and he 'made a deliberate choice, out of his solidarity with Eve' (Wills 2002, p. 61). According to Wills, 'in the scheme Augustine inherited, sin descends from the man', and as such, 'Adam cannot rescue Eve from her death but he can condemn everyone else to it' (2002, p. 62). It is this conscious sin – even though it was born of a seemingly noble loyalty to Eve – that humankind has inherited by way of propagation. Adam's sin, therefore, could itself be seen as the first sin of imitation, one that in Augustine's view engendered original sin.

To return to Augustine's anecdote, what then, Augustine asks, was his 'state of mind' when he stole the pears (1991, pp. 33; bk 2, sec. 9)? What caused him to act in this way – to irrationally follow his friends in stealing something he did not want, to do something he would not have done alone, and to succumb to social influence? The Latin heading for this section (bk. 2, sec. 9) provides us with some sense of an answer to Augustine's rhetorical question, namely '*contagiosa res, sodales mali*', which roughly translates as 'contagious thing, companion of evil' (Augustine 1540, p. 22r).[10] Moreover, it is certainly not coincidental that Augustine describes the playful activities of the group of youths as 'pestilent' ('*quousque ludum de pestilientiae more in areis produxeramus*'). Through his metaphors of contagion and infection, Augustine not only invokes the primal scene in the Garden of Eden, but also once more the concept of the 'contagion of example'. His anecdote not only reinforces his doctrine of original sin, it also suggests that humanity is compelled to imitate, to re-enact, Adam's originary sin of imitation. John Milton, strongly influenced by the Augustinian account of the fall of Adam and Eve,[11] intimates as much in book ten of his *Paradise Lost* (1667) when he describes the fall of Adam and Eve: 'Down fell both spear and shield, down they as fast, / And the dire hiss renewed, and the dire form / Catched by contagion' (2005 [1667], p. 300; bk 10, l. 542–4).

The debate replayed: Erasmus and Calvin on Rom. 5:12

Despite his authority on the matter, Augustine's response to the Pelagians was not the final word on the nature of sin and its relationship to contagion and imitation. Even though Pelagius was labelled a heretic and banished from Rome by the year 418, Pelagianism and Pelagian thought were far from eradicated. Moreover, the question posed by Rom. 5:12 was far from settled. Indeed, in 1516, Erasmus published his own *Annotations on Romans*, effectively reigniting the unresolved fifth-century debate between Pelagius and Augustine.

In his commentary on Rom. 5:12, Erasmus seems to side with Pelagius, arguing that the 'natural propensity to sin ... proceeds from example rather than
from nature' (Erasmus 1994 [1516], p. 140). Augustine's mistake, according to
Erasmus, is that he has attempted to read the passage too literally and has ignored
the figurative in Paul's language. Paul, Erasmus states, citing Pelagian thought,[12]
is not talking about original sin; instead, he 'is talking about the sins that individuals have committed in imitation of Adam'. Further, he maintains, there is
nothing in Paul's language and phrasing 'that cannot be accommodated to the
sin of imitation' (*peccato imitationis*) (Erasmus 1994 [1516], p. 141). Although
Erasmus, as Robert Coogan explains, broadly condemned Pelagianism as heretical, he 'defended [this] central Pelagian tenet' of sin by imitation rather than by
generation (1992, p. 26).

As a result of his defence of free will and his endorsement of the concept
of '*peccato imitationis*', Erasmus was soon accused of being a Pelagian, or a
watered-down semi-Pelagian. More than a millennium after Pelagius's death,
this remained a serious charge, for not only was Pelagianism still considered
a heretical doctrine, it was one that continued to vex the orthodox acceptance
of the doctrines of predestination and original sin. Calvin himself saw fit in
the expanded 1559 version of his *Institutes of the Christian Religion* to directly
counter Pelagian and semi-Pelagian readings of Rom. 5:12. Every descendant of
Adam, Calvin maintained,

> is born infected with the contagion of sin [*peccati contagione nascimur infecti*]
> ... Thus it is certain that Adam was not only the progenitor, but as it were
> the root of mankind, and therefore that all the race were necessarily vitiated
> in his corruption [*corruptione merito vitiatum*]. The Apostle explains this by a
> comparison between him and Christ: "As", says he, "by one man sin entered into
> the world, and death by sin; and so death passed upon all men, for that all have
> sinned": so by the grace of Christ, righteousness and life have been restored to
> us. What cavil will the Pelagians raise here? That the sin of Adam was propa-
> gated by imitation [*peccatum Adae imitatione propagatum*]? Do we then receive
> no other advantage from the righteousness of Christ, than the proposal of an
> example for our imitation? Who can bear such blasphemy? (Calvin 1816 [1559],
> pp. 263–4)

If anything, Calvin went further than Augustine in his insistence on the 'contagion' of original sin. As Michael Heyd explains, in Calvin's doctrine,

> No residue of free will remained to [humanity] after the fall, and the sacrament
> of Baptism (contrary to Augustine's position) did not remit the stain with which

children were born. Indeed, without divine grace, human beings were unable to understand the world properly (as God's creation), and more important – were incapable of any good act, any moral behaviour. They inherited, Calvin emphasized, not just Adam's sin, but his guilt as well; children were born guilty. The question of the precise nature of inheritance, however, Calvin left pretty vague. (Heyd 2005, p. 200)

Pelagianism – a doctrine that espoused the centrality of the contagion of example to understanding the possibility both of good and evil in the world – remained a highly visible and controversial one in the early modern period. Indeed, well into the seventeenth century, theologians and Christian controversialists (predominantly Calvinist ones) regularly described Pelagianism with no hint of irony as a spreading 'infection'[13] or a 'pestilent doctrine'.[14] By the late sixteenth century, the concepts of 'moral contagion' and 'contagion of example' were, therefore, arguably largely commonplace, embedded and promulgated within religious discourse and maxims drawn from biblical and classical sources.

The 'contagion of example' in early modern discourse

One of the earliest print occurrences of a variant of the 'contagion of example' phrase tellingly appears in the elder Henry Peacham's essay on metaphor in the second, expanded edition of his *Garden of Eloquence*, published in 1593. Metaphors, Peacham informs his readers, can be drawn from an 'infinite number' of places, but he suggests a number of common places: from the five senses; from the mind to the body; from non-living things, animals or gods to humans (and vice versa); from the offices and actions of humans; and from the four elements. Remarkably, in this last category the element of air once again signals the link between metaphor, contagion, affect and imitation. When we speak of metaphors from the air, Peacham writes, 'we say, The raging tempests of sedition, the whirlwinds of trouble, the *infection of ill examples*' (1593, p. 11; emph. added). Far from marking a point at which the phrase "contagion" or "infection" of example' begins to enter common discourse, however, Peacham's 'we say' suggests that, by the late sixteenth century, the phrase was, if not a cliché, already a metaphor in common parlance.[15]

Certainly, by the mid-seventeenth century, the phrase 'contagion of example' had become a mainstay in moral and religious discourse. Chief among its English disseminators were the royalist bishop John Gauden (1605–62) and the

Calvinist tract-writer Richard Younge, about whose biography little is known. In one of his *Three Sermons*, published in 1642 (before he became Chaplain to Charles II and Bishop of Exeter and Worcester), Gauden draws attention to the corrupting and contagious power of greatness or prestige:

> There is a *greatnesse* the world applauds, which infinitely lessens a Christian mind . . ., while men measure the greatnesse of their minds, by their boldnesse and daring to sin. Such minds, as Comets (which are *portenta irae Dei*) the higher and greater they are, the more malignant influence they diffuse on the inferiour world, by the contagion of their example. (Gauden 1642, p. 132; emph. in original)

Younge's Calvinist tracts similarly reveal a preoccupation with the contagiousness of example. In his 1655 *Armour of Proof, or a Soveraign Antidote against the Contagion of Evil Company*, he warns against the dangers of fraternizing with the 'spiritually contagious' (1655, p. 32; emph. in original). Still earlier, in his 1638 tract on the dangers of drunkenness, Younge (drawing on Seneca) writes of the importance of worthy examples for imitation: 'True glasses both our deformities and favours tell: and precepts never shine so much, as when they are set in examples; nor examples, as when they are set in curious persons: nor is it easie to finde so fit a person, so meet a patterne for imitation, for incitation' (1638, p. n. pag.) Instead, there are all too many dangerous, contagious examples, notable among which are drunkards, whose 'chiefe delight is to *infect others*' (1638, p. 286; emph. in original). 'Sin', Younge concludes, 'hath an ubiquity; one sinners example infects others, and they spread it broad to more, like a man that dyes of the Plague, and leaves the infection to a whole City' (1638, pp. 496–7).

Although, as I have noted, no extant study examines the ubiquity and significance of the phrase 'contagion of example' in early modern discourse, Marjorie Morgan does devote a passage to the general concept in her 1994 study *Manners, Morals, and Class in England, 1744–1858*. From the start of the early industrial period, Morgan writes,

> moralists expanded the traditional notion of personal influence to include the moral persuasion that all individuals, regardless of rank, were capable of exerting on each other. . . . The outpouring of conduct books was part of a campaign to heighten people's consciousness of their behaviour as a wholesome force for shaping the moral character of individuals and of the present and future society as a whole. According to these works, all members of society had a duty to display exemplary behaviour, because no person was of so inconsiderate a station as to exercise no persuasion over another. (Morgan 1994, p. 61)

Morgan notes the ambivalence with which the eighteenth-century moralists regarded these human capacities for influence and imitation, for they cautioned, 'the contagion of example was equally efficacious whether spreading noxious or wholesome influence' (1994, p. 62). This ambivalence is perhaps drawing on the concerns expressed by earlier moral philosophers, such as Locke. In his late seventeenth-century treatise *Some Thoughts Concerning Education*, Locke writes of the 'inconvenience which children received from the ill examples, which they meet with amongst the meaner servants' (1693, p. 70). Children, Locke maintains, should 'be kept from such conversation: For the contagion of these ill precedents, both in civility and virtue, horribly infects children, as often as they come within reach of it' (1693, p. 70). To ward off the 'infection' of 'vicious' servants, Locke advises that children be kept as much as possible in their parents' company so that they might learn from more positive examples (1693, pp. 70–1).

This emphasis on the contagion of example in moral discourse continues well into the nineteenth century. For instance, in 1855, Rev Edward Thomson, the British-born minister (later Bishop) of the American Methodist Episcopal Church, published an essay titled 'Moral Education' in the Methodist *Ladies' Repository*. In this essay, Thomson portentously warns his presumably impressionable readers that 'The contagion of example, like the malaria of cholera, works silently, insensibly, constantly, widely.... [T]here is no prophylactic against the virus of a bad example' (1855, p. 93). Further, by the mid-eighteenth century, the 'contagion of example' had spread even to the relatively new literary form of the novel. In volume four of the revised and expanded 1742 edition of Samuel Richardson's *Pamela*, the character Mrs B quotes Locke's 'contagion of ill precedents' in a letter to Mr B about the virtues of home schooling (1742, p. 332).[16] In Fanny Burney's 1796 novel, *Camilla*, the eponymous heroine finds it 'hard to resist' the 'contagion of example' when she is asked to join a raffle for a beautiful locket (1796, p. 217). Although the phrase appears only once in the text,[17] Mary Pilkington devoted an entire novel to the concept – her 1797 novel about two orphans titled *The Force of Example*. And, finally, across the Atlantic, the phrase appears in Charles Brockden Brown's 1799 novel, *Edgar Huntly*, whose narrator and protagonist claims that 'no contagious example had contaminated [his] principles' (1799, p. 96).

Invocations of the 'contagion of example' were certainly not, however, confined to the moral literature of the seventeenth, eighteenth and nineteenth centuries. In political discourse, for instance, possibly the most famous example of the phrase 'contagion of example' appears in the 1648/1649 *Eikon Basilike*. The

Eikon Basilike, or 'Royal Portrait', was initially attributed to King Charles I of England, but Gauden himself later claimed to have written it.[18] In Chapter 12, recounting the Irish Rebellion of 1641, the author condemns the Irish rebels who corrupted others with the 'contagion of their Examples':

> I would to God the *Irish* had nothing to alledge for their imitation against those, whose blame must needs be the greater, by how much Protestant Principles are more against all Rebellion against Princes, then those of Papists. Nor will the goodnesse of mens intentions excuse the scandall, and contagion of their Examples. (*Eikon Basilike* 1648, p. 90; emph. in original)

It was not, however, only the spiritually weak, the degenerate and the Irish who were considered susceptible to moral contagion in the mid-seventeenth century. In Hobbes's *Leviathan* of 1651, 'contagion of example' appears as a basic principle, and one of the four ways in which the severity of a crime may be judged. As Hobbes explains, 'The Degrees of Crime are taken on divers Scales, and measured, First, by the malignity of the Source, or Cause: Secondly, by the contagion of the Example: Thirdly, by the mischiefe of the Effect; and Fourthly, by the concurrence of Times, Places, and Persons' (1651, p. 157). In the mid-eighteenth century, David Hume also replays the *Eikon Basilike*'s figuration of the contagiousness of the Irish Rebellion. In volume six of his *History of England*, Hume writes that 'propensity to a revolt was discovered in all the Irish', spurred on by the 'contagion of example, which transports men beyond all the usual motives of conduct and behaviour' (1825 [1754–55], p. 650).

By the late eighteenth century, 'contagion of example' appears to have become a stock phrase in English, French and German political and philosophical discourses. In England, it appears in Burke's *Reflections on the Revolution in France* (1790)[19] and in Edward Gibbon's *History of the Decline and Fall of the Roman Empire* (1788) and posthumously published memoirs (1796).[20] In France, as we have seen, it runs through Primaudaye's *L'Académie Françoise* (1617) and La Rochefoucauld's *Maxims* (1664), but it also finds expression in the work of Olivier Patru, a barrister, lexicographer and elected member of the French Academy. In his 1670 collection of speeches, *Plaidoyers et autres oeuvres*, Patru writes – in a phrase that is strongly reminiscent of La Rochefoucauld – 'les mauvais exemples sont contagieux' (1670, p. 446). A notable eighteenth-century example, moreover, is John-Jacques Rousseau's *Émile*, in which he opines that if only a man could 'guard his heart, his body, his morals from the contagion of bad example', he might be able to become a master of all the 'despicable men produced by early debauchery' (1938 [1762], p. 300).[21] Immanuel Kant, too, employed the phrase in his 1781 *Kritik der reinen Vernunft* (*Critique of Pure Reason*). In his discussion of the discipline of pure reason, Kant looks to the mathematics as an exemplar of the contagious spread of reason. 'Examples', he writes, 'are contagious' (*Beispiele sind ansteckend*), and in this way 'pure reason hopes to be able to expand just as successfully and soundly in its transcendental use as it managed to do in its mathematical use' (1996 [1871], p. 668; sect. B740–1).[22]

Perhaps the strongest indication that the phrase was a commonplace in early modern discourse lies in those vanguards of linguistic and cultural authority, the dictionaries. In the very first monolingual French dictionary – Pierre Richelet's *Dictionnaire François* of 1680 – entries for the words 'contagious' and 'example' demonstrate how entwined the two words were. In the entry for the adjective 'contagieux, contagieuse', the second meaning (marked with an asterisk to indicate its figurative status) is given as follows: 'Qui gâté, qui corrompt les moeurs, ou l'esprit. (L'exemple est contagieux. *M. de la Rochefoucaut* [sic])'. The primary (non-figurative) entry for 'exemple' offers this definition, balancing the La Rochefoucauld quote with one from Patru: 'Action vertüeuse, ou vitieuse qu'on doit imiter, ou qu'on doit fuïr. (Les mauvais éxemples sont contagieux. *Patru, plaidoié* 7)'.[23]

A similar collapsing of contagion and example – and of figurative and literal uses – is apparent in Samuel Johnson's English-language *Dictionary* of 1755. Johnson's entry for 'contagion' provides three meanings for the word: '1. The emission from body to body by which diseases are communicated. . . . 2. Infection; propagation of mischief, or disease. . . . 3. Pestilence; venomous emanations' (Johnson 1755). To illustrate the second of these meanings, the dictionary provides two quotations. The first is the 'contagion of example' passage from the *Eikon Basilike*, which is attributed to 'King Charles'.[24] The second is the passage from Milton's *Paradise Lost*, cited above: 'Down fell they, / And the dire hiss renew'd, and the dire form/Catch'd by contagion'.

The above is by no means intended to be an exhaustive list of printed occurrences of the phrase 'contagion of example' and its variants from the sixteenth to the late nineteenth century. Rather, I have aimed to give a general sense of the phrase's endurance and pervasiveness across moral, political and philosophical discourse in the centuries leading up to the *fin-de-siècle* advent of social contagion theory. Moral contagion was by no means a nineteenth- or even eighteenth-century invention. Indeed, concerns about the relationships among imitation, social influence and group behaviour had been framed in terms of moral contagion for well over a millennium. What we see in the late nineteenth century is a concerted attempt to approach the phenomenon from a scientific standpoint and to identify the mechanisms by which this form of contagion operated. As I briefly noted in the previous chapter, however, by the end of the nineteenth century there seems to be a shift in the rhetoric surrounding the emergent social contagion theory, a shift from 'moral' to 'mental' contagion.

From 'moral' to 'mental' contagion

As we saw in the last chapter, scholars have roundly questioned Le Bon's credibility as a social scientist, and his work faced strong criticism even during his lifetime. However, Le Bon's knack for sensing, as it were, which way the wind was blowing (even if it meant appropriating others' work) and his unselfconscious hyperbole at times make him seem almost prescient rather than a pessimist intent on 'frightening' his readers (McClelland 1989, p. 201). Le Bon was certainly negative about crowds and crowd behaviour, but some of his key statements – the ones most often quoted, the ones that lend themselves to quotation – seem much more ambivalent. When Le Bon writes that 'ideas that have reached a certain stage, in fact, possess a contagious power as intense as that of microbes. Not fear and courage only are contagious; ideas are, too, on condition that they are repeated often enough' (2002 [1895], p. 78), he seems almost to relish this germ theory of ideas. That is, reading this passage out of context, we seem to have left the value-laden realm of morals and entered the realm of ideas and concepts.

Five years before Le Bon published his *Psychologie des foules* and in the same year that Tarde published his *Lois de l'imitation*, the English philosopher Bernard Bosanquet published an article titled 'The Communication of Moral Ideas as a Function of an Ethical Society' in the first issue of the *International Journal of Ethics*. In this article, Bosanquet intimates that contagion is not simply reserved for negative ideas or emotions. In fact, he says, 'Everything is contagious. We are all of us always communicating ideas, and more especially moral ideas' (1890, p. 79). Bosanquet takes great pains to distinguish important 'moral ideas' from more narrow 'ideas *about* morality' (1890, p. 88; emph. added), and the way in which these complex and difficult 'moral ideas' can be communicated is, he argues, by way of contagion. 'Contagion', he says, 'perhaps, after all is said and done, remains the only certain way'; contagion 'is the real thing' (1890, pp. 89, 93). It bears mentioning here that 1890 was also the year in which James George Frazer published the first edition of his *Golden Bough*, which began to outline his theory of 'contagious magic' based on the law of contact and imitation,[25] and which would influence Freud's *Totem and Taboo* (1913).

By the early years of the twentieth century, the emphasis on 'moral contagion' in social-psychological literature seems to have made way for an emphasis on 'emotional contagion' or 'mental contagion'. Although Le Bon states that emotions (along with ideas, sentiments and beliefs) can be contagious, he does not use the phrase 'emotional contagion'. Psychologist William McDougall takes up Le Bon's work in his 1920 book *The Group Mind*, and posits 'emotional contagion' as an underlying principle of crowd behaviour alongside example, suggestion and 'group spirit' (McDougall 1920, p. 91). In developing his theory of crowd behaviour in *Group Psychology and the Analysis of the Ego* (*Massenpsychologie und Ich-Analyse*), published the following year in 1921, Freud draws heavily both on Le Bon's *Crowd*, which he describes as a 'brilliant psychological character sketch of the group mind' (1922 [1921], p. 101),[26] and McDougall's *Group Mind*. Freud specifically adopts McDougall's concept of emotional contagion (1922 [1921], p. 27), which he translates into German as *Gefühlsansteckung* (Freud 1921, p. 30).[27] In describing this affective form of contagion, Freud writes

> There is no doubt that something exists in us which, when we become aware of signs of an emotion in someone else, tends to make us fall into the same emotion; but how often do we not successfully oppose it, resist the emotion, and react in quite an opposite way? Why, therefore, do we invariably give way to this contagion (*Ansteckung*) when we are in a group? Once more we should have to say that what compels us to obey this tendency is imitation, and what induces the emotion in us is the group's suggestive influence. (Freud 1922 [1921], p. 35)

Although 'emotional' or 'affective' contagion found new and sustained expression in late twentieth-century social psychology, most notably in the work of Elaine Hatfield, John T. Cacioppo and Richard L. Rapson (1994), perhaps more pervasive in the psychological literature of the earlier twentieth century was the phrase 'mental contagion'. In 1905, Vigouroux and Juquelier published their *La contagion mentale*, in which they argue that all the manifestations of psychological life are contagious. Ideas, they maintain, are particularly contagious due to their 'affective' value (1905, p. 243).[28] Similarly, in 1911, psychologist Georges Dumas wrote an article for the *Review Philosophique* titled 'Contagion Mentale', in which he, like Vigouroux and Juquelier, subsumed all previous work on moral and imitative contagion under the heading 'mental' contagion. Dumas notably cites the work of the Russian psychologist Vladimir Bekhterev, whose 1908 book

Suggestion and its Role in Social Life had been translated into French only the year before. In particular, Dumas calls attention to Bekhterev's proposal of a 'contagium psychicum' to parallel 'contagium vivum', or physical infection (1911, p. 233), a concept that underpins both Dumas's analysis and choice of title for his article. Bekhterev himself proposes his 'contagium psychicum' in the opening paragraph of his book on suggestion. He writes:

> Nowadays people talk so much about physical infection [*zaraze*] through "living contact" (*contagium vivum*) or so called microbes that I feel it is useful to consider "psychic contact" as well (*contagium psychicum*), which causes a psychic infection, whose microbes, although invisible with a microscope, nevertheless function here, there and everywhere, similarly to physical microbes, and are transferred through words, gestures, and movements of surrounding people, though books, newspapers, etc.; in a word, wherever we are in the surrounding society, we are exposed to the action of psychic microbes and therefore we are in danger of being psychically infected [*zaražennymi*]. (Bekhterev 1998 [1908], p. 1)

Bekhterev's 'contagium psychicum', further, contains echoes of his compatriot and contemporary Leo Nikolayevich Tolstoy's theory of art as infection, which he outlined in his treatise on aesthetics, *What is Art?* (*Chto takoe iskusstvo?*), published in 1897. According to Tolstoy, art has a power that is at once affective and infective and this 'contagiousness' (*zarazitel´nost´*) distinguishes 'real art' from mere imitation (1989 [1897], p. 214). A true work of art, he argues, causes in its perceiver not so much a loss of individual subjectivity as a merging of subjectivities, a 'mental union' with the artist and with others 'who are also receptive of the artistic production' (1989 [1897], p. 214). Tolstoy describes this 'mental union' in epidemiological terms:

> If a person experiences this feeling, is affected contagiously [*zaražaetsâ*] with the state of mind in which the author was, and feels himself merged in other people, the object which calls forth this condition is art; if there is not this contagion [*zaraženiâ*], if there is no merging in the author, and in those perceiving the production, it is not art. (Tolstoy 1989 [1897], p. 215)

Moreover, he adds, 'not only is that contagiousness the indubitable sign of art, but the degree of contagiousness [*zarazitel´nosti*] is the one measure of the value of art' (1989 [1897], p. 215). In this way, he concludes, the value of art can be assessed in more neutral terms, for the principle of contagion allows the value of art to be defined 'independently of its subject, that is independently of whether it conveys good or bad feelings' (1989 [1897], p. 220). We are, indeed, now far removed from the strongly negative Platonic conception of mimetic contagion and the concept of 'moral' contagion that developed from it. In his book on the 'somatics' of literature, Douglas Robinson argues that what Tolstoy's theory of artistic infection or contagion offers is, in fact,

> a dialectical bridge between the Platonic image of art as the carrier of social disease or disorder (infecting audiences with insurgent feelings and a disinclination to resist or suppress them) and the Aristotelian image of art as the carrier of a cure or therapy for emotional excess (infecting audiences with the excessive feelings *and* their purgation – a dim or distant model for the homeopathic cure the estranging formalists imagine). (Robinson 2008, p. x)

Although I certainly do not wish to suggest that the negative connotations surrounding 'moral' contagion disappeared entirely in the late nineteenth and early twentieth centuries, I would argue there was a developing rhetoric of contagion that was more neutral, or perhaps more ambivalent. Undoubtedly, this was related to the germ theory that was developing from the mid 1850s on, with the microbe offering itself as a novel metaphor for the transmission and spread of ideas. In linking ideas to microbes in 1895, Le Bon was in some ways ahead of his time. As McClelland points out, Le Bon shows he 'had a nose for everything' by beginning 'to play with the analogy between crowds and microbes' in *Psychologie des foules*. And yet, he adds, Le Bon 'did not take the matter very far' (1989, p. 294).

By the second half of the twentieth century, however, evidence across a number of disciplines began to suggest a much stronger articulation between ideas and microbes, germs and viruses. This articulation is apparent not only in the work of the economic geographer Siegfried, who, as we saw in Chapter 2, noted the 'striking parallel between the spreading of germs and the spreading of ideas or propaganda' (1965 [1960], p. 85), but also, a decade and a half later, in Richard Dawkins's idea of the 'meme'. Memetics or meme theory is often characterized as a theory of 'thought contagion', but Dawkins not only draws on virological and epidemiological metaphors in outlining his concept of the meme, but also genetic ones, and it is the complex relationship between meme and metaphor to which I will now turn.

Infectious Ideas: Richard Dawkins, Meme Theory and the Politics of Metaphor

In the late nineteenth century, Gabriel Tarde, Gustave Le Bon and Scipio Sighele – as we saw in Chapter 3 – contributed to a new form of social contagion theory whose underlying mimetic processes began to be figured less as 'moral' contagion than as 'mental' or even 'cultural' contagion. Almost a century later, Richard Dawkins (seemingly unaware of the work of Tarde and his contemporaries) coined a small and rather French-sounding word that seemed to encapsulate the very concept of idea diffusion. Dawkins's neologism – the word 'meme' – has subsequently become a byword for cultural and thought contagion and, in its increasingly predominant incarnation as the 'Internet meme', has become virtually synonymous with more recent catchphrases such as 'viral marketing' and 'contagious media'.[1]

The focus of this chapter is on the *rhetoric* of meme theory, or memetics. As meme theorist and evolutionary psychologist Robert Aunger wryly notes, 'the literature of memetics is hugely infected with epidemiological terms' (2000a, p. 8). The virological and epidemiological metaphors that accrue around the meme, I will argue, raise interesting questions not only about the metaphor of contagion, but also about metaphor itself. However, if we go back to Dawkins's original definition of the 'meme', we can see that these metaphors of contagion were not his primary concern, and indeed came about almost accidentally. What Dawkins was most interested in was developing an analogy between meme and gene rather than between meme and virus; he was interested primarily in proposing a kind of cultural evolutionism or a cultural Darwinism.

Selfish genes, selfish memes

In 1976, Dawkins published his acclaimed and influential first book, *The Selfish Gene*. In the 1960s and early 1970s, Dawkins had published a number of academic articles in the field of ethology, but *The Selfish Gene* marked his first real foray into writing for a broader, crossover audience. Dawkins's hope for *The Selfish Gene*, a desire he expresses in the preface to the first edition, was that it would make biology as 'exciting as a mystery story, for a mystery story is exactly what biology is' (1976, p. ix). As such, he suggests, the book 'should be read almost as though it were science fiction', even though it is definitively a work of 'science' (1976, p. ix). In writing his crossover book, Dawkins states that he imagined three readers whom he would need to satisfy: the general reader, the expert and the student. Of these three, it is the expert reader that Dawkins is most tentative about having satisfied:

> The expert will still not be totally happy with the way I put things. Yet my great-est hope is that even he [sic] will find something new here; a way of looking at familiar ideas perhaps; even stimulation of new ideas of his own. If this is too high an aspiration, may I at least hope that the book will entertain him on a train? (Dawkins 1976, p. x)

Ostensibly, *The Selfish Gene* is devoted to debunking the theory of 'group selec-tion', a theory based on the reassuring (but erroneous, Dawkins is quick to point out) notion that individual members of a group, a population or a species 'are prepared to sacrifice themselves for the welfare of the group' (Dawkins 1976, p. 8). Group selection theory holds that this, in turn, can give the altruistically minded group a distinct evolutionary advantage over a 'selfish' one, leading to a world 'populated mainly by groups consisting of self-sacrificing individuals' (1976, p. 8). Against this outdated position, which he argues 'contravene[s] orthodox Darwinian theory' (1976, p. 9), Dawkins proposes a theory of gene selection. More specifically, he proposes a 'fundamental law [of] *gene selfish-ness*', one that he suggests can explain both the phenomenon of selfishness and that of altruism (1976, p. 7). In his gene-centred view of evolution, Dawkins characterizes genes as 'selfish replicators', existing only to make copies (though not always exact) of themselves. Humans, he says, are simply the selfish genes' 'survival machines' (1976, p. 21).

In the 35 years since its publication, *The Selfish Gene* has become a classic of popular science and an exemplar of the genre. As Soraya de Chadarevian notes in her thirtieth-anniversary essay on the publishing history of *The Selfish Gene*, by 2006 the book had 'sold over a million copies' and had been 'translated into over 20 languages' (2007, pp. 31–2). Further, biologist Alan Grafen makes strong claims for the book's direct and lasting influence on his field, arguing that he is 'convinced that *The Selfish Gene* brought about a silent and almost immediate revolution in biology' (2006, p. 72).

Dawkins's adventurous gene-centred view of evolutionary biology certainly had a profound influence both within the scientific disciplines and more generally. Yet today, the influence of Dawkins's first book is perhaps felt less in his concept of the 'selfish gene' than in a second, correlative concept that Dawkins begins to sketch in the book's final, brief chapter. In this closing think-piece of a chapter, Dawkins later acknowledged, he 'allow[ed] himself a little entertainment' (1978, p. 711) by proposing a cultural correlate for the gene, a concept he called the 'meme'. Dawkins might have presented the 'meme' as, quite literally, an afterthought, but as James Gleick puts it in his most recent bestseller, *The Information: A History, A Theory , A Flood*, the 'meme' became Dawkins's 'most memorable invention, far more influential than his selfish genes or his later proselytizing against religiosity' (2011, p. 312).

What, then, did Dawkins mean by the 'meme'? In concluding *The Selfish Gene*, Dawkins suggests that perhaps, now that we have seen how the gene is a selfish replicator, we can think of culture as operating in a similar way. How do ideas develop and spread? By repetition, Dawkins says. And the idea that goes furthest – that has the most salience – is the one that is easily replicated, indeed is programmed to replicate itself. Ultimately, culture appears to Dawkins as operating on a selectionist basis and, furthermore, in a similar way to biological evolution. As Dawkins argues, 'cultural transmission is analogous to genetic transmission in that, although basically conservative, it can give rise to a form of evolution' (1976, p. 203). This 'cultural' form of evolution does, however, differ from biological evolution in two crucial ways: first, it occurs by 'non-genetic means' and, second, it seems to happen 'at a rate orders of magnitude faster than genetic evolution' (1976, p. 203). Fundamentally, though, both cultural and genetic evolution appear to Dawkins as relying on the same principle of selfish replication. In Dawkins's evolving theory of cultural evolution, the base replicating unit analogous to the gene is the meme, and Dawkins explains in detail the etymology of his neologism. He writes:

> We need a name for the new [cultural] replicator, a noun that conveys the idea of a unit of cultural transmission, or a unit of *imitation*. "Mimeme" comes from a suitable Greek root, but I want a monosyllable that sounds a bit like "gene". I hope my classicist friends will forgive me if I abbreviate mimeme to *meme*.

If it is any consolation, it could alternatively be thought of as being related to "memory", or to the French word *même*. It should be pronounced to rhyme with "cream". (Dawkins 1976, p. 206; emph. in original)

Examples of memes, Dawkins continues,

are tunes, ideas, catch-phrases, clothes fashions, ways of making pots or of building arches. Just as genes propagate themselves in the gene pool by leaping from body to body via sperms or eggs, so memes propagate themselves in the meme pool by leaping from brain to brain via a process which, in the broad sense, can be called imitation. (Dawkins 1976, p. 206)

In his neologism's constructed etymology, Dawkins explicitly locates the meme within a tradition of mimetic (rather than memetic) thought. The Greek 'mimeme' (μίμημα) means 'anything imitated, a counterfeit, a copy' (Liddell and Scott 1846, p. 936), and in his *Timaeus*, Plato uses the word μίμημα to distinguish between the noumenal world of forms and the phenomenal world of appearances or representation.[2] The mimeme is, in Plato's theory of mimesis, a copy, a simulacrum, an imitation of an ideal form. Yet, even though Dawkins consciously invokes classical theories of mimesis, he does not explain in any detail what he means by 'imitation', or rather, he treats the term as being self-explanatory or unproblematic. Rather than proposing (as Tarde did) a theory of imitation and social influence, Dawkins focuses on developing his analogy between memes and genes, explaining where the analogy is strong and where it requires further development. He concludes, suggestively, that 'we are built as gene machines and cultured as meme machines, but we have the power to turn against our creators. We, alone on earth, can rebel against the tyranny of the selfish replicators' (1976, p. 215).

Memes, genes and critiques of *The Selfish Gene*

Dawkins certainly never fully equates the meme to the gene – he employs analogy or simile rather than metaphor – but lurking behind this analogy is a larger, implied metaphor, namely that culture is biological, or, more strongly put, that culture is biology. Although *The Selfish Gene* did attract a number of generous and positive assessments,[3] this cultural biologism perhaps unsurprisingly drew strong criticism from across the academic disciplinary spectrum. In the year of the book's publication, *New Scientist* published an excerpt of Dawkins's exploratory chapter on memes under the title 'Memes and the Evolution of Culture'. In the following issue's letters to the editor, a reader – one A. R. Pitcher of Stevenage, Hertfordshire – wrote, 'Sir – I claim the prize for spotting the spoof article for October 1976' (Pitcher 1976, p. 355), referring to Dawkins's article on memes. Certainly less droll, but no less critical, was sociologist Penelope J. Greene's 1978 review of *The Selfish Gene* for the journal *Contemporary Sociology*. In an otherwise positive review of the book, Greene criticized Dawkins's chapter on memes, suggesting 'the value of the book is not to be found in this final chapter, although I anticipate that both the strongest advocates and the harshest critics of sociobiology will focus on this section' (1978, p. 709).

Where many scientists considered the analogy between memes and genes to be deeply flawed, many humanists disliked what they saw as its inherent biological determinism and its attack on existing theories of human subjectivity and agency. Soon after the publication of *The Selfish Gene*, moral philosopher Mary Midgley wrote a famously stinging review, describing Dawkins's arguments and analysis as, among other things, 'absurdly abstract', 'grossly simplified', 'bogus' and 'crashingly wrong' (1979, pp. 441, 446). Notably, Midgley accuses Dawkins of 'withdraw[ing] into talk of metaphors' whenever logical, scientific 'ruin stares him in the face' (1979, p. 446). For Midgley, Dawkins is entirely too dependent on metaphor, even in his discussion of the gene. 'When the mountains of metaphor are removed', Midgley writes, allowing herself some rhetorical flourishes, 'what we find is not so much a mouse as a mare's nest', a 'vacuous' attempt to find a 'fundamental unit' that explains human evolution (1979, p. 451).

More recently, ethicist Hiram Caton has argued strongly against what he calls the 'dumbed-down behaviorism' of the meme (2000, p. 274), which, he argues, ignores the deliberate manufacturing of consent, and which purports to impart a 'double whammy' to a theory of subjectivity based on free will: 'First', Caton argues, 'subjectivity is robotized by genes; then lobotomized by memes' (2000, p. 273). Summing up the negative reactions to Dawkins's 'meme', cognitive scientist Margaret A. Boden explains,

> Sceptics pointed out that memes – unlike genes – can't be crisply identified. They appear to include concepts, schemata, scripts, theories, cultures, and cultural practices, none of which are easily defined. . . . They aren't always copied faithfully, but are often contaminated by new cultural associations, or by metaphor. (Boden 2006, p. 565)

The constellation of 'meme', 'contamination' and 'metaphor' in Boden's passage is striking. For many scientists – and this is a point I will return to later in this chapter – the meme was not itself an empty rhetorical figure, a metaphor, but was also open to 'contamination' *by* metaphor.

The Lamarckian meme

Faced with early criticism, by the early 1980s Dawkins had toned down his evolutionary claims for the meme, but he was not ready to let go of them completely. In his 1982 book, *The Extended Phenotype*, Dawkins grants that 'memes may partially blend with each other in a way that genes do not' and that, in contradiction to accepted theories of the mechanics of evolution, memetic mutations (unlike genetic ones) may be 'directed' rather than properly 'random' (1982, p. 112). In short, he acknowledges, memes are more 'Lamarckian' than genes (1982, p. 112).

This is a significant stumbling block in the meme–gene analogy, for in granting that memes are 'Lamarckian', Dawkins was invoking an evolutionary hypothesis that had been almost thoroughly discredited by the early decades of the twentieth century. At the turn of the nineteenth century, the French naturalist Jean-Baptiste Lamarck (1744–1829) was developing what has been considered 'the first . . . consistent and comprehensive evolutionary theory' (Gould 2002, p. 174), some 50 years before Darwin published his theory of natural selection. Lamarck's theory relied on 'soft inheritance', or the idea that a species can pass on to its offspring certain attributes that it has developed over time in response to the physical environment.[4] The well-worn example inevitably supplied to illustrate soft inheritance is Lamarck's account of giraffe physiology. In his 1809 work *Philosophie zoologique*, or *Philosophical Zoology*, Lamarck provides this brief description of the giraffe:

> It is interesting to observe the result of habit in the peculiar shape and size of the giraffe (*Camelo-pardalis*): this animal, the largest of the mammals, is known to live in the interior of Africa in places where the soil is nearly always arid and barren, so that it is obliged to browse on the leaves of trees and to make constant efforts to reach them. From this habit long maintained in all its race, it has resulted that the animal's fore-legs have become longer than its hind legs, and that its neck is lengthened to such a degree that the giraffe, without standing up on its hind legs, attains a height of six metres (nearly 20 feet). (Lamarck 1914 [1809], p. 122)

This account, often reduced in accounts of the development of evolutionary theory to a kind of 'how the giraffe got its long neck' fable, relies on a bidirectional communication between the genes or germ line cells (the geno-type) and the bodily cells (the phenotype) of an organism. In other words, it presumes the gene has a certain amount of plasticity or permeability and is able to be acted upon and modified by bodily phenomena. In the soft inheritance account of the giraffe, the animal develops a long neck by reaching for leaves, a phenomenon that occurs at the level of the phenotype. The animal is then able to pass this trait developed in its bodily cells on to its offspring by way of its germ line cells, or genes. As Lamarck explains,

> every change that is wrought in an organ through a habit of frequently using it, is subsequently preserved by reproduction, if it is common to the individuals who unite together in fertilisation for the propagation of their species. Such a change is thus handed on to all succeeding individuals in the same environment, without their having to acquire it in the same way that it was actually created. (Lamarck 1914 [1809], p. 122)

It was not long before this idea that the phenotype can effect change in the genotype was extended into the social realm, and indeed what has become known as 'Social Darwinism' was undergirded by the concept of soft inherit-ance. According to neurobiologist Kenan Malik,

> It is easy to see why Lamarck's theory [of inheritance] should appeal to reform-minded social scientists. Lamarckism provided the bridge between the biologi-cal and the social, and afforded a mechanism for social and cultural factors to affect human evolution. Whereas Darwinian theory implied that evolutionary change occurred accidentally and spontaneously, Lamarckism allowed for con-sciousness and will in evolution. (Malik 1996, p. 158)

It is also, then, easy to see why Dawkins felt compelled to admit that his memes were somewhat Lamarckian and that the evolution of memes could be 'directed' (Lamarckian) rather than entirely random, as a staunchly 'hard' inheritance approach would require.

By the late nineteenth century, however, the German evolutionary biolo-gist August Weismann (1834–1914) refuted soft inheritance by positing the 'Weismann barrier', a move that effectively discredited Lamarckism within evolutionary biology. Weismann's barrier asserts that hereditary information can be transmitted only in one direction: from the genotype to the phenotype, and never from the phenotype to the genotype. That is, changes in the soma or bodily cells cannot affect the germ line cells or genes. Weismann established his theory of 'hard' inheritance in a series of experiments on rats that provided a conceptual counterpoint to Lamarck's giraffe. As systems theorist Graeme Donald Snooks explains, Weismann conducted 'mutilation experiments (most famously by removing the tails of rats soon after birth) to discover whether these bodily modifications could be passed on to their progeny' (2003, p. 86). Weismann's experiments, Snooks continues, were certainly a 'rather naive test of Lamarckian theory', but they 'were taken seriously at the time' and his resulting 'barrier' has since 'become part of the dogma of modern biology' (2003, p. 86). Indeed, Snooks notes that Dawkins has avowed himself an 'extreme Weismannist' and has 'offered to eat his hat if anyone is able to demonstrate that this part of the central dogma is not true' (2003, p. 86). In the light of his tenacious endorsement of the Weismann barrier, then, Dawkins's concession that memes might be considered 'Lamarckian' is a significant and a problematic one.

By describing memes as 'Lamarckian', Dawkins in effect allows for two-way interaction between bodies and memes – between the phenotype and, in this case, the *memotype*. In order to operate, the meme must break the Weismann barrier because otherwise there could be no human agency determining which memes are picked up and passed on in its cultural evolutionary model. If memes were not 'Lamarckian', we might be powerless to resist or reject (as Dawkins would have us do) religious memes, or the 'God delusion'. As an aside, not all Dawkins's followers agree with this. Susan Blackmore in her book *The Meme Machine*, for instance, argues that humans are nothing but memeplexes or meme machines and that as a species we need to move beyond the idea of human agency (Blackmore 1999). Further, contra Dawkins, historian and philosopher of science David Hull argues that memetic transmission cannot be considered to be Lamarckian, because 'memes are analogous to genes, not phenotypic characteristics' (2000, p. 56).

As Boden explains, Lamarckism is one of the forms of 'contamination' that the idea of the meme opens itself up to:

> [Memes] don't have separate lineages, for while one can imitate one's parents' or neighbours' ideas one can also (thanks to books and other media) imitate ideas far away in time and space. They can be discarded and replaced by others, whether voluntarily or not .... And whereas genes are clearly distinct from the phenotypic characters they "cause", memes are seen sometimes as the brain mechanisms that underlie a concept or cultural practice and sometimes as those phenomena themselves. (Boden 2006, p. 565)

Even though researchers have suggested that the Weismann barrier is not as impermeable as previously thought,[5] from a biological perspective these questions pose significant hurdles for Dawkins's meme–gene analogy. Indeed, by 1982, Dawkins was starting to resile somewhat from his strong analogy between memes and genes, stating that

> These differences may prove sufficient to render the analogy with genetic selection worthless or even positively misleading. My own feeling is that its main value may lie not so much in helping us to understand human culture as in sharpening our perception of genetic natural selection. This is the only reason I am presumptuous enough to discuss it, for I do not known [sic] enough about the existing literature on human culture to make an authoritative contribution to it. (Dawkins 1982, p. 112)

The contagious meme

Even though there was – and continues to be – trenchant criticism of Dawkins's meme, at the same time it gathered just as many followers as critics. The meme seemed to appeal to a range of writers and thinkers: from academics interested in applying the concept of the meme to their object (usually cultural) of study to techno-determinists and independent researchers with an interest in New Age humanism. The meme also caught the eye of Douglas Hofstadter and Daniel Dennett, two cognitive scientists who worked the concept of the meme into their own research and contributed to a developing 'meme theory' in the early 1990s.[6] Since Dawkins first introduced the meme in 1976, more than 20 books have been devoted to the meme and to meme theory,[7] as well as hundreds of articles. The word 'meme' has also been recognized in the *Oxford English Dictionary*, staking its place in the third edition of 2001 after first appearing in the 1997 supplementary 'Additions' to the second edition. Replaying the original meme–gene analogy, the *OED* entry defines a meme as

> A cultural element or behavioural trait whose transmission and consequent persistence in a population, although occurring by non-genetic means (esp. imitation), is considered as analogous to the inheritance of a gene. ('Meme' 2001)

This rapid cultural uptake of the meme – despite the trenchant criticisms leveled against it – is quite remarkable. In short, there seemed to be something sexy, something catchy about the meme, so that by the late 1990s it began to seem like a self-fulfilling prophecy: the *meme* meme.

At the same time as Dawkins was backing away from his gene–meme analogy and playing down the link to evolutionary theories, the meme increasingly began to be figured in terms of contagion. As we have seen, this was not Dawkins's original intent; in *The Selfish Gene*, he is clearly most interested in the analogy between gene and meme. However, in *The Selfish Gene*, Dawkins briefly hints at the epidemiological metaphors that the meme would soon accrue. Immediately after Dawkins defines his meme and provides his list of examples, he states that

> If a scientist hears, or reads about, a good idea, he passes it on to his colleagues and students. He mentions it in his articles and his lectures. If the idea catches on, it can be said to propagate itself, spreading from brain to brain. (Dawkins 1976, p. 206)

Dawkins then does something a little unusual. He includes a comment that one of his colleagues, N. K. Humphrey, made in response to reading a draft of the chapter:

> As my colleague N. K. Humphrey neatly summed up in an earlier draft of this chapter: ". . . memes should be regarded as living structures, not just metaphorically but technically. When you plant a fertile meme in my mind you literally parasitize my brain, turning it into a vehicle for the meme's propagation in just the way that a virus may parasitize the genetic mechanism of a host cell. And this isn't just a way of talking – the meme for, say, 'belief in life after death' is actually realized physically, millions of times over, as a structure in the nervous systems of individual men the world over". (Dawkins 1976, pp. 206–7)

Dawkins not only implicitly concurs with Humphrey's virological metaphor, he soon after reasserts it by describing certain dominant and long-lasting memes (such as the 'idea of God') as having an 'infective power' (1976, p. 207). Humphrey's statement is worth looking at closely for the way in which it problematizes an easy distinction between the literal and the metaphorical.

Humphrey argues that the meme should be thought of as parasitic in a *literal* sense. And, as though wary of being accused of mistakenly using the term 'literally' when he means 'metaphorically' – the sort of common error grammarians might jokingly describe as literally a hanging offence – Humphrey spells out that he means it 'technically' and not just 'metaphorically', and then reiterates that 'this isn't just a way of talking'. Of course, the only thing that can 'literally' be parasitic is a parasite itself; therefore, if we are to take Humphrey at his word (if we are, in other words, to take him literally), then he must also mean us to accept that the meme is (literally) a parasite. Further, Humphrey describes the meme/parasite's operation as, in turn, perfectly analogous to a virus. In (literally) parasitizing human brains, he argues, the meme operates in 'just the same way' as a (literal) virus.

This is the only point in *The Selfish Gene* at which Dawkins employs the virological metaphor with reference to memes,[8] and yet, from the mid 1980s, the meme-as-virus or meme-as-contagion metaphor begins to assert its dominance over the meme–gene analogy. Undoubtedly instrumental in this rhetorical and conceptual shift was Douglas R. Hofstadter. In the early 1980s, Hofstadter wrote a series of articles on what he termed 'metamagical themas' for *Scientific American*. In a 1983 issue, Hofstadter devoted one of these articles to exploring the 'viral' nature of the meme. In this article, titled 'Virus-like Sentences and Self-Replicating Structures', Hofstadter engages with two thought-provoking letters he had received from readers of an earlier article he had published on self-referential sentences. These letters were, according to Hofstadter, 'remarkably similar' in that both authors 'saw self-replicating sentences as being similar to viruses' (1983, p. 14). Hofstadter is taken by one letter in particular. Its author, a New York-based *Scientific American* reader named Stephen Walton (who had also, apparently, read Dawkins's *Selfish Gene*), pithily described these self-referential, self-replicating sentences as 'viral sentences' (Hofstadter 1983, p. 14).

Hofstadter relates Walton's concept of 'viral' sentences to the work of a number of scientists and thinkers who had already remarked on the evolutionary or 'infective' nature of ideas. Hofstadter briefly mentions the work of neurophysiologist R. W. Sperry, who, in 1965, suggested that 'ideas cause ideas and help evolve new ideas', before turning to Jacques Monod's 1970 description of the 'spreading power' or 'infectivity' of ideas,[9] both of which he sees encapsulated in Dawkins's 1976 concept of the meme (1983, p. 14). Hofstadter does refer to Dawkins's gene–meme analogy, but, in his reading, the viral metaphor appears more apt, more suggestive of the mechanics of self-replicating structures. He writes,

> I found Walton's phrases "viral sentence" and "viral text" to be exceedingly catchy – little memes in themselves, definitely worthy, in my opinion, of republication some 700,000 times in print, and who knows how many times orally beyond that? Walton's own viral text, as you can see before your eyes, has managed to commandeer the facilities of a powerful host: an entire printing press and magazine and distribution service. It has leaped aboard and is now – even as you read this viral sentence – propagating itself madly through the ideosphere. (Hofstadter 1983, p. 18)

In other words, by dint of its very contagiousness, the virological metaphor enacts what it describes: it is explicitly both self-reflexive and self-replicating. And, perhaps predictably, from there the virological metaphor caught on, appearing also in Daniel Dennett's provocative book of 1991, *Consciousness Explained*. Dennett dedicates a section of *Consciousness Explained* to memes, arguing that they may provide a key to understanding the evolution of consciousness. Even though his focus is on the *evolutionary* aspect of meme theory as cultural evolution, he nevertheless seems compelled to employ a metaphor drawn from epidemiology. 'Memes', Dennett writes,

> now spread around the world at the speed of light, and replicate at rates that make even fruit flies and yeast cells look glacial in comparison. They leap promiscuously from vehicle to vehicle, and from medium to medium, and are proving to be virtually *unquarantinable*. (Dennett 1991, p. 205; emph. added)

By the early 1990s, Dawkins himself was foregrounding the meme's accrued and increasingly predominant viral metaphors. In 1993, he published an essay on memes titled 'Viruses of the Mind', which was included in an essay collection devoted to Dennett's work. In this essay, Dawkins initially turns his attention to computer viruses, suggesting they might be considered as a 'model for an informational epidemiology' (1993, p. 14). Viruses, he says, 'aren't limited to electronic media such as disks and data lines' (1993, p. 15) and further, he argues, 'at the very least the mind is a plausible *candidate* for infection by something like a computer virus, even if it is not quite such a parasite's dream-environment as a cell nucleus or an electronic computer' (1993, p. 20; emph. in original).

Dawkins acknowledges that his virological analogy 'is not that precise', but states that it 'is nothing to get worked up about'; rather, he argues, 'what matters is that minds are friendly environments to parasitic, self-replicating ideas or information, and that minds are typically massively infected' (1993, p. 20). Yet, despite this, Dawkins does go to some lengths to quarantine science itself from his epidemiological analogies and metaphors. In a section of his 'Viruses of the Mind' essay, Dawkins poses the question 'Is Science a Virus?' and he responds with a resounding 'no'. The spread of scientific ideas might, he grants, 'look superficially virus-like', but, unlike the faith-based spread of religion, 'the selective forces that scrutinize scientific ideas are not arbitrary or capricious. They are exacting, well-honed rules, and they do not favor pointless, self-serving behavior' (1993, p. 26). Dawkins adds,

> You may find elements of epidemiology in the spread of scientific ideas, but it will be largely descriptive epidemiology. The rapid spread of a good idea through the scientific community may even look like a description of a measles epidemic. But when you examine the underlying reasons you find that they are

good ones, satisfying the demanding standards of scientific method. In the history of the spread of faith you will find little else but epidemiology, and causal epidemiology at that. . . . For scientific belief, epidemiology merely comes along afterwards and describes the history of its acceptance. For religious belief, epidemiology is the root cause. (Dawkins 1993, p. 26)

Beginning with Hofstadter and Dawkins's foregrounding of epidemiological analogies and metaphors, a clear virological line begins to develop, running through the literature on meme theory. The rhetoric of memetics substantially shifts from an evolutionary/genetic focus to an epidemiological one. Aunger argues that it is the 'diffusionist perspective' of epidemiology from which 'memetics gets its almost obsessional concern with the transmission of information', and he suggests that meme theorists' enthusiastic and wholesale adoption of epidemiological metaphor is 'most readily seen in the titles of meme articles and books' (Aunger 2000a, p. 8). These epidemiological metaphors are evident also in the stock phrases that begin to accrue around meme theory, including 'viral sentences', 'viruses of the mind',[10] 'thought contagion',[11] 'contagious ideas'[12] and 'religious infection'.[13] The last one of these replays Dawkins's figuration of religion as a 'bad' contagion, but the thought contagion metaphor is a generally neutral one. Contagion is the way in which all ideas – good and bad – are transmitted and shared, for, as Dawkins explains in 'Viruses of the Mind', 'the virus principle could, in theory, be used for non-malicious, even beneficial purposes' (1993, p. 16).

However, when we look at the titles of meme books and articles that make direct reference to genes and to evolution, it appears that these are far less metaphorical. Titles such as Stephen Shennan's *Genes, Memes and Human History: Darwinian Archaeology and Cultural Evolution* (2002), Alister E. McGrath's *Dawkins' God: Genes, Memes, and the Meaning of Life* (2004) and Leigh Hoyle's *Genes, Memes, Culture, and Mental Illness: Toward an Integrative Model* (2010) suggest a syndetic relationship among the terms rather than a metaphorical one. In other words, the titles of these books suggest their content will focus on memes *and* genes or memes *and* evolution, not on memes *as* genes or memes *as* evolution.

In short, although genetics and evolution remain as *analogies* for the meme, contagion, I would argue, becomes the primary *metaphor* for the meme. Interestingly, this shift from analogy to metaphor in discourse around the meme appears to invert the predominant linguistic shift that Dedre Genter and Michael Jeziorski have identified in the history of Western science. Genter and Jeziorski argue that Western scientific discourse broadly has witnessed an 'evolution' from the alchemists' 'pluralistic use' of metaphor to contemporary science's 'austere modern focus on structural analogy' (1993, p. 448). Analogy, they argue, was '(re)discovered in Western science in about 1600' (1993, p. 475), and since that time has become the dominant scientific mode of explanation by similarity.

Although analogical reasoning has its critics, as we will see below, this shift away from a more controlled, controllable and scientifically sanctioned form of reasoning towards a more slippery, wayward and above all *pre-scientific* form of metaphorical reasoning may well underlie criticisms of the meme's accretion of epidemiological metaphors. At the same time, however, the increasing predominance of the contagion metaphor in meme discourse could be read as strategic, and as part of the efforts of meme theorists to situate memetics in relation to existing models of culture or knowledge diffusion – models that, as we have seen, have inevitably drawn on the language of contagion and infection. That is, critics and supporters alike of meme theory regularly acknowledge Dawkins was not the first to propose a diffusion-based form of cultural evolutionism, and they take care to place memetics within this tradition. Most research that traces the history of memetics customarily notes two main precursors of this form of cultural evolutionism: Gabriel Tarde's nineteenth-century socio-psychological theory of contagious imitation and anthropologist F. Ted Cloak's concept of 'cultural ethology', a biological/genetic approach to studying culture that Cloak first proposed in the late 1960s.

French social and cognitive scientist Dan Sperber was one of the first to articulate the links between Tarde's theory of imitation and Dawkins's theory of memes. In his 1996 book *Explaining Culture*, Sperber writes that Tarde's is the 'first serious attempt at a scientific cultural epidemiology', and that Dawkins's meme theory, among others, is a more recent, Darwinian response to the same problem (Sperber 1996, pp. 2–3).[14] Six years later, Bruno Latour criticized Blackmore for 'ignoring' Tarde in her 1999 book-length study of memetics, *The Meme Machine*, an omission he argued was 'unfair since mimetics [sic] is a simplified version of [Tarde's] monadology' (2002, p. 131; n. 8). Social psychologist Paul Marsden has also claimed that Tarde is a 'forefather' of memetics (2000, passim) and that memetics and social contagion theory are, in fact, 'two sides of the same epidemiological coin' (1998, n. pag.). Where memetics is, Marsden argues, 'a theory rich version' of social contagion, social contagion is an 'evidence-rich' version of memetics (1998, n. pag.). Certainly, Tarde's notion – expressed in his 1898 work, *Les lois sociales* (*Social Laws*) – of 'imitative rays' that emanate contagiously outward from strong concepts shares some similarities with Dawkins's concept of the meme. As Tarde writes,

> It is through imitative repetition that invention, the fundamental social adaptation, spreads and is strengthened, and tends, through the encounter of one of its own imitative rays with an imitative ray emanating from some other invention, old or new, either to arouse new struggles, or (perhaps directly, perhaps as a result of these struggles) to yield new and more complex inventions, which soon radiate out imitatively in turn, and so on indefinitely. (Tarde 1907 [1898], p. 135)

Moreover, Tarde's argument that 'invention, the fundamental social adaptation' is the direct result of the encounter and interactions of two contagious 'imitative rays' that emanate from different sources has some resonance with those interactionist theories of metaphor outlined earlier in this book.[15]

Dawkins was apparently unaware of Tarde's epidemiological theory of imitation – and of the social-psychological field of social contagion more broadly – when he first formulated his concept of the meme. He was, on the other hand, familiar with Cloak's case for a 'cultural ethology'. Although Dawkins cites Cloak's 1975 article 'Is a Cultural Ethology Possible?' in passing in *The Selfish Gene*, he does acknowledge it further in *The Extended Phenotype*. In this later book, Dawkins acknowledges that, unlike Cloak, he had been 'insufficiently clear about the distinction between the meme itself, as replicator, on the one hand, and its "phenotypic effects" or "meme products" on the other' (1982, p. 109). In effect, in *The Extended Phenotype*, Dawkins attempts to submerge his distinction between the phenotype and the memotype into Cloak's distinction between what he calls *m-culture* and *i-culture*. Cloak's *m-culture*, which refers to material structures and relationships among them, Dawkins says, is roughly analogous to the phenotype in his theory of the meme. *I-culture*, which Cloak describes as the 'set of cultural instructions [humans] carry in their central nervous systems' (Cloak 1975, p. 168) is roughly analogous to Dawkins's memotype.

Cloak's distinction between *m-culture* and *i-culture* has been considered an important influence on Dawkins's Lamarckian meme theory.[16] But what is rarely remarked on by meme theorists is that Cloak, like Tarde and Dawkins, himself employed virological analogies and metaphors. In his seminal article of 1975, Cloak writes:

> In a human carrier, then, a cultural instruction is *more analogous to a viral or a bacterial gene* than to a gene of the carrier's own genome. It is like an active parasite that controls some behavior of its host. It may be in complete mutual

symbiosis with the human host, in which case the behavior it produces has survival value for itself through the value it has for the survival/reproduction of the host. On the other hand, it may be like the gene of a flu or "cold" virus; when the virus makes the host behave, e.g., sneeze, that behavior results in extraorganismic self-replication of the virus gene but not in survival or reproduction of the host or his conspecific. From the organism's point of view, the best that can always be said for cultural instructions, as for parasites of any sort, is that they can't destroy their hosts more quickly than they can propagate. In short, "our" cultural instructions don't work for us organisms; we work for them. At best, we are in symbiosis with them, as we are with our genes. At worst, we are their slaves. (Cloak 1975, p. 172; emph. added)

In both Cloak's and Dawkins's diffusionist theories of culture, then, we appear to end up with two interlinked but competing analogical models: an evolutionary/genetic analogy and a contagion/epidemiological one, the latter of which progressively takes on a metaphorical form and function and increasingly suffuses memetic discourse.

Memes and metaphors

According to Aunger, this argument by analogy is the result of the 'absence of a well-founded model' for the meme (2000a, p. 8), and has provided critics with some of their strongest arguments against meme theory. Social anthropologist Adam Kuper, for instance, warns against the risks of a strong analogy between memes and genes. At one level, the question is a political one. Darwin himself might have used analogy in framing natural selection; however, for some biologists, analogies from evolution should be off limits. As Kuper writes, 'a good case can be made for avoiding the whole business of neo-Darwinian metaphors, if only because they always seem to muddy the waters' (2000, p. 185). To demonstrate, Kuper quotes biologist Steve Jones's straight-talking strong opinions about evolutionary analogies: 'Evolution is to analogy', according to Jones, 'as statues are to birdshit' (qtd. in Kuper 2000, p. 185).

However, Kuper maintains that there is yet a 'more fundamental difficulty' with the meme/gene analogy. Memes, he says, 'are rather shadowy entities, which acquire a certain solidity only by virtue of a metaphorical relationship with genes. (I may not be sure what a meme is, but I think I know what it is like.)' (2000, p. 187). Kuper acknowledges the irony that the *gene* itself was once thought to be invisible – a 'notional entity' rather than a material thing.

Indeed, Kuper adds, a number of scholars, Dawkins included, consider the gene to remain a 'theoretical artefact', a fact that has led Dawkins to be criticized by a number of geneticists (2000, pp. 185–6).

Dawkins is certainly not the only one to question the literality and materiality of the gene. As medical anthropologist Theresa MacPhail has noted, Bruno Latour also considers genes to be effectively 'quasi-objects; things produced by the constant interplay of the material and semiotic, at once both natural/cultural productions' (2004, p. 327). From this constructivist perspective, genes exhibit as much ontological and semantic instability as do memes. In other words, the gene may be no less metaphorical than the meme, but, MacPhail argues, over time, and particularly as a result of the Human Genome Project, the metaphor of the gene has become a dead one – it became 'the only way anyone could talk about genes' and so effectively became literal (2004, p. 329).

Kuper acknowledges that 'perhaps Dawkins's notion of the gene will triumph', but he concludes that 'one does not have to be an overcautious empiricist to feel uneasy when confronted with a Platonic idea of a thing, which can be grasped only by imagining another idea' (2000, p. 186). Ultimately, Kuper argues, Dawkins's memes do not help us, and 'the analogy between memes and genes is fanciful and flawed' (2000, p. 187). Similarly, writing about the meme as metaphor, Mark Jeffreys has noted the problems that emerge from 'the confusion of virology and genetics as base domains for the meme metaphor' (2000, p. 228). Jeffreys is nothing short of scathing in his criticism of the meme's mixing of virological and genetic metaphors when he argues that

> Either the phenomenon of culture evolves or it does not – and if it does evolve, it either does so by a separate system of Darwinian selection or it does not – but in no case is it contagious, or viral, or parasitic, at least not from the point of view of individual humans and their brains. If cultural viruses exist, they infect other cultural entities, and describing the entire process of cultural replication itself in virological terms, as if ideas replicated as germs that fever our vulnerable, but otherwise coolly reasoning brains, takes us steadily further away from understanding how any cultural entities might actually be said to replicate and evolve. (Jeffreys 2000, pp. 230–1)

At base, Jeffreys maintains, 'contagions, hosts, etc., are hopelessly inadequate tropes for discussing a presumed second replicator and a presumed second process of natural selection' (2000, p. 228). Moreover, just as the meme's Lamarckism rendered the meme-as-gene analogy a problematic, if not false, one, it also causes trouble for the meme-as-virus metaphor. If Dawkins's Lamarckian meme allows for even a small amount of human agency in determining which memes are propagated, then, as Francis Heylighen and Klaas Chielens point out, humans cannot be considered 'passive "vehicles" or "carriers" of ideas and beliefs, the way they may carry viruses' (2009, p. n. pag.).

Why then, if contagion is such an inapt metaphor for cultural evolutionism, did it become the predominant metaphor for it? Indeed, going back to the starting point of this chapter, when we consider those now ever-present, 'virally' spreading internet memes, the question of evolution or genetics barely comes into it. If nothing else, the internet meme exemplifies the triumph of the trope of contagion in the struggle between the meme's epidemiological and genetic analogies. Further, I am interested in the meme's potential for self-reflexively highlighting the problem of metaphor. Metaphor is, as I have argued elsewhere, central to questions of disciplinarity, interdisciplinarity and knowledge formation more generally in that it exposes both the poetics and politics of language (Mitchell 2011, pp. 80–1). Metaphors are where resonances between disciplines are most marked, but they are also often where disciplinary skirmishes take place. For instance, when Alan Sokal and Jean Bricmont took what they call postmodern philosophy's 'abuse' of science to task in their book *Intellectual Impostures*, which was based on their notorious *Social Text* hoax of 1996,[17] their argument, in part, hinged on metaphor.

In their introduction to *Intellectual Impostures*, Sokal and Bricmont argue that 'postmodern' philosophers such as Deleuze and Guattari, Baudrillard, and Lacan have misused scientific concepts *as* metaphors. '[W]hat is the purpose of these metaphors?' Sokal and Bricmont ask. 'After all, a metaphor is usually employed to clarify an unfamiliar concept by relating it to a more familiar one, not the reverse' (Sokal and Bricmont 1998, p. 9). In other words, while the humanities provide familiar concepts for use by the sciences, the natural sciences should not be considered as 'a mere reservoir of metaphors ready to be used in the human sciences' (Sokal and Bricmont 1998, p. 177). Literary scholars, rhetoricians and cognitive linguists interested in the question of metaphor might argue that Sokal and Bricmont's attitude towards allowable uses of scientific metaphor merely reflects an overly simplistic and outdated understanding of metaphor. However, Sokal and Bricmont's charge against figural applications of scientific concepts cannot simply be dismissed out of hand, for it not only reflects a relatively common attitude to metaphor within science,[18] but it also unambiguously exposes the politics of metaphor.

Stephen Jay Gould has called the meme 'a meaningless metaphor' (qtd. in Blackmore 1999, p. 17), but whether or not a 'science' of memetics is possible or even desirable, I believe that the meme can have interesting things to say *about* metaphor, about how metaphors develop and spread, and how new scientific metaphors, such as the meme, can call into question the literality of other scientific constructs, such as the gene. In this sense, I want to sidestep the debate over whether memes really do or do not exist or whether culture really does or does not evolve. What I want to do is to suggest that the potential self-reflexivity of the meme-as-contagion metaphor means that it may offer itself as a singularly useful tool for considering the very workings of metaphor.

Having said this, I do not mean to suggest that anything goes with metaphor, or that false analogies should not be held up for critique. Sontag's forceful critique of certain disease metaphors in *Illness as Metaphor* might be too quick to condemn metaphor entirely (a point Sontag concedes in the introduction to *AIDS and Its Metaphors*), but she does dramatically illustrate metaphor's potential for harm. Metaphor should not be taken lightly. But the paralogy at the heart of many critiques of metaphor – particularly critiques of the use of 'scientific' metaphors outside the domain of science – is that metaphor is treated not only as being self-evident, but also as simultaneously both superficial and dangerous. As such, the 'meme' and its accreted epidemiological metaphors can be considered at once 'meaningless' and damaging. In this case, however, inapt metaphors are not so much considered damaging in the sense that Sontag meant, but rather, they are considered damaging to the linguistic precision demanded by science.

More nuanced studies of scientific metaphor, on the other hand, have demonstrated an understanding of the complexities of metaphor and its underlying cognitive nature. Philosopher Richard Boyd, for instance, argues that linguistic precision does not in itself exist; indeed, he maintains, 'there is only one sort of scientific precision – methodological or epistemological precision', and that any perceived linguistic precision is a function of methodological precision (1993, p. 523). Boyd admits that this kind of precision is necessary for science, and he goes so far as to suggest a set of 'realist standards of precision' that might govern the pedagogical or exegetical use of metaphor in science (1993, pp. 523–4). However, Boyd also identifies a special case of scientific metaphor that goes beyond pedagogical or exegetical application, and these types of metaphors he calls 'theory-constitutive metaphors'. These metaphors, he argues, are 'an irreplaceable part of the linguistic machinery of a scientific theory'; they are '*constitutive* of the theories they express, rather than merely exegetical' (1993, p. 486; emph. in original). The primary example Boyd gives of a theory-constitutive metaphor is the mind-as-machine metaphor used in cognitive psychology.

Tarde's imitation-as-contagion or Dawkins's meme-as-contagion metaphors would similarly fall into this theory-constitutive category.

What is interesting about Boyd's theory-constitutive metaphors is that they inherently lack the precision usually demanded of scientific metaphor: in one sense, they are science's *best* metaphors (in that they *constitute* a scientific theory rather than just describe it), but in another sense, they tend to be more inde-terminate and more vague, and therefore fail the test of precision. This lack of precision, however, does not in Boyd's analysis render the theory-constitutive metaphor a poor or inadequately scientific one. Rather, he states, 'the vagueness of scientifically useful theory-constitutive metaphors may serve to remind us of both the actual vagueness of some natural phenomena and the deep limitations of the empiricist conception of linguistic precision' (1993, p. 530).

Sabine Maasen and Peter Weingart have also suggested Earl MacCormac's cognitive approach to metaphor 'places metaphor in a broader biological-cultural context' and argue that metaphors 'mediate between cultural and bio-logical evolution' (2000, p. 143). According to MacCormac,

> As an expression of the cognitive activity of the brain, metaphor interacts with culture not only because it depends on societies' stocks of language acquired by the individual and stored in long-term memory but also because new met-aphors change the language. New metaphors change the stock of language used by society, which in turn becomes stored in long-term memory, thereby changing human conceptual activity. Changes in culture can change the envi-ronment, thereby affecting the biological adaptability of the human organism. Thus, through conceptual metaphoric changes in language, biological evolution may be influenced. (MacCormac 1985, p. 150; qtd. in Maasen and Weingart 2000, p. 143)

MacCormac's metaphor, like Dawkins's Lamarckian meme, can effect changes in the world. Although Maasen and Weingart argue that meme theory is 'seem-ingly senseless' (2000, p. 149) and contains 'fundamental flaws' (p. 150), they too draw out the relationships between meme and metaphor. Indeed, at one point they collapse memes into metaphors – 'memes', they write '(that is, metaphors) . . .' (p. 148) – and suggest that a true evolutionary approach to understand-ing the dynamics of knowledge would entail a shift 'from memes to metaphors, from memetics to an evolutionary metaphorology' (Maasen and Weingart 2000, p. 150). Yet, this response to the meme-metaphor problem ignores what places the meme within the continuum of theories of knowledge diffusion: that is, the seeming inevitability of the contagion metaphor. Unlike the meme-as-gene analogy, when the meme-as-contagion metaphor has been held up for criticism, the historical context of contagion metaphors has been largely, if not completely, ignored. Setting the meme within what is, as we have seen, a long tradition of contagion metaphors related to affect or knowledge further exposes the complexity of metaphor, as well as the lack of contextualization that often characterizes debates around uses of 'scientific' metaphor.

Moreover, as we saw in Chapter 1, contagion also complicates the idea of metaphor, disrupting any simple mapping – in the cognitive linguistic sense – of the source domain onto the target domain, and blurring the edges of the domains themselves. While critics of the meme-as-contagion metaphor appear to want a clear, literal, denotative source domain based on late nineteenth-century medical theories of contagious disease transmission, the history of contagion suggests the concept cannot be so simply quarantined. Critiques of the genetic analogy are on firmer ground here, considering the term *gene* was only coined in 1909 by Wilhelm Johannsen (Keller 2000, p. 1); however, *contagion*, as I have demonstrated, has a much longer provenance and cannot be separated from theories of mimesis, affect and social influence. As a result, the meme's accretion of epidemiological metaphors begins to seem inevitable, articulating its links between the biological and the social, as well as its relationship to Tardean social contagion theory and earlier theories of moral contagion and mimesis. As Matthew Potolsky points out, Dawkins's memetics is 'unthinkable without the philosophical concept of mimesis', but he also suggests mimesis can be cast in terms of the meme, describing mimesis itself as a 'memeplex' that has 'found yet another willing host' in Dawkins and his fellow meme theorists (2006, p. 106).

The meme, perhaps, is simply the most recent attempt to formulate the relationship between contagion and culture, but it is one that, more than any other, I believe highlights the role that language plays. Moreover, the meme-as-contagion metaphor seems to resist clear categorization, leaving us with the question of whether the meme is a metaphor, or metaphor is a kind of meme.[19] In proposing the meme, Dawkins's intent was to suggest that culture is biological, but metaphor, and particularly the contagion metaphor, has a way of switching the terms of the game. Perhaps – using his own logic – Dawkins was simply an unwitting host for the contagion meme, which continues to blur the line between the literal and the metaphorical and between science and culture.

Networks of Contagion

The age of globalization is the age of universal contagion.
Michael Hardt and Antonio Negri, Empire. 2000.[1]

The rise of what Manuel Castells has termed the 'network society' has brought with it an assemblage of so-called viral phenomena. Computer viruses, financial contagion, contagious media, viral marketing – all of these emergent phenomena of the network rely at once on an epidemiological and a networked understanding of transmission. In these recent formations, 'contagion' always-already invokes a second concept, that of the 'network'. Indeed, in recent decades these two concepts – both of which sit in a grey area between the material and the metaphorical – have become so inseparable that they now seem co-constitutive.

In an increasingly technologized and globalized world, Castells argues, networks 'have become the predominant organizational form of every domain of human activity' (2010, p. xliv). Indeed, the network has become so pervasive that it has come to 'constitute the new morphology of our societies' (2010, p. 500). The idea of the network is, of course, not new, and Castells grants that the 'networking form of social organization has existed in other times and spaces' (2010, p. 500). In the twentieth and twenty-first centuries, however, the 'new information technology paradigm' has enabled the 'pervasive expansion throughout the entire social structure', culminating in the rise of the 'network society' (2010, p. 500).

Earlier in this book, I noted that research in epidemiology had undergone a kind of 'network' turn, with topological approaches to understanding the transmission of infectious disease coming to the fore. This relatively new approach to the study of infectious disease has been termed 'network epidemiology'.[2] And yet, as the emergent 'viral' network phenomena of the past 30 years indicate, the correspondence between contagion and the network in the twentieth and twenty-first centuries has by no means been a one-way street. Just as a network perspective has reshaped the study of epidemiology, an epidemiological perspective has transformed understandings of the network. As a result, within the last few decades, we have witnessed the appearance of both a network epidemiology and an epidemiology of networks, both a 'network' turn in the study of infectious disease and an 'epidemiological' turn in network theory.

Contagion and the 'network society': The rise of 'network epidemiology'

In the mid-twentieth century, André Siegfried foresaw the future of infectious disease in an ever more globalized and networked world. Although his *Routes of Contagion* (1965 [1960]) stresses the importance of geography and topography in the spread of infectious disease, Siegfried's description of the relationship between transport and trade routes, networks of communication, and contagion suggests also an increasingly topologized understanding of global flows of capital, goods, information and disease. In Siegfried's account, these are interpenetrating, relational networks of communication or transmission: diseases have traditionally followed established trade routes, and these routes, in turn, are the result of 'numerous and complex' factors, including 'geographical structure, techniques of construction, economic conditions, revolutions in transport methods, political disputes, and the changes which take place in the balance of continents' (1965 [1960], p. 15).

In the twentieth century, Siegfried argues, these 'routes of contagion' have been subjected to a rapid compression of time and space. The result of an 'astonishing increase in speed of communications', this time–space compression has led to a situation in which 'the means of penetration are becoming more and more subtle and more and more unexpected' (1965 [1960], p. 17).[3] Of greatest concern for Siegfried was, as I mentioned in Chapter 2, the development of global air transport networks, which opened up previously isolated spaces and places to increased communication in all its forms. Although he was not the first scholar to raise concerns about the epidemiological consequences of air travel, in his speculations on the role communications and air transport networks might play in the future of disease transmission, Siegfried seems particularly prescient.[4]

Indeed, some 50 years later, epidemiology is only now explicitly responding in a concentrated way to the challenge of Castells's 'network society' through the development of analytical frameworks based on a 'network perspective' of epidemiology. Sociologist Martina Morris's 2004 edited collection, *Network Epidemiology*, is one key text that scopes the terrain of this new network approach and provides it with a name. In her introduction, Morris explains that, although network analysis has its theoretical roots in 'the classic works of anthropology' and has been developing as a method over the past half-century, it has only been taken up in an applied way within epidemiology in 'the last decade or so' (2004a, p. 1). In their 2008 collection, *Networked Disease: Emerging Infections in the Global City*, Harris S. Ali and Roger Keil also advance the case for a network perspective on the study of epidemiology. Post-SARS, Ali and Keil argue, the study of infectious disease necessitates a network perspective: 'global forces and networked relations of all types (e.g., economic, cultural, political, and spatial)', they maintain, 'now need to be taken into account when investigating questions related to the spatial diffusion of a virus under contemporary conditions' (Ali and Keil 2008, p. 3). Finally, in a recent essay on network approaches to epidemiology, J. Shin Teh and Harvey Rubin also argue that a 'networks perspective' is necessary for understanding the spread of infectious disease in current times. But they add to this that infectious disease itself exemplifies the concept of the network. 'Infectious diseases', they explain,

> are excellent examples of complex network systems in motion, from the molecular level right up to the societal and global: Pathogens elaborate complex networks of genetic elements, the interplay of which determines metabolism, survival, and virulence; networks of environmental niches in turn naturally select animal and human reservoirs; and finally, networks of humans and human activities predict risk of disease establishment and spread. (Teh and Rubin 2009, p. 475)

Intersecting networks of contagion in Soderbergh's *Contagion*

The complex interplay of these intersecting networks is nowhere more dramatically portrayed than in Soderbergh's *Contagion* (2011). I have mentioned already that Soderbergh's film emphasizes emotional or affective contagion as much as it does the virus that gives rise to it. Yet, the film also deftly shows how, in the context of an infectious disease outbreak, a multitude of national and global networks – health, transport, economic, communication and media, and security – interact to create 'viral' network phenomena that seem to parallel, if not outstrip, the spread of the literal virus itself.

The hybrid 'novelty' of the film's 'MEV-1' virus, its ability to rapidly mutate, and its access to human bodies whose immune systems are not equipped to resist it are three important factors in its accelerated spread outward from the 'index' patient, Beth Emhoff (Gwyneth Paltrow). However, a fourth factor, the international air transport network, is what ensures the virus's attainment of pandemic status. The virus travels by plane to the USA, to Japan, to the UK and to Europe. Outbreak clusters form across the globe almost simultaneously, and those clusters themselves bleed outward, with the film again emphasizing the role of transport networks in the virus's spread. Urban mass-transport networks not only contribute to the spread of the virus, but also to the spread of information about the outbreak. In Tokyo, a man collapses on a bus. His convulsions are filmed by a passenger, and the video comes to the attention of Alan Krumwiede (Jude Law), a conspiracy-obsessed science blogger. Krumwiede ensures the video goes viral on his blog, aptly named 'Truth Serum Now'. 'You wait', he tells newspaper editor Lorraine Vasquez (Monique Gabriela Curnen), 'this will be tweeted, YouTubed all over the planet. . . . Print media is dying, Lorraine. It's dying. I'll save you a seat on the bus'.

In the early stages of the virus's spread, conspiracy is also not too far from the minds of the US authorities attempting to control the outbreak. Government official Dennis French (Enrico Colantoni) speculates whether the virus has been deployed by terrorists as an airborne biological weapon, and nervously asks Dr Ellis Cheever (Laurence Fishburne), Deputy Director of the US Government's Centers for Disease Control (CDC), 'Is there any way someone could weaponize the bird flu? Is that what we're looking at?'. Cheever, in response, plays down suggestion the virus might be part of a coordinated attack: 'Someone doesn't have to weaponize the bird flu', he tells French. 'The *birds* are doing that'.

Cheever is, however, concerned that social panic will 'tip over', making the virus 'the least of our worries'. The film singles out Krumwiede as a principal *agent provocateur* of this social contagion. When the two characters go head-to-head on a news programme, Krumwiede accuses the CDC and the World Health Organization of a cover-up and of being in bed with the major pharmaceutical companies, which, he claims, are profiting from the outbreak. Cheever, in return, accuses Krumwiede of scaremongering, indeed of being like a virus himself: 'What we do know', Cheever tells the television audience,

> is that in order to become sick you have to first come in contact with a sick person or something that they touched. In order to get scared, all you have to do is to come in contact with a rumour, or the television or the Internet. I think what Mr Krumwiede is spreading is far more dangerous than the disease.

Although Krumwiede is one of the first to recognize the signs of a possible infectious disease outbreak and to alert the public, he is also depicted as hampering 'real' or practical efforts to contain the outbreak and to develop a vaccine. Far from being the administrator of a 'truth serum', he is portrayed as a kind of snake oil salesman, a liar and a hypocrite who is profiteering from the virus as much as those he accuses of the same.[5] On his blog, Krumwiede peddles not only what the authorities consider to be misinformation, but also an apparently clinically useless homeopathic remedy. The film shows Krumwiede touting the herb Forsythia (a staple in traditional Chinese medicine) as a lucrative investment to a hedge fund manager, lying about its benefits on his blog, and causing mass panic-buying sprees of the herb. By the end of the film, the authorities have arrested him for securities fraud, conspiracy and, French informs him, most likely manslaughter.

Through the figure of Krumwiede, *Contagion* also casts 'viral' media in a decidedly critical light, summed up neatly in epidemiologist Dr Ian Sussman's (Elliott Gould) observation that 'Blogging is not writing; it's graffiti with punctuation'. In its desire to limit Krumwiede's viral transmissions, the CDC exemplifies the need to control transmission of the virus in all its forms. As Eugene Thacker has pointed out, since the 1990s, organizations such as the CDC have developed a range of information networks – or 'disease surveillance networks' (DSNs) – to track infectious disease. As Thacker explains, the emergence of these DSNs across the globe marks a significant turning point in the control of infectious disease, for it signals an increased awareness of the role of the network in the spread *and* control of disease. In effect, Thacker argues, the DSNs are based on the concept of 'networks fighting networks', and, more specifically, on the idea of a centralized control network fighting a decentralized disease network (2005, n. pag.). Almost paradoxically, the 'strategy' of the DSNs is to exploit information networks in order to 'canalize transmission', which in turn enables them to 'fight the decentralization of contagion' (Thacker 2005, n. pag.). Krumwiede's blog, for the CDC, is, in an informational respect, no less a threat to its control than an infected person on an aeroplane; it is an infected node in a distributed and decentralized network, transmitting contagion.

Interestingly, perhaps even ironically, despite *Contagion*'s strongly negative depiction of the 'viral' possibilities of social media, its Canadian distributors, Warner Bros. Canada, came up with a (quite literally) viral media strategy to promote the film's release. They commissioned a group of scientists led by mycologist Patrick Hickey to create a 'living billboard'. In the windows of a downtown Toronto storefront, Hickey and his team installed what are potentially the largest

Petri dishes ever built, containing some 35 different microbes. Chosen because they 'would look dangerous', the microbes, as they spread and multiplied, spelt out the name of the film (Travis 2011, n. pag.). In these many and layered ways, Soderbergh's *Contagion* both taps into and vividly illustrates the bidirectional relationship between contagion and the network. In other words, the film not only proposes a network epidemiology (the view that infectious disease is now predicated on the concept of the network), but also an epidemiology of the network (the view that network dynamics are similarly predicated on the concept of contagion).

Epidemiologies of the network: Contagion and network theory from tarde to financial contagion and viral network theory

As network theorist Jussi Parikka has argued, since the 1970s and 1980s, a particular 'logic' of contagion has arisen that is connected both to the 'mathematics of epidemics and [to] network organization theories' (2007a, p. 288). This 'viral logic' has in turn 'present[ed] itself as a key tactic in commercial, security and technological contexts' (2007a, p. 288). Although this convergence between contagion and the network has become self-evidently manifest in the financial and digital contagions of the network era, it is not a uniquely twenty-first- or even twentieth-century phenomenon. Indeed, this convergence is apparent even in Tarde's late nineteenth-century social theory. That is, Tarde's theory of social influence and invention relies not only on the notion of contagious imitation, but also on the idea of society as a complex and productive network of objects, actors and influences. In his essay on monadology, for instance, Tarde describes the 'social elements' as being held within a 'dense, infinitely extensible network' (*réseau serré qui s'étend sans cesse*) from which, he maintains, are born the 'wonders of civilization' (1895, p. 376).

Tarde's concept of society-as-network is, as Bruno Latour would have us understand, a subtle and a multifaceted one that differs in important ways from other current definitions and theories of the network, such as that proposed by Castells. In *Reassembling the Social* (2005), Latour states that the word 'network' suffers from a particular ambiguity because it calls upon distinct 'traditions' of theorizing or approaching the idea of the network. In its most physical sense, Latour explains, the word 'network' can refer to built-environment or 'technical' networks, such as 'electricity, trains, sewages, internet, and so on' (2005, p. 129).

In a sociological sense, it can refer to a way of conceptualizing the relationships among human agents. Or, as Latour points out, in the case of Castells, it can refer to the interrelationship of both of these network levels – the material and the conceptual.

However, in respect of his own use of the word 'network' (and particularly in relation to his Actor-Network Theory[6]), Latour explains that he is 'always referr[ing]' to yet another tradition, one that constellates around the French word for network, *réseau*. In the work of Deleuze and Henri Bergson, Latour argues, the word 'network' means something beyond material networks or networks of human agents (or even a basic understanding of the interaction between the two). Rather, the word 'network' represents an 'active and distributed materialism' that refuses a simple separation of society and social agent, of network and actor (Latour 2005, p. 129). Traces of this tradition, he continues, lie in Denis Diderot's use of *réseau* to develop his 'network philosophy of nature' in the eighteenth century, a tradition that is also apparent in Tarde's nineteenth-century network-based microsociology (Latour 2005, p. 129). After quoting an extended example from Diderot's *Le rêve d'Alembert*, Latour argues that '[i]t's clear . . . that *réseau* has nothing to do with the social as normally construed, nor is it limited to human ties. But it's certainly close to Tarde's definition of "society" and "imitative rays"' (2005, p. 130).

It is, perhaps, unsurprising that contagion and the network become such pivotal structuring metaphors in Tarde's sociological theory. Just as nineteenth-century sociology was increasingly turning to the concept of contagion to explain otherwise inexplicable social phenomena, so too was it turning to the network. Where contagion offered a conceptual theory for explaining imitation and social influence, the network offered a conceptual model for those phenomena, one that promised to reveal hitherto concealed lines of influence and points of connection.

As Kai Eriksson explains, by the mid-nineteenth century, the network 'constituted a generic model for considering societal phenomena', but, he adds, this conception of the network drew mainly on 'biological analogies . . . , thus preventing any direct comparison to the currently prevailing topological metaphor of the network' (2005, p. 595). The biological analogy provides an obvious point of connection between the manifestations of contagion and the network in nineteenth-century sociological theory, and certainly across his major works, Tarde's use of *réseau* and *contagion* is at times inflected by biological analogy.[7] More often than not, however, in Tarde's writing the biological has given way to or has been submerged by a more explicitly topological sense of the network.

Indeed, in a telling passage in *Les lois sociales*, Tarde raises, perhaps deliberately, a decidedly topological network metaphor against what he suggests is evolutionary sociology's too-narrow biological reading of the social:

> The [modern evolutionists], in discussing the transformations of laws (particularly the laws of family and of property) and the transformations of language, religion, industry, and art, have ventured to formulate general laws that would confine the progress of society, under these different aspects, to a constant passing and repassing along successive portions of the same arbitrary path. It remained to be discovered later that these supposed rules are honeycombed with exceptions, and that evolution, whether linguistic, legal, religious, political, economic, artistic, or moral, is not a single road, but a network of routes [*réseau de voies*] with many intersecting cross-ways. (Tarde 1907 [1898], p. 26)

With his topological understanding of society and his epidemiological understanding of social influence, Tarde himself stands at a kind of crossroads in the history of these two concepts. From the late nineteenth century onwards, the term 'network' has increasingly taken on its contemporary topological meaning, while 'contagion' has become attached more firmly to complex, network-based social phenomena. With the rise of the network society, new 'viral' phenomena have emerged and, with them, new epidemiological theories of the network. Here, I wish to focus on two of these recent formations – financial contagion and digital contagion – and the theoretical discourse that has developed around them over the past 30 years.

Financial contagion: Between models and metaphors

Of all contemporary uses of the contagion metaphor, financial contagion is, in a political sense, the most salient. The term has been in widespread use in economic discourse about currency crises since the mid 1980s, but, since the 2007 subprime mortgage crisis, 'financial contagion' has become a commonplace, having crossed over into the public domain via finance reporting. Despite the prevalence of the term in both academic and popular discourse, the growing body of literature on financial contagion has had very little indeed to say on the implications or history of its epidemiological rhetoric or on the remarkable (dare we say, contagious) spread of the term itself.

Over the past two decades, dozens of books and scores of articles have been published on financial contagion, many of them proposing refined definitions and models for 'contagious' currency crises and calling for further empirical research. However, this research has not yet, in any sustained way, turned its gaze inward to critically examine the implications of the contagion metaphor or the relationship between financial contagion and other epidemiological network models. Indeed, in the literature on financial contagion, the term appears to have been accepted at face value – almost as a kind of self-evident meme – with very little critical apparatus attached.

Where the economic literature on financial contagion historicizes, contextualizes and develops explanatory models for 'contagious' financial crises, financial contagion as a concept is itself rarely contextualized in relation to other cultural forms of contagion, such as social, emotional, mimetic or cultural contagion, or indeed to network epidemiology.[8] Economist Sebastian Edwards is, perhaps, alone in his attempt to track the emergence of the term 'contagion' within the economic literature. In fairness to Edwards, he makes clear that his overview of 'contagion' within economics is limited to a search of the term within titles and abstracts of the *EconLit* database between 1969 and 2000 (2000, p. 873). However, his conclusion that contagion is a 'relatively new concept in economics' that has 'surged' in the economic literature since the mid 1990s (2000, p. 873) has led at least one subsequent researcher to conclude, in a somewhat less qualified way, that contagion 'was scarcely mentioned' in the economic literature before 1990 (Kolb 2011b, p. 3).

Certainly, references to 'financial contagion' have dramatically if not exponentially increased in economic and public discourse since the last decade of the twentieth century, and this increase has been fuelled in no small part by the Asian financial crisis of 1997 and the Global Financial Crises of the late 2000s. And yet, the mention of contagion was by no means 'scarce' in the economic literature prior to 1990. Indeed, the contagion metaphor has a long history within economic literature, and one that is clearly linked to earlier traditions of moral and social contagion. From the mid-nineteenth century to the early twentieth century, seemingly irrational economic phenomena, such as speculative 'bubbles' or 'manias' and inflation crises, were commonly described in terms of contagion.

These references to contagion in the economic literature or economic commentary, moreover, strongly invoked psychological theories of emotional or social contagion as well as tapping into more general understandings of imitative contagion or the contagion of example. For instance, in his 1848 *Principles of Political Economy*, John Stuart Mill describes speculation as operating, more generally, on principles of contagious imitation, which when unchecked can result in credit crises. According to Mill, credit crises occur when '[s]ome accident, which excites expectations of rising prices, such as the opening of a new foreign market, or simultaneous indications of a short supply of several great articles of commerce, sets speculation at work in several leading departments at once' (1848, p. 55). The ensuing rise in prices brings about a particular 'state' of the 'public mind' that is characterized by a 'contagion' of imitative speculation (1848, p. 55):

> such examples of rapid increase of fortune call forth numerous imitators and speculation not only goes much beyond what is justified by the original grounds for expecting rise of price, but extends itself to articles in which there never was any such ground: these, however, rise like the rest as soon as speculation sets in. At periods of this kind, a great extension of credit takes place. Not only do all whom the contagion reaches, employ their credit much more freely than usual; but they really have more credit, because they seem to be making unusual gains, and because a generally reckless and adventurous feeling prevails .... (Mill 1848, p. 55)

Similarly, an article published in an 1890 issue of *Iron and Machinery World* opens with this dire warning, linking speculation to the contagion of example: 'The spell of speculation is insidious and epidemic. It is a mania by contagion and a craze by example' ('Foreign Furor' 1890, p. 9). As a final illustrative example, in his 1911 standard text, *The Principles of Economics*, William Taussig emphasizes the connections between speculation, market contagion, psychology and social contagion theory. In financial crises, Taussig explains, 'the psychological factor comes into play' (1911, pp. 404–5). 'Business men', he explains, tend to be suffused by and to pass on whatever 'pervading spirit' is economically current: an optimistic one during 'times of activity' and a pessimistic one during 'times of depression'. As a rule, he continues, 'business men respond to the influences that surround them', and only a 'few very sagacious and sober persons' are immune to this 'contagion' of imitation (Taussig 1911, pp. 404–5). And yet, Taussig continues, '[t]his contagion is not merely contagion; it rests on a real interdependence' (1911, p. 405). That is, market contagion not only relies upon psychological notions of imitative contagion or crowd dynamics, but also on the network of relations that constitute the economy:

> The maker of iron and steel sells to the maker of machinery, he to the manufacturer, he to the wholesale agent or jobber, he to the retailer. Every one of these, unless possessed of almost unlimited capital or credit on his own account, necessarily depends on what others will buy of him. Whatever be his own opinion

of the source or extent of ultimate demand, the direct influence on him comes from those who stand next in the long chain of apparently separate, yet essentially interdependent, operations. (Taussig 1911, p. 405)

Taussig's chosen metaphor for this system of interdependences, this conduit for contagious phenomena, is the 'chain'. In the economic literature of the last two decades, the metaphor of the chain, with its emphasis on the *serial* nature of interdependence, has largely made way for the metaphor of the network, with its emphasis on the *distributed* nature of interconnectedness and influence. Franklin Allen and Ana Babus have, for instance, recently called for the development of a sustained 'network perspective' in economics that will aid in the understanding of financial crises and enable the development of 'new regulations that better meet the challenge of an increasingly networked world' (2009, p. 379).

What has remained a constant in the economic literature of the past century is the link between metaphors for connectedness (the 'chain', the 'network') and metaphors of influence ('contagion', 'infection'). Over the past few decades, however, there has been a marked shift in the 'career' of contagion within economics. In the late nineteenth and early twentieth centuries, 'contagion' inevitably appealed to social-psychological theories of emotional or social contagion based on the 'contagion of example'. By the mid-twentieth century, these appeals to social contagion theory had largely been replaced by a focus on developing models to explain 'contagion effects' and putting forward a 'contagion hypothesis'.[9] By the early 1980s, 'contagion' had begun featuring in the titles of economic literature, and, by the late 1990s, it had become a focal term in the literature.[10] Indeed, by the 2000s, both 'contagion' and the 'network' had become such commonplaces as to be treated as dead metaphors, if not completely literal expressions.

In the economic literature on contagion, references to its own epidemiological rhetoric are so rare as to be virtually non-existent. Barry Eichengreen and Richard Portes's 1987 essay on the 'anatomy of financial crises' is one of only a handful of texts to note that 'epidemiological metaphors like fever and contagion feature prominently in the literature on financial crises' (1987, p. 10). More recently, however, Robert Kolb has gone to some lengths to place 'flesh on the bare bones of the contagion metaphor' in the field of economics (2011a, p. xiii). Kolb's analysis of the contagion metaphor – following, as it does, that of Edwards – is confined to the last 20 years, and does not account for its connection to earlier theories of social contagion. Kolb does, however, point out that, since the late twentieth century, the concept of financial contagion has been plagued by ambiguity, with researchers proposing numerous and varied definitions and models.

If these theories have a point of commonality, according to Kolb, it lies in the way they tend to view 'contagion' as 'a departure from the normal, the expected, or the rational' (2011b, p. 5). Although, he continues, this 'line of thought has seemed attractive to quite a few researchers' it has distinct drawbacks, for 'it threatens implicitly to define contagion as that which is inexplicable on our ordinary understanding' (2011b, p. 5). To operate effectively as an economic concept, Kolb argues, financial contagion must be explainable: contagious financial episodes, for instance, must be able to be distinguished in nature and degree from non-contagious episodes, and this distinction should be 'discernible in economic data' (2011b, pp. 6, 9). Kolb argues, effectively, for a more self-aware use of the contagion metaphor, which, he says, '[l]ike almost all metaphors ... has the power to illuminate and mislead' (2011b, p. 3). In Kolb's account, it is the 'disorder, dislocation, or disease' implied in the contagion metaphor that threatens to derail attempts to identify, define and rationally model financial contagion (2011b, p. 3). Once again, contagion – like metaphor – is seen both to assist and to thwart attempts to explain the seemingly inexplicable.

As this very brief survey demonstrates, 'contagion' does indeed have an extensive history within economic discourse. Understandably, and quite rightly, the primary focus of economic researchers working in the field of financial contagion is on developing practical models that can predict, inhibit or even prevent the spread of financial crises. And yet, unlike other sociocultural formations of contagion, financial contagion remains strangely under-theorized, other than in an insular sense. Moreover, the field's general disinclination to interrogate its epidemiological rhetoric, its submerged links to social contagion theory and its relationship to other newly emergent epidemiological network models is in marked contrast to another form of contagion that emerged in the late twentieth century – digital contagion – and the 'viral' network theory that developed in response to it.

Digital contagion and 'viral' network theory

In 1983, a strange viral outbreak occurred: the word 'contagion' appeared for the first time in the title of a published piece of economic research;[11] two computer scientists at the University of Southern California – graduate student Fred Cohen and his dissertation advisor Len Adleman – ran a computer security seminar in which they described, for the first time, a self-replicating computer program as 'computer virus';[12] and Douglas Hofstadter published his article on 'viral' sentences, thereby launching the meme-as-virus metaphor. This cross-disciplinary discursive outbreak of epidemiological metaphors in and around 1983 must be understood in relation to what Jeffrey Weinstock has called the 'viral culture' of the twentieth-century *fin de siècle*, a culture in which the dual phenomena of AIDS and the computer virus

> came to the fore of national consciousness at almost the exact same cultural moment and which are figured in identical terms – an identification resulting in the subsumption and problematic conflation of the mechanical and biological under the larger generic term Virus. (Weinstock 1997, n. pag.)

In other words, as Parikka points out, 1983 marked not just the advent of the computer virus, but also the year AIDS researchers declared that the syndrome was caused by a virus – what would later be named the human immunodeficiency virus (HIV) (2007b, p. 130). Parikka is careful to qualify that '[t]here is no direct and linear cause–effect pattern from AIDS to computer viruses' and that 'AIDS discourse was not the sole reason viruses became an issue in computer discourse and other cultural platforms' (2007b, p. 130). Rather, he maintains, the viral discourse that emerged in the 1980s

> should be approached as a feedback system where causalities are multidirectional. AIDS sparked the use of viral concepts, but at the same time various events and processes in different cultural contexts, for example, the rise of self-reproductive software or the economic emphasis on global vectors of movement of people, goods, and money, all contributed to the rising concern over the viral qualities of culture. (Parikka 2007b, p. 130)

Thirty years after the advent of the computer virus and the discovery of the viral cause of AIDS, Weinstock's 'virus culture' has not so much been supplanted by as it has mutated into a viral *network* culture. The viral trope that attached itself to self-replicating computer programs, to self-replicating memes and to 'viral' capital in the early 1980s has, in the twenty-first century, spread most notably to those phenomena born of social networking, such as viral internet memes, viral videos, viral marketing and viral media.

These 'viral' phenomena of the network have also, in the last half-decade, generated a critical, broad ranging and epidemiologically aware 'viral' network theory that has developed around the work of Parikka (2005, 2007a,b), Roberta

Buiani (2005), Tony Sampson (2004, 2011) and Thacker (2005, 2009). Just as economic discourse in the twenty-first century has increasingly become redolent with epidemiological metaphors, so too has the discourse surrounding new/digital/networked media, as this passage from Galloway and Thacker's 'epidemiological' approach to network theory, *The Exploit: A Theory of Networks*, exemplifies:

> For the last decade or more, network discourse has proliferated with a kind of epidemic intensity: peer-to-peer file-sharing networks, wireless community networks, terrorist networks, contagion networks of biowarfare agents, political swarming and mass demonstration, economic and finance networks, online role-playing games, personal area networks, mobile phones, "generation Txt", and on and on. (Galloway and Thacker 2007, p. 25)

In Galloway and Thacker's account, not only are the phenomena of the network 'contagious' or 'viral', thereby lending themselves to an epidemiological approach (2007, p. 88), the *discourse* about viral networks is itself figured in terms of contagion. Where financial contagion theory has, as I have argued, largely overlooked or occluded its own rhetoric, viral network theory has, from the very outset, been attentive to the question of metaphor, if only to argue against it.[13] Sampson, for instance, argues that 'humanist perspectives' that attempt to understand 'viral' digital networks 'by recourse to metaphor, signification and resemblance' are essentially damaging in that they 'do little more than reproduce the biologically inspired analogies that the antivirus industry uses to effectively scare net-slaves into buying costly hygiene products' (2007, n. pag.).

Parikka, too, has argued that considering digital 'viruses', 'contagions' and even 'networks' as purely discursive or linguistic phenomena can obscure material and structural relations that are vital to digital network culture. 'We should not', Parikka maintains,

> talk merely about the metaphorics of computer culture (as a cultural studies perspective so often does), but see the biology of computers also as organizational in that a certain understanding of biological organisms and ecological patterns and characteristics of life is entwined as part of the design and implementation of digital culture. (Parikka 2005b, n. pag.)

In their *Spam Book* of 2009, Parikka and Sampson again warn against the 'constraints' of metaphor. When 'contemplating the metaphor of contagion', they write,

> it is important to acknowledge two constraining factors at work. First, the analytical focus of metaphorical reasoning may well establish equivalences, but

these resemblances only really scratch the surface of an intensive relation established between a viral abstraction and concrete contagious events. Second, it is important to recognize the political import of the analogical metaphor in itself. It has an affective charge and organizational role in the spaces, practices, and productions of digital network culture. . . . In light of the often-divisive imposition of the metaphor in the materiality of digital network culture, it is important that . . . this volume provides a potential escape route out of the analytical constraints of representation. (Parikka and Sampson 2009, pp. 19–20)

In this passage, 'metaphor' performs two limiting functions that are essentially at odds with one another. Metaphor, on the one hand, is presented as a mere surface effect. It can 'establish equivalences', but these superficial equivalences operating at the level of discourse can only 'scratch the surface' of the 'intensive relation established between a viral abstraction and concrete contagious events'. On the other hand, however, metaphor is damaging, 'divisive'; it generates an 'affective charge' and plays an 'organizational role' in the formations of network culture that obscures their more-than-representationality. How can metaphor at once be immaterial and material, abstract and concrete, unless it too, like network culture, is more than 'mere' representation? In an argument *against* metaphor, we are provided a clear instance of metaphor's own materiality and more-than-representationality, its continued fluctuation between the abstract and the concrete, between representation and enactment.

Thacker seems to recognize this problematic – namely, that this form of strident argument against metaphor may itself be falling into the same trap of oversimplification – and, in attempting to define the network against a simplistic 'metaphorical' reading of the concept, he has highlighted the impossibility of fully disavowing the question of rhetoric in an analysis of network culture. As I stated at this chapter's outset, the concept of the network, like contagion, exists in a liminal zone between the metaphorical and the material. Also, like contagion, the network is transgressive, transmissive, epidemic. As Thacker writes, 'the very nature of networks is to pass – to pass between, to pass across, to pass over, to pass through'; the network's 'topological form of transgression seems to know no limits, passing across species, boundaries, national boundaries and social boundaries' (2009, p. 137).

Despite this clear oscillation – between contagion and the network – that crosses semantic, semiotic, structural and material levels, Thacker, too, cautions against a simplistic 'metaphorical' understanding of the network. In his foreword to Alexander Galloway's edited collection on network theory, *Protocol*, Thacker states that 'the first point' about networks is that they 'are not metaphors'; they are, rather, 'material technologies, sites of variable practices, actions, and move-ments' (2004, p. xiii). And yet, Thacker immediately qualifies his otherwise cat-egorical stance: 'this is', he explains 'perhaps, stated too strongly', for 'metaphors do materialize and corporealize, and, in some sense, metaphor is consonant with language itself' (2004, p. xiii). Thacker's main argument is (as it is for Parikka and Sampson) with what he calls 'vapor theory' – theory that ignores the mate-riality of networks and simply treats them as 'tropes for notions of "intercon-nection"' (2004, p. xiii). Networks are 'abstract', he grants, but they are also, and at the same time, 'real', and this 'abstract-but-real is the network that is always enacted and always about to enact itself' (2004, p. xiv).

Digital contagions, viruses and even networks, then, both *are* and *are not* metaphorical in the discourse of network theory. As Parikka has pointed out, they are, in effect, 'quasi-objects' that display a kind of 'parasite' logic (2005b, n. pag.; 2007b, p. 30). Both of these concepts – the 'quasi-object' and the 'parasite' – are drawn from Michel Serres's *The Parasite* (1982 [1980]). For Serres, the quasi-object is in constant flux between subject and object: it 'is not an object, but it is one nevertheless, since it is not a subject, since it is in the world; it is also a quasi-subject, since it marks or designates a subject who, without it, would not be a subject' (1982 [1980], p. 225). Latour further develops Serres's con-cept of the quasi-object in *We Have Never Been Modern*, arguing that it presents itself as a hybrid form that does not belong to nature, society, or discourse taken separately, but to all three at once (1993 [1991], pp. 64–5). In Serres's reading, quasi-objects also display a form of 'parasite' logic, a logic that is exemplified, according to Parikka, by digital contagions. 'Contagions are', Parikka explains in the introduction to his 2007 book, *Digital Contagions*,

> to be understood in the ambiguous sense Michel Serres gives to parasites: para-sites are not actually disconnectors of communication, but thirds-excluded that guarantee the interconnectivity and movement of a system. Communication cannot go on without the element of miscommunication, of contagion, at its center .... Contagion is a jump cut, an open-ended system, an experiment. (Parikka 2007b, p. 20)

However, just as the 'viral' phenomena of the network can be seen to exemplify Serres's 'parasites', so too can metaphor. As Serres points out in *The Parasite*, 'metaphors', like parasites, 'move around, metamorphose' (1982 [1980], p. 25). Metaphor might even be the ultimate parasite, or perhaps even the ultimate met-aphor for a parasite. As we saw in Chapter 1, Derrida has similarly drawn out the relationship between metaphor, viral rhetoric and the parasite, arguing that rhetoric is both parasitic and viral in nature. The viral rhetoric of the network age, according to Derrida, has exploded the possibility of any neat separation between the metaphorical and the proper. 'In the case of computers', he asks, 'is the use of the word "virus" simply a metaphor?' and, he continues, 'we might pose the same question for the use of the word "parasite"' (Derrida 1993 [1989], p. 23). Derrida's answer is not to suggest that metaphor is suddenly irrelevant; rather, it is to argue that rhetoric itself is essentially viral and parasitic. Rhetoric, Derrida argues, 'always obey[s] a logic of parasitism', while the 'virus' comes to mean that which (like metaphor) 'comes to affect the proper' (1993 [1989], pp. 23–4). The increasing convergence between contagion and network culture does not render metaphor, or rhetoric more broadly, obsolete. Instead, it renders starkly visible the enduring problem of metaphor, a problem that, I have argued, has also always been the problem of contagion, of the virus and the parasite – of communication in all its forms.

Coda: Language is a virus

In concluding, I wish to draw out further the complex interplay between the concepts of metaphor, virus, contagion and communication in the age of networks. In his 2002 essay on the history of virology, Joost van Loon argues that '[t]he virus has always functioned as a label for that which cannot be named otherwise, a remainder of the known world, and a reminder of nature's unintelligibility' (2002, p. 108). Not only does the virus stand in for unintelligibility, it also, as Parikka suggests, appears as an active 'disruptor' that threatens the ideal of a 'perfect equilibrium of communication, or the frictionless state of economical transactions' (2005a, n. pag.). For sociologist and media theorist Thierry Bardini, contemporary culture has, since the 1980s, become infected by a communicative/informational 'hypervirus' that has effectively 'redefin[ed] culture as a viral ecology' (2006, n. pag.). The dominant trope of this 'postmodern' viral ecology is, Bardini continues, the notion of the language virus, a notion contained in the 'postmodern master equation': 'LANGUAGE = VIRUS = INFORMATIONAL PARASITE' (2006, n. pag.).

In Chapter 1, I examined cognitive scientist Mark Turner's 1992 analysis of what he considered to be a particularly strange metaphor: the metaphor 'language is a virus'. Interestingly, in his article, Turner briefly explains how this 'unconventional metaphor' came to his attention; it was, he says, 'once the refrain of a not very popular song' that in turn 'allegedly quot[ed] a line in a novel by William Burroughs' (1992, p. 732). The 'not very popular song' that Turner leaves unnamed is, of course, performance artist Laurie Anderson's homage to Burroughs, 'Language is a Virus from Outer Space', which was first released on her 1984 album, *United States Live.*

The phrase 'language is a virus' is often unproblematically attributed to Burroughs as though it were an individual aphorism locatable – as Turner puts it – in one of his novels, and Anderson's song has almost certainly amplified and perpetuated this misconception. Burroughs's 'language is a virus' meme is much less a singular quote from a singular Burroughs novel than a trope that underlies a number of his fictional and non-fictional works, notably among them his novels *The Naked Lunch* (1959) and *The Ticket that Exploded* (1962), and his essay collection *The Electronic Revolution* (1970). Turner would, undoubtedly, be the last person to admit he might have been 'infected' by Burroughs's viral language meme, for, as we saw in Chapter 1, his aim is ultimately to demonstrate the conventionality of this unconventional metaphor, to return it to a stable and rule-bound system of metaphorical signification. Burroughs's intention in proposing that language is a virus is, on the other hand, diametrically opposed to Turner's attempt to 'stabilize' language. Instead, by forcing a literal reading of the apparently metaphorical statement, Burroughs paradoxically makes a claim for the inherent instability of the act of communication, for the impossibility of literal or proper meaning.

In his essay collection of 1970, *The Electronic Revolution*, Burroughs directly posits his thesis (a thesis explicitly influenced by L. Ron Hubbard's *Dianetics* and Alfred Korzybski's theory of general semantics) that 'the written word was *literally* a virus that made the spoken word possible' (1970, p. 6; emph. added). The inherently viral nature of language, Burroughs argues, is only now becoming apparent, because the state of 'stable symbiosis with the host' that has allowed the viral nature of language to remain hidden, or at least obscured, is beginning to break down (1970, p. 6). In a rhetorical move that must now seem familiar, Burroughs maintains that this adequation of language and virus 'is not an allegorical comparison'; rather, he asserts, the 'falsifications of syllabic western languages are in point of fact actual virus mechanisms' (1970, p. 56). Bardini argues that Burroughs, in his prescience, is '*patient 0*', 'the original vector' of the postmodern 'hypervirus', for his viral ruminations pre-empt not only the computer virus but also Derrida's 'virology' and Dawkins's concept of the 'viral' meme (2006, n. pag.).

Numerous scholars have also drawn parallels between Burroughs's explorations of the language virus meme within his fiction and Neal Stephenson's 1992 novel, *Snow Crash*, which depicts a language-based 'metavirus' that infects computers and human beings alike.[14] Unlike Burroughs's extraterrestrial language virus, however, Stephenson's 'snow crash' virus has a terrestrial origin in the ancient and extinct language of Sumer. Now known only through surviving written sources, the Sumerian language emerged in ancient Mesopotamia in the fourth millennium BCE, and is thought to have produced the earliest known writing system (Comrie 2005, p. 569). In *Snow Crash*, the novel's ironically named protagonist, Hiro Protagonist, is a freelance hacker whose friends begin succumbing to a 'snow crash' virus that leaves them in a vegetative, zombie-like state. The virus has been released by the novel's villain, L. Bob Rife, an information monopolist and founder of the 'Church of Happyology', in what is no doubt an intentional reference to Hubbard's influence on Burroughs.[15]

Rife's 'snow crash' virus is, however, more properly called the 'Asherah' virus, a linguistic virus released by the goddess Asherah that infected the ancient Sumerian language and its speakers, but has since lain dormant for millennia. Sumerian is, in Stephenson's novel, a language radically unlike any currently in existence and one that is 'ideally suited to the creation and propagation of viruses' (Stephenson 1992, p. 261). In her reading of the novel, N. Katherine Hayles explains that Asherah's virus infected the 'vulnerable' Sumerian language, thereby

> reduc[ing] neurolinguistic functioning to the lowest level of subcortical processing, the machine language of the brain. . . . According to the interpretation that Hiro gives to a Sumerian myth, this system changed when the god Enki pronounced his nam-shub, a performative speech that enacts what it describes. The nam-shub acted as a benign virus that counteracted the first virus and thus freed the neocortical structures, allowing higher neurolinguistic pathways to develop. (Hayles 1999, pp. 273–4)

The 'snow crash' virus undoes Enki's 'nam-shub' and 'convert[s] modern humans into the equivalent of ancient Sumerians – devoid of agency, individuality, and autonomy' (Hayles 1999, p. 274). In this way, Hayles argues, Stephenson's novel 'writes binary code and viral engineering back into history, making the reduction of conscious humans into automata the recapitulation of an ancient struggle' (1999, p. 274).

A more recent, multifaceted instantiation of the language virus meme occurs in Bruce McDonald's 2008 film, *Pontypool*. Based on the 1998 novel *Pontypool Changes Everything* by Tony Burgess (who also wrote the film script), *Pontypool* is, along with Danny Boyle's *28 Days Later* (2002) and the *Resident Evil* video game and film franchise (1996–), one of a new breed of 'viral' narratives that blend elements of the outbreak narrative with elements of the zombie film genre. In these 'viral' zombie narratives, the 'zombies' are not reanimated corpses (as the term would properly require)[16]; they are not 'undead', but have instead been infected with a virus that has essentially dehumanized them. Stephanie Boluk and Wylie Lenz have recently argued *28 Days Later* represents a new kind of zombie and that this new 'viral' zombie in turn represents a new kind of plague. Moreover, they suggest, in the comparisons that can be drawn between early modern plague narratives (such as Defoe's *Journal of the Plague Year*) and the new zombie narratives, '[t]here seems to be an underlying link that formally binds together the rhetoric of plague to the notion that rhetoric itself operates by a model of contagion' (Boluk and Lenz 2011, p. 143).

This implicit link between rhetoric and infection is rendered vividly explicit in McDonald and Burgess's *Pontypool*, for, like *Snow Crash*,[17] *Pontypool* literalizes the 'language is a virus' metaphor, and does so in rich and productive ways. As a late winter storm rages outside, former big-city shock jock Grant Mazzy (Stephen McHattie) begins his Valentine's Day morning shift at CLSY Radio 660 in the small Canadian town of Pontypool, Ontario. Mazzy has only recently begun work at Radio 660, having been fired from his job in Toronto for his 'take no prisoners' approach. Reduced to reporting small-town news and obituaries, Mazzy attempts to bring some of his hard-boiled cynicism and black humour to his morning programme, much to the displeasure of station manager Sydney Briar (Lisa Houle), who vainly tries to keep him under control. Mazzy's idiosyncratic style is evident in the voice-over that opens the film – a 'pre-record' public service announcement about a missing cat, named Honey, in which he draws out a network of strange-seeming, almost ominous coincidences:

> Mrs French's cat is missing. The signs are posted all over town. "Have you seen Honey?" We've all seen the posters, but nobody has seen Honey the cat. Nobody. Until last Thursday morning, when Miss Colette Piscine swerved her car to miss Honey the cat as she drove across a bridge. Well, this bridge, now slightly damaged, is a bit of a local treasure, and even has its own fancy name: Pont du Flaque. Now, Colette, that sounds like "culotte"; that's "panty" in French. And "piscine" means "pool". "Panty pool". "Flaque" also means "pool" in French. So Colette Piscine (in French, "panty pool") drives over the Pont du Flaque (the Pont du Pool, if you will) to avoid hitting Mrs French's cat that has been missing in Pontypool. . . . Pontypool. Pont du Pool. Panty pool. Pont de Flaque. What does it mean? . . . Well, Norman Mailer, he had an interesting theory that he used to explain the strange coincidences in the aftermath of the JFK assassination.

In the wake of huge events – after them and before them – physical details, they "spasm" for a moment. They sort of unlock, and when they come back into focus they suddenly coincide in a weird way. Street names and birthdates and middle names, all kind of superfluous things appear related to each other. It's a ripple effect. So, what does it mean? Well, it means something's going to happen. Something big. But then, something's always about to happen.

And something does happen. All too soon, it becomes apparent to those holed up in the Radio 660 studio – the film's action takes place almost entirely within its confines – that Pontypool's townspeople are acting strangely. Ken Loney (Rick Roberts), the station's roving weather and transport reporter phones in, clearly shaken, from his viewpoint in the 'Sunshine Chopper' (in actuality, a car on a hill overlooking Pontypool) to report that a riot appears to be taking place in the township. Reports come in to the station, which are then broadcast by Mazzy, that groups of 'babbling' people (the film credits them as 'conversationalists', rather than zombies) are attacking other residents. As Loney calls in with updates, the viewer gradually learns more about the chaos developing unseen beyond the station's walls. Before he, too, becomes 'infected', Loney, now hiding in a silo, describes the frightening homicidal scenes outside: 'They're biting them!', he exclaims. 'It really looks like these people are trying to climb or eat their way inside [their victims]. They're so desperate, like they have to be inside'.

When the town's GP, Dr Mendez, crawls through one of the radio station's windows, seeking refuge from the marauding groups of babbling killers, he joins Mazzy on air to shed more light on the mysterious outbreak of violence. 'It's viral', Mendez says, 'that much is clear'. But this virus is not 'of the blood' or 'in the air'. Rather, as Mendez explains, the virus that causes the 'zombie' outbreak in the small Ontarian town of Pontypool is a linguistic or, more specifically, a *semantic* one. The virus has inhered itself in particular 'infected' words: only words in the English language have apparently been infected, and then predominantly only terms of endearment, such as 'honey' or 'sweetheart'. Although the infection is semiotic, the transmission of the virus occurs semantically; that is, the virus is spread only when an uninfected person understands the *meaning* of an infected word. 'We are witnessing', Mendez proclaims, 'the emergence of a new arrangement for life, and our language is its host'.

The film is not explicit about the origin of the viral outbreak; however, it does strongly intimate that the original viral meme, as it were, came from Mazzy himself. At one point, Mazzy seems to realize that his repeatedly broadcast announcement about Honey the cat – the voice-over that opens the film – may have triggered and intensified the viral outbreak. The virus, then, is less 'in the air', than 'on the air'. When, at the conclusion of the film, Sydney herself succumbs to the infection and becomes fixated on the word 'kill', Mazzy must discover a vaccine for the linguistic virus – he must find a way to 'disinfect' the infected words. 'Dr Mendez', Mazzy muses, 'said that understanding a word copies the virus, so how do you . . . how do you not understand a word? . . . How do you make it strange?' He hits on the answer: 'You kill the word that's killing you'. He forces Sydney to disassociate the infected word from its meaning by making her repeat the phrase 'kill is kiss'. Mazzy disinfects language via an extreme form of metaphor – a metaphor that is only effective if it does not return to the proper. Mazzy gets back on the air, broadcasting his 'vaccine'. 'You have to stop under-standing what you are saying, and listen to me', he tells whoever may be listening: 'The sky is a person, laughter is walking, yellow is crowded, friends are verbs, teeth are enteric'.

In a 2009 interview with Ian Daffern, Burgess explains the concept that drove his vision of a linguistic virus. 'Everyone', he says, 'talks about *Night of the Living Dead*, or *Dawn of the Dead*, or *Day of the Dead*, or *28 Days Later*' as 'meta-phors' for something else. Zombie films, he continues, are always talked about in terms of 'A is B', as though they are 'really metaphor[s] for . . . communism, or the red menace, or global warming'. In *Pontypool*, however, he says, his aim was slightly different. Instead of the film being a metaphor for something else, something more concrete, *Pontypool* is a meta-metaphor. Certain metaphors, Burgess explains, 'keep coming at you', and this is what *Pontypool* dramatizes: it is a 'metaphor for metaphors that keep haunting you long after . . . their mean-ings as figures of speech have left the stage'.

Contagion is one of these metaphors, these concepts that continue to 'haunt' us down the millennia, just as metaphor itself does. My attempt in this book has been to show just how closely interwoven these two concepts have been throughout history. Metaphor, so often metaphorized as an 'infective', 'parasitic' and 'viral' form of language, is virtually unthinkable without contagion, while contagion has never been able to be contained within the literal or the proper. The cultural forms of contagion that have been my focus here are at once novel and age-old, metaphorical and yet strangely literal, and, as always, they highlight the very contagiousness of contagion.

Notes

Introduction

1 The English translation is Clara Bell's, from the 1896 English edition of Balzac's *Comédie humaine* (1896, p. 164). Balzac's text in the original French is as follows: 'La vie semble ne plus être en nous; elle en sort et jaillit, elle se communique comme une contagion, se transmet par le regard, par l'accent de la voix, par le geste, en imposant notre vouloir aux autres'.

2 As psychoanalyst Salomon Resnik explains, Cotard's syndrome is typified by a 'delusion of negations' (2001, p. 44). Jules Cotard (1840–89), the French psychiatrist who first defined Cotard's syndrome in the late nineteenth century, divided these negations into three groups: 'negation of physical aspects of the individual – the existence of certain organs is denied', 'negation of the psyche – there are neither thoughts nor ideas' and 'negation of the external world – neither people nor things exist'. The 'conjunction of all three', Resnik continues, 'gives rise to what is known as "universal negation", in which neither the world nor the individual concerned exists' (2001, p. 44).

Chapter 1

1 Derrida (1981 [1972], p. 149). © 1981 by The University of Chicago. Reprinted with permission by The University of Chicago Press. Derrida's text in the original French is as follows: 'La métaphoricité est la contamination de la logique et la logique de la contamination'.

2 Sobolev (2008, p. 927). © 2008 New Literary History, The University of Virginia. Reprinted with permission by The Johns Hopkins University Press.

3 See, for instance, Peter Baldwin's *Contagion and the State in Europe, 1830–1930* (2008, p. 927), Andrew Robert Aisenberg's *Contagion: Disease, Government, and the "Social Question" in Nineteenth-century France* (1999) and Lawrence I. Conrad and Dominik Wujastyk's collection *Contagion: Perspectives from Pre-Modern Societies* (2000).

4   See, for instance, Pamela Gilbert's 'Ingestion, Contagion, Seduction: Victorian Metaphors of Reading' (1997), Heather Schell's 'Outburst! A Chilling True Story about Emerging-Virus Narratives and Pandemic Social Change' (1997), Barbara Browning's *Infectious Rhythm: Metaphors of Contagion and the Spread of African Culture* (1998) and David Farrell Krell's *Contagion: Sexuality, Disease, and Death in German Idealism and Romanticism* (1998).

5   See Mitchell (2008).

6   See *Poetics* (1984a, p. 2332; sec. 1457b1) and *Rhetoric* (1984b, p. 2240; sec. 1405a).

7   See Rousseau (1781).

8   Writing in 1981, Johnson may have been unaware of the dramatic resurgence of interest in and uptake of Nietzsche's essay in the late 1960s and early 1970s by philosophers and literary theorists such as Angèle Kremer-Marietti, Sarah Kofman, Jacques Derrida, Paul Ricoeur and Paul de Man (see the section devoted to this renewal of interest in Nietzsche later in this chapter). Considering Johnson is well known to have 'studied with Ricoeur' (Keesing 1985, p. 216; Pires de Oliveira 2001, p. 24), this does, however, seem unlikely.

9   'Über Wahrheit und Lüge im aussermoralischen Sinne' was first published in 1903, in volume ten of the second edition of *Nietzsche's Werke* (*Grossoktavausgabe*). The first English translation ('On Truth and Falsity in their Ultramoral Sense') was published in 1911, in volume two of Oscar Levy's *Complete Works of Friedrich Nietzsche*. See also Breazeale (1979) for an overview of the composition and publication history of Nietzsche's planned *Philosophenbuch*.

10 In his *Principles of Literary Criticism* (1924), Richards argued that metaphor 'is the supreme agent by which disparate and hitherto unconnected things are brought together in poetry' and a 'semi-surreptitious method by which a greater variety of elements can be wrought into the fabric of the experience' (p. 240).

11 A decade later, Genette would ask a similar question of figurative language: 'why does the figure signify more than the literal expression? Where does its surplus of meaning come from and, for example, how can it designate not only an object, a fact, a thought, but also their affective value or their literary dignity?' Semiology proffers an answer to these questions, Genette suggests, in the concept of the 'connotation' (1982 [1966], pp. 56–7).

12 In his review of *Metaphors We Live By*, Booth points out that 'the main thrust of [Lakoff and Johnson's] critique is perhaps not as new as the authors believe' (1983, p. 619) and that their study 'neglect[s] traditions of literary and rhetorical theory' (1983, p. 621). Booth, nonetheless, maintains that the 'details' of Lakoff

and Johnson's argument are 'both new and important' (Booth 1983, p. 619). See also J. P. Thorne, who, in his review of *Metaphors We Live By*, notes that 'Lakoff and Johnson do not mention [Max] Black's book, despite the fact there are certain quite striking similarities between their ideas and his . . . . It is difficult to believe that they do not know Black's work but it is easy to understand why they should be anxious in giving the impression that their work is in any way derivative' (Thorne 1982, p. 246).

13 See, for instance, Swiggers (1984) and Kirby (1997).

14 Lakoff defines the 'invariance principle' thus: 'Metaphorical mappings preserve the cognitive topology (that is, the image-schema structure) of the source domain, in a way consistent with the inherent structure of the target domain' (1993, p. 215).

15 In 1996, Charles Forceville drew attention to the importance of 'extended context' in the analysis of metaphor, arguing that incorporating a broader context can reveal a 'subsidiary transfer' from target to source domain (1996, p. 706). More recently, Peter Stockwell has critiqued the notion of directional 'invariance' in metaphor. Although he grants that 'in general' the movement of metaphor goes from source to target, in 'literary discourse' metaphor 'works differently' (2002, p. 111). Indeed, Stockwell maintains, '[s]ome very striking or defamiliarizing metaphors (as in some literature, but not exclusively so) seem to be so strong that they make the reader re-think the source model in the light of its mapping with the target' (2002, p. 111). From an artificial intelligence perspective, John A. Barnden et al. have sought to counter the prevailing, one-way 'source-to-target' model of interdomain influence by analysing the 'reverse influence' of metaphor; that is, when meaning is transferred from target to source (2004; passim). Additionally, Alice Deignan's corpus research presents a 'challenge' to the unidirectional hypothesis, for her findings 'suggest that the inherent structure of the target domain does not only constrain the mapping, it helps to shape it' (2008, p. 292). These corpus data, she adds, 'suggest a rich, dynamic, and context-bound view of figurative language' (2008, p. 293).

16 As Earl R. MacCormac has pointed out, in subordinating metaphorical statements to underlying conceptual metaphors, 'Lakoff and Johnson seem to be searching for a way to avoid linguistic relativity', and have thereby 'robbed metaphor of its distinctive cognitive feature, that of creating new categories through a complex cognitive process of change in the associations of words' (1985, pp. 68, 75).

17 In his interview with Pires de Oliveira, Lakoff strongly disavows any connection
    between CMT and the interactionist and continental traditions (embodied for
    him by Black and Ricoeur, respectively). When asked to what extent his theory
    was influenced by the earlier rejection of logical positivist approaches to figura-
    tive language, Lakoff replies categorically:

>   I had read Black and I had no interest in what Black was doing. Black
>   had accepted the basic tenets of analytic philosophy and he saw meta-
>   phor as external to ordinary everyday language of meaning, which
>   was the heart of what I was interested in. Mark Johnson had studied
>   with Paul Ricoeur. So he knew the Ricoeur tradition and the conti-
>   nental tradition and had come to the conclusion, through working
>   with Ricoeur, that metaphor was central to thought. But I wasn't at all
>   influenced by that tradition. (Pires de Oliveira 2001, p. 24)

18 Turner notes that he has drawn this 'unconventional metaphor' from the
    'refrain of a not very popular song (allegedly quoting a line in a novel by
    William Burroughs . . .' (Turner 1992, p. 732). The popular song Turner
    references is performance artist Laurie Anderson's homage to Burroughs,
    'Language is a Virus from Outer Space – William S. Burroughs', first released
    on her 1984 album, *United States Live*.

19 Lakoff and Turner outline the GREAT CHAIN metaphor in Chapter Four of
    More than Cool Reason (1989).

20 In his 1970 essay 'La rhétorique restreinte' ('Rhetoric Restrained'), Genette
    argues that metaphor's 'promotion to the rank of figure of analogy *par excellence*
    is the result of a sort of takeover' and is 'detrimental not only to comparison, but
    also to several forms of figure the diversity of which does not seem to have been
    entirely appreciated until now' (1982 [1970], pp. 113, 111).

21 See also Genette, who writes that '[t]he age-old tendency of rhetoric to reduc-
    tion seems, then, to have culminated in an absolute valorization of metaphor,
    bound up with the idea of the essential metaphoricity of poetic language – and
    of language in general' (1982 [1970], p. 118).

22 See Deleuze and Guattari (1987 [1980], pp. 69, 77) and Baudrillard (1988
    [1987], pp. 102–3; 1993, pp. 50–1).

23 Although his theory of metaphor largely precedes the 'Nietzschean turn' I have
    been mapping out, Jacques Lacan, too, considers figurative language to be much
    more than mere ornament. Instead, in Lacan's view, metaphor enacts the proc-
    esses of rupture and displacement that are the very nature of language. In his
    1961 essay 'Metaphor of the Subject', Lacan describes metaphor and metonymy

as 'the two fundamental facets of the play of the unconscious' (2006 [1961], p. 755). Moreover, he maintains that 'the most serious reality, and even the sole serious reality for man, if one considers its role in sustaining the metonymy of his desire, can only be retained in metaphor' (2006 [1961], p. 758).

24 See, for instance, Kofman (1993 [1972], p. 12), Blondel (1985 [1971], p. 173) and Mitchell (2008, pp. 153–4).

25 See also the discussion of the related word νότος (Notos), Greek god of the pestilential south wind, in Chapter 2.

26 See Else (1958, p. 74) and Gebauer and Wulf (1995, p. 27).

27 See, for instance, Golden (1975, pp. 124–5), Ricoeur (1986 [1975], pp. 36–41) and Gebauer and Wulf (1995, p. 32).

28 It is, of course, ironic that Plato critiques imitation by way of imitating Socrates.

29 Jonathan Holmes and Adrian Streete, for instance, conclude that, in Plato's view, mimesis is 'contagious', noting that this is 'a Platonic idea that Jacques Derrida has famously expanded upon' (2005, p. 5). Gebauer and Wulf, too, explain that 'the relevance of mimesis is not restricted to the aesthetic, that its effects press outward into the social world, taking root, as Plato saw it, in individual behavior like a contagion' (1995, p. 310).

Chapter 2

1 See, for instance, Priscilla Wald (2008), who repeatedly refers to the 'geography of disease', and Bewell (1999).

2 See, for instance, Barrett (2000) and Koch (2005).

3 See also Irigaray's essays 'The Age of Breath' and 'Spiritual Tasks for Our Age' in her collected *Key Writings* (2004). In these essays, Irigaray argues that we need to cultivate a feminized 'creative breath' (2004, p. 166), for breath is what connects us to the world and to others within the world. Breath, she writes, is 'the universal principle of natural and spiritual life' (2004, p. 184).

4 See, for example, Cooke (2009) and Leavy (1992).

5 See Beagon (2005, p. 387), who traces the assumption that epidemics spread from the south to Thucydides's account of the plague of Athens, and Grigsby (2004, p. 106), who notes the medieval medical assumption that contagious disease was carried on the south-west wind. A rare positive portrayal of a southern wind occurs in Samuel Taylor Coleridge's 'Rime of the Ancient Mariner', yet it is important to note that Coleridge's 'good' southern wind blows northwards from the Antarctic region rather than from the miasmatic tropics.

6 The Hippocratic linking of air and disease is most evident in the text 'Breaths' (1923a) and 'Nature of Man' (1931).

7 See, for instance, Pelling (1978), Vinten-Johansen et al. (2003, pp. 179–81) and Carmichael and Fleming Moran (2002, pp. 23–5) for an overview of the nineteenth-century contagionist versus miasmatist (anti-contagionist) debate. According to Frank M. Snowden, earlier studies that stressed a strong distinction between the stances of nineteenth-century contagionism and anti-contagionism were overturned in the late 1970s by revisionist scholars such as Margaret Pelling, whose research 'established that the terms of this debate were complex; that the lines of division were fluid and shifting; and that there was room for a wide spectrum of intermediate positions. The profession was not neatly split into two clearly demarcated and warring camps' (1995, p. 67). Magner similarly argues that 'sharp distinctions between contagion and miasma models might be considered rather misleading and anachronistic when applied to the period between Fracastoro's publication of *On Contagion* in 1546 and the triumph of microbiology at the end of the nineteenth century' (1992, p. 305).

8 See Morse (2006, pp. 17–18) and Nutton (1983, p. 13).

9 See Byrne (2006, p. 267) and Nutton (1983, p. 18).

10 In contemporary epidemiology, the word 'fomite' is still used to refer to any object (such as a door handle) that can carry and transmit infectious organisms.

11 See also Magner (2009, p. 21) and Magner (1992, p. 305).

12 An example of the continuing influence of miasma theory in the latter half of the nineteenth century is the 1875 International Sanitary Conference, held in Brussels, which was dedicated to methods for the prevention of cholera. Rollo Russell, in his 1892 *Epidemics, Plagues, and Fevers*, states the 1875 conference made the following resolutions: that 'the cholerigenic miasma is spontaneously developed in certain conditions in India, notably in the Delta of the Ganges and the flat lands which surround Madras and Bombay'; that 'cholera is contagious [and] can be dissolved in water and diffused in air', although it can be 'easily destroyed, especially when the air is strongly ozonized'; that people 'exposed to the miasma' may become acclimatized to it; that the contagion has its source in 'ejecta, the corpse, linen, clothes, ships, rooms, carriages, latrines, contaminated water, the air at a short distance only, animals and merchandise'; and finally that 'the miasma penetrates by the pulmonary and digestive passages' – that is, via the respiratory and digestive systems (1892, p. 35). Therefore, according to Russell, by 1875 – 20 years after Snow's discoveries – the scientific community

considered cholera to be, to some degree, still miasmatic in origin: although cholera could be 'propagated by drinks, particularly by water' and could not be transmitted great distances by air, the 'surrounding air is the chief vehicle of the generative agent of cholera' (1892, p. 34).

13 See, for example, Jan P. Vandenbroucke's discussion of the tendency of twentieth-century epidemiologists to 'make John Snow a "hero"' of epidemiology (2004, p. 144).

14 *Sirocco* is the modern name for the auster (Brewer 1898), which in turn is the equivalent of Notus or Notos, Greek god of the south wind. According to Saint Isidore of Seville in his seventh-century *Etymologies* (*Etymologiae* or *Origines*), '*Auster* is named from gathering (*aurire*, i.e. *haurire*) waters, with which it makes the air thick and feeds the rain-clouds. It is called νότος [Notos] in Greek because it sometimes corrupts the air (cf. νοθεύειν, "corrupt, adulterate") for when *Auster* blows, it brings to other regions pestilence, which arises from corrupted air' (Isidore of Seville 2006, p. 275).

15 See Ovid's description of the plague at Aegina: 'My people were struck by a terrible plague, through the anger of cruel Juno . . . In the beginning the sky weighed down on the earth in a thick, black fog which trapped the prostrating heat in a blanket of clouds; and throughout the time that it took four moons to wax and to wane, the south winds [*flatibus Austri*] blew with their sweltering currents of toxic air' (Ovid 2004, p. 274).

16 See, for example, L. Cohen (1825, pp. 114–38); Martin (1835, pp. 333–4); Alison (1839, pp. 162–3); and Jameson (1855, pp. 181–2).

17 Koch was not, however, the first to isolate the cholera bacterium. In 1854, the Italian microscopist Filippo Pacini identified a bacterium in cholera patients' stool samples, which he named the cholera *Vibrio*, following Otto Frederic Müller's late eighteenth-century use of the term 'vibrio' to designate a certain curved or comma-shaped type of 'animalcule', or microorganism. Due to the prevailing miasmatic theory of disease, Pacini's discovery and subsequent publications were largely ignored, and Koch is understood to have been unaware of Pacini's work when he independently isolated the bacillus 30 years later, naming it the 'comma bacillus'. According to Gerry Greenstone, Koch's research found greater traction in the scientific community because, by 1884, 'the scientific world was ready to accept microorganisms rather than the so-called miasmata as the cause of [cholera]' (2009, p. 165).

18 Camus quotes Defoe in French, and the epigraph is often absent from English translations of the novel.

19 See also Camus's description of Oran in his essay 'The Minotaur, or Stopping in Oran': 'You expect a town opening on the sea, washed and refreshed by the evening breezes. But except for the Spanish district, you find a city with its back to the sea, built turning in upon itself, like a snail' (1970 [1954], p. 116).
20 See Brée (1961, p. 119) and Lottman (1979, p. 256).
21 See Defoe (1998 [1722], pp. vii–ix).

Chapter 3

1 See, for example, the models of social contagion developed by James and Lawrence Hamilton (1981) and by Ronald S. Burt (1987) in the 1980s and by Joseph L. Rodgers and David C. Rowe (1993) in the early 1990s.
2 See, for instance, social psychologists Elaine Hatfield, John T. Cacioppo and Richard L. Rapson's influential 1994 book, *Emotional Contagion*, which defined the phenomenon of emotional contagion as the human 'tendency to automatically mimic and synchronize expressions, vocalizations, postures, and movements with those of another person's and, consequently, to converge emotionally' (Hatfield et al. 1994, p. 5).
3 See David P. Phillips, who proposes a form of cultural contagion based on a 'sociological theory of imitation and suggestion' (1980, p. 1002) and Dan Sperber's *Explaining Culture* (1996), which proposes an 'epidemiological' approach to culture and anthropology. The links between 'cultural contagion' and meme theory will be explored in greater detail in the following chapter.
4 See Jan Goldstein (1984, p. 201) and Beer (2007, pp. 534–5).
5 Translation is author's own. Jolly's original text is as follows: 'L'imitation, comme on l'a dit, est une véritable contagion, une contagion qui a son principe dans l'exemple comme la variole a son contage dans le virus qui la transmet: et de même qu'il existe dans l'intimité de notre organisation, des maladies qui n'attendent pour se développer que la plus légère cause, de même aussi il est en nous des passions qui restent muettes dans l'exercice de la raison et qui peuvent se prononcer, s'éveiller par le seul effet de l'imitation. . . . C'est en cela que l'expression de contagion morale n'est plus seulement une vaine image, mais la représentation d'un fait physiologique de la plus haute importance dans l'étiologie de certaines maladies.' (1869, p. 369)

6 See also Scipio Sighele, who cites N. Ebrard (1870), Prosper Despine (1870) and Paul Moreau de Tours (1875) as writers who claimed, along with Jolly, that 'moral contagion' – particularly in the case of suicide – was as real as some physical illnesses (1892, pp. 38–9).

7 See Nye (1975, p. 11), McClelland (1989, p. 17) and van Ginneken (1992, p. 132).

8 See also Le Bon's original French text: 'Dans les foules, les idées, les sentiments, les émotions, les croyances possèdent un pouvoir contagieux aussi intense que celui des microbes.' (1895, p. 113)

9 See also Le Bon's original French text: 'Dans une foule, tout sentiment, tout acte est contagieux, et contagieux à ce point que l'individu sacrifie très facilement son intérêt personnel à l'intérêt collectif.' (1895, p. 18)

10 See also Le Bon's original French text: 'Lorsqu'il s'agit d'entraîner une foule pour un instant, et de la déterminer à commetre un acte quelconque: piller un palais, se faire massacrer pour défendre une place forte ou une barricade, il faut agir sur elle par des suggestions rapides, dont la plus énergique est encore l'exemple . . .'. (1895, p. 111)

11 See also Le Bon's original French text: 'Ce n'est pas avec des arguments, mais avec des modèles, qu'on guide les foules' (1895, p. 114).

12 See also Le Bon (1895, pp. 114, 116).

13 According to van Ginneken, it is 'highly improbable that Le Bon was unaware of [Sighele's] book' (1985, p. 376).

14 Le Bon does provide a very brief, passing reference to Tarde in Chapter two of *Psychologie des foules.*

15 Sighele also accused Tarde of drawing on his work without due acknowledgement; however, as van Ginneken notes, Sighele's main argument was with Le Bon's wholesale and unabashed appropriation (1985, p. 376).

16 It should be noted that *Les lois de l'imitation* does not mark Tarde's first or only use of the term contagion to explain social behaviour. In Tarde's first book, *Criminalité comparée* (1886), he relates increases in crime and recidivism to 'imitative contagion' (*contagion imitative*) (p. 85). In this early work, Tarde also argues that statistical trends can reflect an 'imitative spread, a mental and moral contagion from man to man' ('*une propagation imitative, une contagion mentale et morale d'homme à homme*') (p. 175), and he warns of the danger of the contagion of example (*contagion de l'exemple*) (pp. 105, 143, 179). In 1890, a second edition of *Criminalité comparée* was published, alongside *Les lois de l'imitation* and a second new book, *La philosophie penale*. In *La philosophie*

penale, Tarde again refers frequently to contagious imitation and to the contagion of example or influence, but he is also somewhat more forthcoming in contextualizing his use of the term 'contagion' than in either *Criminalité comparée* or *Les lois de l'limitation*. In *La philosophie penale*, for instance, Tarde quotes Charles Féré on the relationship between degeneracy and susceptibility to the 'contagion' of suicide and murder (1890, p. 238). He also notably provides a reference to Paul Aubry's *La contagion du meurtre* (1887), a text that is critical to Scipio Sighele's historical overview of the concept of moral contagion in his *La folla delinquente* (1891).

17 See also Taine's *De l'intelligence* (1870, p. 324).

18 See also Taine's original French text: 'Ce sont là désormais les nouveaux chefs: car, en tout attroupement, c'est le plus audacieux, le moins embarrassé de scrupules, qui marche en tête et donne l'exemple du dégât. L'exemple est contagieux: on était parti pour avoir du pain, on finit par des meurtres et des incendies' (1878a, p. 20).

19 See also Taine's original French text: '[S]'il y a pour les corps des maladies épidémiques et contagieuses, il y en a aussi pour les esprits, et telle est alors la maladie révolutionnaire. Elle se rencontre en même temps sur tous les points du territoire, et chaque point infecté contribue à l'infection des autres. Dans toute ville ou bourgade, le club est un foyer inflammatoire qui désorganisé émet au loin ses exemples comme des miasmes. De toutes parts la même fièvre, le même délire et les mêmes convulsions indiquent la présence du même virus, et ce virus est le dogme jacobin' (1881a, pp. 313–14).

20 See also Terry N. Clark's 1969 introduction to Tarde's *oeuvre* and his place in the history of sociology. Clark explains that the debate between Durkheim and Tarde revolved around the question of imitation and the role of psychology in sociology. Contra Tarde, Durkheim 'refused to accept that sociological principles should be grounded in psychology' and posited that the basic 'social fact' was not imitation, 'but that which was exterior to the individual and imposed on him through a sort of constraint' (1969, p. 16).

21 Tarde's influential essay on monadology was originally published as 'Monades et science sociale' in the first volume of the *Revue Internationale de Sociologie* (Tarde 1893), and republished two years later as 'Monadologie et sociologie' in his collection *Essais et mélanges sociologiques* (Tarde 1895).

22 See, for instance, Paul Marsden (2000) and H. B. Schmid (2009), who have also traced Dawkins's concept of memetic cultural evolution to Tarde's *Les lois de l'imitation*.

23 According to van Ginneken, however, *La folla delinquente* was translated into French, German, Russian, Polish and Dutch (1992, p. 83).

24 Subsequent citations will refer to the French edition of *La folla delinquente*.

25 '[T]ous concordément affirmèrent que la contagion morale est aussi certaine que celle de certaines maladies physiques' (Sighele 1892, p. 39).

26 I will return to La Rochefoucauld in the following chapter.

27 '. . . comme toutes les maladies nerveuses, elle se propage par une sorte de contagion morale et par la force de l'imitation' (Esquirol 1838, p. 247).

28 Ebrard's text is as follows: 'Devenu en Europe, par sa constitution épidémique, un fléau social, le suicide offre tous les signes d'un état pathologique habituel et semble incurable. On dirait que ses progrès sont soumis à une loi inconnue; il s'avance d'une façon constante et régulière, et d'année en année, il voit augmenter le pâle troupeau de ses victimes. Pareille à la peste asiatique exhalée des vapeurs du Gange, l'affreuse *désespérance* marche à grands pas sur la terre. C'est en un mot une *mal'aria*, espèce de maladie morale nouvelle de notre siècle, qu'il faut constater *comme telle* et à laquelle il faut pourvoir' (1870, pp. 83–4; emph. in original).

29 See Ginneken (1992, p. 119, n. 24).

30 Aubry similarly cites Lucas, Brierre de Boismont, Despine and Moreau de Tours in his overview. Further, Aubry is cited not only by Sighele, but also by Tarde in *La philosophie penale*, by Émile Durkheim in his famous 1897 treatise on suicide and by Auguste Vigouroux and Paul Juquelier in their 1905 essay on 'mental contagion'.

31 See, for instance, Beer (2007, p. 541, n. 34) and van Ginneken (1992, p. 119, n. 24).

32 Hecquet does not refer to 'moral contagion' in his pamphlet. He does, however, employ the phrases 'contagion des convulsions', 'contagion Convulsionnaire' and 'contagion d'imaginations' (1733, pp. 112, 119, 180).

33 See, for instance, Goldstein (1984), van Ginneken (1992), Forth (2001) and Beer (2007).

34 In a rare example of a study that moves beyond the confines of the French *fin de siècle*, Daniel Beer (2007) has examined the emergence of sociological theories of moral and mental contagion in late Imperial Russia. Although these theories were strongly influenced by the example of the French crowd psychologists and the theories of Espinas, they nonetheless formed a distinctly Russian tradition, encapsulated in the work of such writers as Victor Kandinskii, Pavel F. Kapterev and Vladimir Bekhterev.

Chapter 4

1 It is important to note again here that the terms 'infection' and 'contagion' were often used interchangeably both in medical and non-medical discourse throughout the early modern period (Gilman 2009, p. 138; Kinzelbach 2006, passim). For this reason, I will treat phrases such as 'infection of ill example' as an instance of a broader 'contagion of example' trope.

2 Primaudaye's *L'académie Françoise* was translated into English and German before the close of the sixteenth century, and, as Frances Amelia Yates notes in her study of the sixteenth-century French academies, it 'had a very great vogue in England' (1988, p. 124).

3 See also Montaigne's French text: 'la contagion est très dangereuse en la presse. Il faut ou imiter les vitieux ou les haïr: Tous les deux sont dangereux; et de leur ressembler, par ce qu'ils sont dissemblables' (1588 [1580], p. 98 v). Montaigne is quoting from Seneca's seventh epistle to Lucilius: 'Necesse est aut imiteris, aut oderis. Utrumque autem devitandum est; ne vel similis malis fias, quia multi sunt; neve inimicus multis, quia dissimiles sunt' (Seneca 1825, p. 6). Or, in Thomas Lodge's first English-language translation, 'What thinkest thou may become of those manners, which are violently laid hold on, followed and applauded by the multitude? These of force must thou either imitate or hate; but both the one and the other of these ought to be avoided, for fear lest thou be either like unto the wicked, by reason there are many, or enemy to diverse, because they are unlike to thee' (Seneca 1620, p. 175).

4 See also Cicero's Latin text: 'neque solum obsunt ipsi quod corrumpuntur, sed etiam quod corrumpunt, plusque exemplo quam peccato nocent' (1824, bk III, sec. 13–14).

5 In his late nineteenth-century edition of the *Moralia*, Gregorius N. Bernardakis gives a Latin title for Plutarch's essay on flattery, namely 'Quomodo adulator ab amico internoscatur'. Scholars have since tended to refer to the essay simply as 'Adulator'.

6 See also the entries for ἀνάχρωσις and συνανάχρωσις in George Liddell and Robert Scott's *Greek–English Lexicon* (1940).

7 Sighele, Tarde and Le Bon, for instance, all note the 'contagiousness' of the act of yawning, as does Malcolm Gladwell – much more recently – in the introduction to his bestselling popular book on social contagion, *The Tipping Point* (2000, pp. 9–10).

8 Specifically, the quoted line is from Menander's lost comic play *Thaïs*.

9   As Tyler Graham explains in his essay on Augustine's conversion, 'the problem of grace and free will is separate from Augustine's depiction of mimetic desire. While we can become aware of our imitation of others, we cannot be sure where we get the power to stop imitating bad models, start imitating good ones, or begin to search for better ones. In other words, one can be late Augustinian, semi-Pelagian, or Pelagian without forfeiting the knowledge of mimetic desire' (1998, p. 145).

10 Most contemporary English-language translations of the *Confessions* omit the text's section headings altogether; however, William Watts in his seventeenth-century English edition translates 'contagiosa res, sodales mali' as 'bad company is infectious' (1631, p. 94).

11 See, for instance, Fiore (1981, passim), Wills (2002, p. 62) and Colebrook, (2008, p. 21).

12 Erasmus was citing a Pelagian document attributed to Jerome (pseudo-Jerome), which was later accepted as having been written by Pelagius himself.

13 See, for instance, Burhil (1602, n. pag.), Fuller (1655, p. 28) and Cressy (1668, pp. 168, 172).

14 See, for instance, Featley (1626, p. 3).

15 Fulke Greville's (Lord Brooke) unfinished 'Letter to an Honourable Lady' suggests also the commonality of the phrase 'infection of example' in the sixteenth century. Most likely written in 1588 (J. Rees 1971, p. 175), the letter warns the 'Honourable Lady' that 'though Authority may cut off the *infection of ill example* from others, yet can it no more take away the devil's part in us, than call up the dead' (Fulke Greville 1870, p. 245).

16 Richardson's *Pamela* was originally published in two volumes in 1740–1. However, Richardson continued to revise and expand the novel, publishing a sixth edition in 1742 that ran to four volumes. Despite the novel's popularity, the intensely moralizing tone of the latter two volumes saw the continuation fall out of favor with later critics. As nineteenth-century literary critic Henry J. Nicoll explained in his *Landmarks of English Literature*, Richardson's 'spurious continuation' of *Pamela* 'shared the common fate of continuations in turning out a failure' (1886, p. 211). Nicoll also noted that *Pamela*'s final two chapters 'are now seldom if ever read by Richardson's most enthusiastic admirers' (p. 211), a point reinforced by contemporary editions, which inevitably publish only the first two volumes.

17 The character Henry is described as displaying 'the *contagion of bad example*' in his conduct (Pilkington 1797, p. 20; emph. in original).

18 See Madan (1950) and Wilcher (1991) for an account of the authorship controversy surrounding Gauden's claim to have written the *Eikon Basilike*.

19 Burke describes the Christian statesmen of England as 'sensible, that religious instruction is of more consequence to them than to any others; from the greatness of the temptation to which they are exposed; from the important consequences that attend their faults; from the contagion of their ill example' (1790, p. 151).

20 In Volume six of his *History*, first published in 1788, Gibbon writes of the pilgrimage to Rome in the year 1300: 'The calculation of [the number of pilgrims] could not be easy nor accurate; and they have probably been magnified by a dexterous clergy, well apprised of the contagion of example' (1788, p. 558). In his memoirs, which Gibbon wrote in 1789 but which were published in 1796, two years after his death, he writes of his own susceptibility to the contagion of example: 'The pleasures of a town life are within the reach of every man who is regardless of his health, his money, and his company. By the contagion of example I was sometimes seduced; but the better habits which I had formed at Lausanne, induced me to seek a more elegant and rational society; and if my search was less easy and successful than I might have hoped, I shall at present impute the failure to the disadvantages of my situation and character' (1796, p. 80).

21 See also Rousseau's original French text: 'Tels sont les méprisables hommes que forme la crapule de la jeunesse: s'il s'en trouvait un seul qui sût être tempérant et sobre, qui sût, au milieu d'eux, préserver son coeur, son sang, ses moeurs, *de la contagion de l'exemple*, à trente ans il écraserait tous ces insectes, et deviendrait leur maître avec moins de peine qu'il n'en eut à rester le sien' (1866 [1762], p. 384; emph. added).

22 In a similar rhetorical move, Georg Wilhelm Friedrich Hegel describes the diffusion and spread of 'pure insight' as a form of infection or contagion in his 1807 *Phänomenologie des Geistes* (*Phenomenology of Spirit*). Hegel writes, 'the communication of pure insight . . . is a penetrating infection [*durchdringende Ansteckung*] that gives no prior indication that it is something opposed to the indifferent element into which it insinuates itself; hence it cannot be warded off' (2001 [1807], pp. 78–9). See also Michael Pfister's detailed examination of this passage, in which he argues that, for Hegel, the word *Ansteckung* (contagion, infection – see also note 27) becomes a privileged metaphor for Enlightenment thought (Pfister 2005, passim).

23 It is perhaps not surprising that Patru is quoted here, considering he was one of the major contributors to Richelet's dictionary, along with 'the translators Maucroix and Cassandre . . . and the Jesuits Rapin and Bouhours' (Bray 1986, pp. 13–14).

24 The phrase 'contagion of example' appears again in Johnson's *Dictionary* in the entry for 'Immersion'. To illustrate the word's sense of '[t]he state of being overwhelmed or lost in any respect', Bishop Francis Atterbury (1663–1732) is cited: 'Many persons, who, through the heat of their lusts and passions, through the contagion of ill example, or too deep an immersion in the affairs of life, swerve from the rules of their holy faith; yet would, upon extraordinary warning, be brought to comply with them. *Atterbury*' (Johnson 1755). Johnson, indeed, appears to be particularly partial to contagion metaphors. 'Contagion of example' also appears in his *Rambler* (see no. 14, Saturday, 5 May 1750 and no. 175, Tuesday, 19 November 1751), along with other contagion metaphors such as 'instantaneous contagion' (no. 50, Saturday, 8 September 1750), 'contagion of misery' (no. 59, Tuesday, 9 October 1750), 'contagion of impatience' (no. 73, Tuesday, 27 November 1750), 'contagion of vanity' (no. 95, Tuesday, 12 February 1751), 'the natural contagion of felicity' (no. 148, 17 August 1751) and 'contagion of his peculiarities' (no. 164, Saturday, 12 October 1751). In *The Adventurer*, we find the 'contagion of diligence' (no. 45, Tuesday, 10 April 1753), the 'contagion of desire' (no. 119, 25 December 1753) and the 'contagion of his defects' (no. 131, Tuesday, 5 February 1754). In Johnson's 1749 poem, 'The Vanity of Human Wishes', we find 'the strong contagion of the gown' (1749, p. 13) and in his 1759 *History of Rasselas*, we find 'the contagion of his confidence' (1759, p. 42).

25 Frazer's treatment of magical contagion is fairly slight in the first, two-volume edition of *The Golden Bough* (1890). He develops his theory of contagious magic more fully in Lectures II and III of his *Lectures on the Early History of the Kingship* (1905), and incorporates it into volume one of the third edition of the *Golden Bough* (1911–15).

26 Freud's unquestioning acceptance of Le Bon's theory of the crowd has not gone unnoticed in psychoanalytic research. Hugh Veness (1971), for instance, argues that Freud's *Group Psychology* relies too heavily on Le Bon's suspect data and descriptions, and attempts to reconcile Freud's theory of mass psychology with more current historical research. Veness also draws a parallel between Freud's use of Le Bon in *Group Psychology* and existing criticism of Freud's reliance on James George Frazer's discredited research in his earlier *Totem and Taboo*.

27   The term *Gefühlsansteckung* has its own history in German thought and
     expression. Most notably, philosopher Max Scheler employs the term in his
     1923 book *Wesen und Formen der Sympathie* to describe an involuntary and
     self-generating but relatively superficial form of inter-subjective understanding
     that stands in contrast to 'true emotional identification' (1970 [1923], p. 12).
     Gefühlsansteckung, Scheler argues, 'occurs only as a transference of the *state* of
     feeling, and does *not* presuppose any sort of *knowledge* of the joy which others
     feel' (1970 [1923], p. 15; emph. in original). In the only extant English-language
     translation of Scheler's book, *The Nature of Sympathy* (1970 [1923]), Peter Heath
     translates *Gefühlsansteckung* as 'emotional infection'. Where *Gefühl* can simply
     be translated as 'feeling' or 'emotion', *Ansteckung* can variously mean 'infection',
     'contamination' or 'contagion'. As Annemarie Kinzelbach notes:

> in modern German–English dictionaries, "Ansteckung" is translated
> as contagion. Literal translation would add further meanings to those
> already mentioned: "to stick on", as well as "to pass on", or "to set fire to".
> The medieval root of "anstecken" is "stechend befestigen", to fasten sting-
> ing. Modern German–German or etymological dictionaries explain the
> word "Infektion" with "Ansteckung". (Kinzelbach 2006, p. 374).

28   Vigouroux and Juquelier's original text is as follows:

> Toutes les manifestations de la vie psychique sont contagieuses: les actes
> réflexes simples ou complexes ont une tendance à être reproduits du fait
> qu'ils sont perçus: les états affectifs sont contagieux par l'intermédiaire
> des modifications organiques (élément moteur) qui les traduisent et les
> constituent: les idées sont contagieuses lorsqu'elles ont une valeur affec-
> tive, le plus grand nombre de nos actions dites volontaires, parce qu'elles
> ne sont qu'une résultante d'états affectifs à propos desquels la contagion
> peut faire sentir son influence. (Vigouroux and Juquelier 1905, p. 243).

Chapter 5

1   See, for instance, Jean Burgess's essay 'All Your Chocolate Rain are Belong to Us'
    (2008), which examines the relationships between meme theory, 'viral' video,
    marketing and internet-based participatory culture, and Joshua Green and
    Henry Jenkins's 'Spreadable Media: How Audiences Create Value and Meaning
    in a Networked Economy' (2011).

mimemaμίμημα

2 See Alfred Edward Taylor who, in his commentary on Plato's *Timaeus*, explains that μίμημα refers to a '*reproduction* . . . which is not the "thing in itself", but a reduced model from it' (1928, p. 245).

3 See, for instance, the British evolutionary biologist W. D. Hamilton's 1977 review of *The Selfish Gene* for *Science*, in which he anticipates the term 'meme' will 'soon be in common use by biologists and, one hopes, by philosophers, linguists, and others as well and that it may become absorbed as far as the word "gene" has been into everyday speech. I suspect, too, that this chapter will do much to stimulate interest in processes of cultural evolution per se' (1977, p. 759). Hamilton's positive review is perhaps not surprising, considering Dawkins draws heavily on his research in *The Selfish Gene*. Indeed, Dawkins describes two of Hamilton's papers as 'among the most important contributions to social ethology ever written', and argues for greater recognition of his 'neglected' work (Dawkins 1976, p. 97).

4 Although he did not coin the term 'soft inheritance', Ernst Mayr is credited as the first to have defined it in his prologue to his 1980 edited collection *The Evolutionary Synthesis: Perspectives on the Unification of Biology* (Lamb 2011, p. 110). According to Mayr, use of the term 'soft' refers to 'whether the author [of the evolutionary theory] believed that the genetic basis of characters could be modified either by direct induction by the environment, or by use and disuse, or by an intrinsic failure of constancy, and that this modified genotype was then transmitted to the next generation' (Mayr 1980, p. 4).

5 See, most notably, molecular immunologist Ted Steele's neo- or meta-Lamarckian research (Steele 1981; Steele et al. 1998). More generally, see articles such as Roger Lewin's 'Lamarck Will Not Lie Down' (1981) and Michael Balter's 'Was Lamarck Just a Little Bit Right?' (2000), published in *Science*.

6 See, in particular, Hofstadter's article on 'viral sentences', published in a 1983 issue of *Scientific American* (and republished in his 1985 collection *Metamagical Themas*); Dennett's *Consciousness Explained* (1991) and *Darwin's Dangerous Idea* (1996); and Hofstadter and Dennett's edited collection *The Mind's Eye* (1981), which contains a Dawkins essay titled 'Selfish Genes and Selfish Memes'.

7 See, for instance, Robert Aunger's edited collection *Darwinizing Culture: The Status of Memetics as a Science* (2000b) and his *Electric Meme: A New Theory of How We Think and Communicate* (2002), Peter Baofu's *Beyond Nature and Nurture: Conceiving a Better Way to Understand Genes and Memes* (2006), Susan Blackmore's *The Meme Machine* (1999), Thorsten Botz-Bornstein's edited collection *Culture, Nature, Memes* (2008), Richard Brodie's *Virus of the Mind: The New Science of the Meme* (1996), Andrew Chesterman's *Memes of Translation: The*

Spread of Ideas in Translation Theory (1997), Kate Distin's *The Selfish Meme: A Critical Reassessment* (2005), Michael C. Drout's *How Tradition Works: A Meme-based Cultural Poetics of the Anglo-Saxon Tenth Century* (2006), John Gunders and Damon Brown's *Complete Idiot's Guide to Memes* (2010), Leigh Hoyle's *Genes, Memes, Culture, and Mental Illness* (2010), Steven B. Jan's *The Memetics of Music: A Neo-Darwinian View of Musical Structure and Culture* (2007), Maria Kronenfeldner's *Darwinian Creativity and Memetics* (2011), Alister E. McGrath's *Dawkins' God: Genes, Memes, and the Meaning of Life* (2004), Evan Louis Sheehan's *The Mocking Memes: A Basis for Automated Intelligence* (2006), Stephen Shennan's *Genes, Memes and Human History: Darwinian Archaeology and Cultural Evolution* (2002) and Yuzuru Tanaka's *Meme Media and Meme Market Architectures* (2004).

8   Earlier in *The Selfish Gene*, however, Dawkins does link *genes* with viruses, but this time in a less rhetorical sense. He states that viruses may themselves be 'rebel' genes that 'have broken loose from "colonies" such as ourselves' and 'evolved' in such a way that they 'travel from body to body directly through the air, rather than via the more conventional vehicles – sperms and eggs'. 'If this is true', Dawkins eagerly continues, 'we might as well regard ourselves as colonies of viruses!' (1976, p. 196).

9   Hofstadter appears to have been the first to draw attention to Monod's description of ideas as 'infectious' as a kind of precursor to Dawkins's thinking about the meme. Since then, references to Monod's *Chance and Necessity* (a translation of his 1970 *Le hasard et la nécessité*) have become standard in the literature on memes. It is, however, important to note that, in his original French text, Monod does not employ virological/epidemiological metaphors to explain how ideas replicate and spread; instead, he uses metaphors of invasion and expansion. Where Austryn Wainhouse's English translation gives 'the "spreading power" – the infectivity, as it were – of ideas' (Monod 1972, p. 166), the original text gives simply 'le pouvoir d'invasion' (1970, p. 182).

10 See Dawkins's 1993 essay titled 'Viruses of the Mind', and also Richard Brodie's 1996 book, *Virus of the Mind: The New Science of the Meme*.

11 See, for instance, Aaron Lynch's *Thought Contagion: How Belief Spreads through Society: The New Science of Memes* (1996).

12 See, for instance, Hugh T. Miller's chapter on memes, titled 'Idea Contagion', in his *Postmodern Public Policy* (2002) and Ben Cullen's *Contagious Ideas: On Evolution, Culture, Archaeology, and Cultural Virus Theory* (2000). Although Cullen is not focused on memes – in *Contagious Ideas* he proposes his own 'cultural virus theory' – he does discuss meme theory in the same terms.

13 See, for instance, Darrel W. Ray's *The God Virus: How Religion Infects Our Lives and Culture* (2009).

14 Before this, Alan Wolfe briefly noted in 1993 that Dawkins, in putting forward his concept of the meme, 'reminds one of the nineteenth-century social theorist Gabriel de Tarde' (Wolfe 1993, p. 48).

15 Latour also suggests a connection between Tarde's 'imitative rays' and later metaphors for the transmission of ideas and information. Latour states that it is 'unfortunate' that Tarde 'did not have the allegory of information technologies to materialize his web of connections and instead had to rely on the loose metaphor of "imitative rays"' (2005, p. 216).

16 See, for instance, Rose (1998, n. pag.), Boden (2006, pp. 564–5) and Blackmore (1999, pp. 31–2).

17 The Sokal hoax effectively divided the academy and spawned scores of broadly polarized critical responses. A sample of these overviews and responses include Mara Beller's 'The Sokal Hoax: At Whom Are We Laughing?' (1998), Paul A. Boghossian's 'What the Sokal Ought to Teach Us' (1996), Marie Secor and Lynda Walsh's 'A Rhetorical Perspective on the Sokal Hoax' (2004) and Lynn Bennett's 'Boundaries and Frontiers: Metaphor and the Rhetoric of Interdisciplinarity in Literary Studies' (2004).

18 See Robert R. Hoffman's 'Metaphor in Science' (1980) for an historical overview of scientific attitudes towards metaphor.

19 As we have seen, analysis of the meme-metaphor relationship tends to focus almost exclusively on the first form of the question: that is, is the meme a metaphor? In his essay on 'Literary Memetics', Daniel Rancour-Laferriere approaches the question from the reverse perspective, asking whether metaphors are themselves memes. Because literary devices, such as metaphor, metonymy, synecdoche and so forth, have not 'evolved' over time – because they are 'basic mechanism[s] of language itself' – they cannot themselves be memes, although 'the content of such devices may in fact be memetic' (1981, p. 83). However, he grants that, as a device, metaphor can provide 'a kind of skeleton through which fragile memetic traditions may pass' (1981, p. 83).

Chapter 6

1 Hardt and Negri (2000, p. 136). Reprinted by permission of the publisher from EMPIRE by Michael Hardt and Antonio Negri, p. 136, Cambridge, Mass.: Harvard University Press, Copyright © 2000 by the President and Fellows of Harvard College.

2 See Morris (2004b).

3 Although Siegfried emphasizes the role technological developments are likely to play in the future of infectious disease, he is by no means technologically deterministic in his argument. When he turns to the relationship between germs and ideas – between infectious disease and thought contagion – he explains that time–space compression has been ever-present in the concept of communication: 'The world is infinitely more permeable than one could believe, and in order to be so it has not had to wait for the telephone, the telegraph or the aeroplane to conquer distance and time for us' (1965 [1960], p. 87).

4 As early as 1933, Arthur Massey drew attention to the question of air travel and disease transmission in his *Epidemiology in Relation to Air Travel* (1933).

5 It may be a happy accident, but Krumwiede's name also suggests he should be understood as a fundamentally 'crooked' character. Translated into English, the German 'krumwiede' means a bent or crooked (*krumm*) willow (*wiede*). The German 'krumm' also carries connotations of dishonesty. See 'Krumm' (1857) and 'Wiede' (1857).

6 Specifically in relation to ANT, Latour explains that the word 'network'

> does not designate a thing out there that would have roughly the shape of interconnected points, much like a telephone, a freeway, or a sewage "network". It is nothing more than an indicator of the quality of a text about the topics at hand. It qualifies its objectivity, that is, the ability of each actor to make other actors do unexpected things. (Latour 2005, p. 129)

7 For instance, in *Les lois de l'imitation*, Tarde refers to the 'social germ' (*germe social*) as emerging through 'a network of contrary habits and beliefs' (*un réseau d'habitudes et de croyances contraires*) (1903 [1890], p. 141).

8 Rare exceptions to this are André Orléan's 'Mimetic Contagion and Speculative Bubbles' (1989), which links speculation to Girardian theories of mimetic contagion, and Prasanna Gai and Sujit Kapadia's 'Contagion in Financial Networks' (2010), which compares the epidemiological analysis of financial networks with network epidemiology.

9 See, for instance, Perry (1975), Gordon (1975) and Flanagan et al. (1976).

10 See, for instance, Saunders (1987), Doukas (1989), Orléan 'Mimetic Contagion and Speculative Bubbles' (1989), Gerlach and Smets (1994), Eichengreen et al. (1996), Glick and Rose (1999) and Masson (1999).

11   According to the *EconLit* database and the broader literature on financial conta-
     gion, the word 'contagion' first appears as a title keyword in Joseph Aharony and
     Itzhak Swary's 1983 article 'Contagion Effects of Bank Failures'.

12   In a conference paper published in 1984, Cohen credited Adleman with coining
     the phrase 'computer virus' (F. Cohen 1984, p. 146).

13   For an examination of 'virus' as metaphor, see Lupton (1994), van Loon (2002)
     and Buiani (2005); for 'contagion', see Thacker (2005) and Parikka and Sampson
     (2009); for 'epidemic', see Thacker (2009); and for 'network', see Thacker (2004)
     and Sampson (2007).

14   See, for instance, N. Katherine Hayles's analysis of *Snow Crash* in *How We
     Became Posthuman* (1999) and Kelly Wisecup's '"Let's Get Semiotic": Recoding
     the Self in Neal Stephenson's *Snow Crash* (1992)' (2008).

15   As a number of commentators have pointed out, the character of L. Bob Rife is
     an amalgam of such 'initialized luminaries' (as Hayles puts it) as L. Ron Hub-
     bard, H. Ross Perot, L. B. Johnson and H. L. Hunt – with Hubbard inevitably at
     the fore (Hayles 1999, p. 273; Moulthrop 1997, p. 285).

16   There is some debate in the zombie fan community as to whether the infected
     within these 'viral' narratives can or should be called 'zombies'.

17   Stephenson's novel even makes an appearance in *Pontypool*. In one scene, a copy
     of *Snow Crash* can be seen sitting on a table in the radio station.

Bibliography

Aharony, Joseph and Swary, Itzhak (1983), 'Contagion effects of bank failures: Evidence from capital markets'. *Journal of Business*, 56(3), 305–22.

Ali, S. Harris and Keil, Roger (2008), 'Introduction: Networked disease', in S. Harris Ali and Roger Keil (eds), *Networked Disease: Emerging Infections in the Global City*. Malden: Blackwell, pp. 1–7.

Alison, Somerville Scott (1839), *An Inquiry into the Propagation of Contagious Poisons, by the Atmosphere*. Edinburgh: Maclachlan, Stewart and Co.

Allen, Franklin and Babus, Ana (2009), 'Networks in finance', in Paul R. Kleindorfer and Yoram Wind (eds), *The Network Challenge: Strategy, Profit, and Risk in an Interlinked World*. New Jersey: Pearson, pp. 367–82.

Ames, Fisher (1809 [1799]), 'Laocoon, no. 1', in *Works of Fisher Ames*. Boston: T. B. Wait and Co., pp. 94–103.

Aristotle (1961), *Problems* (trans. W. S. Hett, vol. 1). London: Heinemann.

—(1984a), 'Poetics', in Jonathan Barnes (ed.), *Aristotle: The Complete Works* (vol. 2). Princeton: Princeton University Press.

—(1984b), 'Rhetoric', in Jonathan Barnes (ed.), *Aristotle: The Complete Works* (vol. 2). Princeton: Princeton University Press.

Artaud, Antonin (1958 [1934]), 'The theater and the plague' (trans. of 'Le Théâtre et la peste', trans. Mary C. Richards), in *The Theater and Its Double*. New York: Grove, pp. 15–32.

Aubry, Paul (1887), *La contagion du meurtre: étude d'anthropologie criminelle*. Paris: Faculté de Médecine de Paris.

Augustine, Saint, Bishop of Hippo (1540), *D. Aurelii Augustini Hipponensis Episcopi Confessionum libri tredecim*. Paris: Petrum Regnault.

—(1913), *De Peccatorum Meretis et Remissione et de Baptismo Parvulorum ad Marcellinum Libri Tres*, Carl Franz Vrba and Joseph Zycha (eds). Vindobonae: F. Tempsky.

—(1991), *Confessions* (trans. Henry Chadwick). Oxford: Oxford University Press.

—(1997), *Answer to the Pelagians I* (trans. S. J. Teske). New York: New City Press.

Aunger, Robert (2000a), 'Introduction', in Robert Aunger (ed.), *Darwinizing Culture: The Status of Memetics as a Science*. Oxford: Oxford University Press, pp. 1–23.

—(ed.) (2000b), *Darwinizing Culture: The Status of Memetics as a Science*. Oxford: Oxford University Press.

—(2002), *The Electric Meme: A New Theory of How We Think and Communicate*. New York: Simon and Schuster.

Bacon, Francis (1858 [1622]), 'History of the winds' (trans. of 'Historia ventorum'), in James Spedding, Robert Leslie Ellis and Douglas Denon Heath (eds), *The Works of Francis Bacon* (vol. 5). London: Longman, pp. 137–200.

Baldwin, Peter (1999), *Contagion and the State in Europe, 1830–1930*. Cambridge: Cambridge University Press.

Balter, Michael (2000), 'Was Lamarck just a little bit right?', *Science*, 288, (5463), 38.

Balzac, Honoré de (1896), 'Colonel Chabert' (trans. Clara Bell), in George Saintsbury (ed.), *The Atheist's Mass and Other Stories. Vol. 3 of Comédie Humaine*, London: J. M. Dent, pp. 109–81.

Baofu, Peter (2006), *Beyond Nature and Nurture: Conceiving a Better Way to Understand Genes and Memes*. Newcastle: Cambridge Scholars Press.

Barcelona, Antonio (2003), 'Introduction: The cognitive theory of metaphor and metonymy', in Antonio Barcelona (ed.), *Metaphor and Metonymy at the Crossroads: A Cognitive Perspective*. The Hague: Mouton de Gruyter, pp. 1–28.

Bardini, Thierry (2006), 'Hypervirus: A clinical report'. *CTheory*, td031, www.ctheory.net/articles.aspx?id=504.

Barnden, John A., Glasbey, Sheila R., Lee, Mark G. and Wallington, Alan M. (2004), 'Varieties and directions of interdomain influence in metaphor'. *Metaphor and Symbol*, 19, (1), 1–30.

Barrett, Frank A. (2000), *Disease and Geography: The History of an Idea*. Atkinson College: Department of Geography.

Barrows, Susanna (1981), *Distorting Mirrors: Visions of the Crowd in Late Nineteenth-Century France*. New Haven: Yale University Press.

Bashford, Alison and Hooker, Claire (2001a), 'Introduction: Contagion, modernity and postmodernity', in Alison Bashford and Claire Hooker (eds), *Contagion: Historical and Cultural Studies*. London: Routledge, pp. 1–12.

— (eds) (2001b), *Contagion: Historical and Cultural Studies*. London: Routledge.

Baudrillard, Jean (1988 [1987]), *The Ecstasy of Communication* (trans. of *L'Autre par lui-même*, trans. Bernard Schutze and Caroline Schutze). New York: Semiotext(e).

—(1993), 'Forget Baudrillard. Interview with Sylvere Lotringer', in Mike Gane (ed.), *Baudrillard Live: Selected Interviews*. London: Routledge, pp. 99–127.

Beagon, Mary (2005), *The Elder Pliny on the Human Animal: Natural History Book 7*. Oxford: Oxford University Press.

Beecher, Donald (2005), 'An afterword on contagion', in Claire L. Carlin (ed.), *Imagining Contagion in Early Modern Europe*. Houndmills: Palgrave Macmillan, pp. 243–60.

Beer, Daniel (2007), ' "Microbes of the mind": Moral contagion in late imperial Russia'. *Journal of Modern History*, 79, 531–71.

Bekhterev, Vladimir Mikhaïlovich (1998 [1908]), *Suggestion and its Role in Social Life* (trans. of *Vnushenie i evo rol' v obshchestvennoĭ zhiani*, trans. Tzvetanka Dobreva-Martinova). Piscataway: Transaction.

Beller, Mara (September 1998), 'The Sokal hoax: At whom are we laughing?'. *Physics Today*, pp. 29–34.

Bennett, Lynn (2004), 'Boundaries and frontiers: Metaphor and the rhetoric of interdisciplinarity in literary studies'. *Genre*, 37, (3–4), 505–29.

Bewell, Alan (1999), *Romanticism and Colonial Disease*. Baltimore: Johns Hopkins University Press.

Black, Max (1954-5), 'Metaphor'. *Proceedings of the Aristotelian Society*, 55, 273–94.

Blackmore, Susan (1999), *The Meme Machine*. Oxford: Oxford University Press.

Blondel, Eric (1985 [1971]), 'Nietzsche; Life as metaphor' (trans. of 'Nietzsche: La vie et la métaphore'), in David B. Allison (ed.), *The New Nietzsche: Contemporary Styles of Interpretation*. Cambridge, MA: MIT Press, pp. 150–75.

Blumenberg, Hans (2010 [1960]), *Paradigms for a Metaphorology* (trans. of *Paradigmen zu einer Metaphorologie*, trans. Robert Savage). Ithaca: Cornell University Press.

Boden, Margaret A. (2006), *Mind as Machine: A History of Cognitive Science* (vol. 1). Oxford: Oxford University Press.

Boghossian, Paul A. (September 1996), 'What the Sokal Hoax Ought to Teach Us: The Pernicious Consequences and Internal Contradictions of "Postmodernist" Relativism'. *Times Literary Supplement,* pp. 14–15.

Bogue, Ronald (1984), 'Introduction', in Ronald Bogue (ed.), *Mimesis in Contemporary Theory* (vol. 2). Philadelphia: John Benjamins, pp. 1–12.

Boluk, Stephanie and Lenz, Wylie (2011), 'Infection, media, and capitalism: From early modern plagues to postmodern zombies'. *Journal for Early Modern Cultural Studies*, 10, (2), 126–47.

Booth, Wayne C. (1983), 'Review: *Metaphors We Live By*'. *Ethics*, 93, (3), 619–21.

Bosanquet, Bernard (1890), 'The communication of moral ideas as a function of an ethical society'. *International Journal of Ethics*, 1, (1), 79–97.

Botz-Bornstein, Thorsten (ed.) (2008), *Culture, Nature, Memes*. Newcastle upon Tyne: Cambridge Scholars Publishing.

Boyd, Richard (1993), 'Metaphor and theory change: What is a "metaphor" a metaphor for?', in Andrew Ortony (ed.), *Metaphor and Thought* (2nd edn). Cambridge: Cambridge University Press, pp. 481–532.

Boyle, Danny (2002), *28 Days Later* [Film].

Braun, Bruce (2008), 'Thinking the city through SARS', in S. Harris Ali and Roger Keil (eds), *Networked Disease: Emerging Infections in the Global City*. Malden: Blackwell, pp. 250–66.

Bray, Laurent (1986), 'Richelet's "Dictionnaire François" (1680) as a source of "La Porte des Siences" (1682) and Le Roux's "Dictionaire Comique" (1718)', in Reinhard Hartmann (ed.), *The History of Lexicography*. Amsterdam: John Benjamins, pp. 13–21.

Breazeale, Daniel (1979), 'Introduction', in Daniel Breazeale (ed.), *Philosophy and Truth: Selections from Nietzsche's Notebooks of the Early 1870s*. Sussex: Harvester, pp. xiii–xlix.

Brée, Germaine (1961), *Camus*. New Brunswick: Rutgers University Press.

Brewer, E. Cobham (1898), 'Auster', in *Dictionary of Phrase and Fable*. Philadelphia: Henry Altemus.

Brierre de Boismont, Alexandre (1856), *Suicide et de la folie suicide*. Paris: Germer Baillière.

Brodie, Richard (1996), *Virus of the Mind: The New Science of the Meme*. Seattle: Integral.

Brown, Charles Brockden (1799), *Edgar Huntly* (vol. 1). Philadelphia: H. Maxwell.

Browning, Barbara (1998), *Infectious Rhythm: Metaphors of Contagion and the Spread of African Culture*. New York: Routledge.

Buiani, Roberta (2005), 'Marginal networks: The virus between complexity and suppression'. *Fibreculture*, 4, www.four.fibreculturejournal.org/fcj-020-marginal-networks-the-virus-between-complexity-and-suppression/.

Burgess, Jean (2008), '"All Your Chocolate Rain are Belong to Us"?: Viral Video, YouTube, and the dynamics of participatory culture', in Geert Lovink and Sabine Niederer (eds), *Video Vortex Reader: Responses to YouTube*. Amsterdam: Institute of Network Cultures, pp. 101–10.

Burgess, Tony (2009 [1998]), *Pontypool Changes Everything*. Toronto: ECW.

Burhil, Robert (1602), 'The epistle dedicatorie', in *A Learned and Godly Sermon Preached at Worcester, at an Assise* by Miles Smith. Oxford: Joseph Barnes.

Burke, Edmund (1790), *Reflections on the Revolution in France and on the Proceedings in Certain Societies in London Relative to that Event* (2nd edn). London: J. Dodsley.

Burney, Fanny (1796), *Camilla: Or, A Picture of Youth* (vol. 1). London: T. Payne.

Burnham, John C. (1999), 'A brief history of medical practitioners and professional historians as writers of medical history'. *Health and History*, 1, (4), 250–73.

Burroughs, William S. (1959), *Naked Lunch*. Paris: Olympia.

—(1962), *The Ticket that Exploded*. Paris: Olympia.

—(1970), *The Electronic Revolution*. Göttingen: Expanded Media Editions.

Burt, Ronald S. (1987), 'Social contagion and innovation: Cohesion versus structural equivalence'. *American Journal of Sociology*, 92, (6), 1287–1335.

Byrne, Joseph Patrick (2006), *Daily Life During the Black Death*. Westport: Greenwood.

Calmeil, Louis Florentin (1845), *De la folie considérée sous le point de vue pathologique, philosophique, historique et judiciaire* (vol. 1). Paris: Baillière.

Calvin, John (1816 [1559]), *Institutes of the Christian Religion* (trans. John Allen, vol. 1). New Haven: Hezekiah Howe.

Camus, Albert (1960 [1947]), *The Plague* (trans. of *La Peste*, trans. Stuart Gilbert). London: Penguin.

—(1966), *Carnets 1942–1951* (trans. Philip Thody). London: Hamish Hamilton.

—(1970 [1954]), 'The Minotaur, or stopping in Oran' (trans. Ellen Conroy Kennedy), in Philip Thody (ed.), *Lyrical and Critical Essays*. New York: Vintage, pp. 109–33.

Carlin, Claire L. (ed.) (2005), *Imagining Contagion in Early Modern Europe*. Houndmills, Basingstoke: Palgrave Macmillan.

Carmichael, Ann G. and Fleming Moran, Millicent (2002), 'Historical connections between climate, medical thought and human health', in Pim Martens and Anthony J. McMichael (eds), *Environmental Change, Climate and Health: Issues and Research Methods*. Cambridge: Cambridge University Press, pp. 18–51.

Castells, Manuel (2010), *The Rise of the Network Society* (2nd edn). Chichester: John Wiley.

Caton, Hiram (2000), 'Review of *The Meme Machine* by Susan Blackmore and *Thought Contagion: How Belief Spreads through Society* by Aaron Lynch'. *Politics and the Life Sciences*, 19, (2), 272–5.

Chadarevian, Soraya de (2007), '*The Selfish Gene* at 30: The origin and career of a book and its title'. *Notes and Records of the Royal Society of London*, 61, (1), 31–8.

Chesterman, Andrew (1997), *Memes of Translation: The Spread of Ideas in Translation Theory*. Amsterdam: J. Benjamins.

Church, Alfred John and Brodribb, William Jackson (trans.) (1864), *The History of Tacitus Translated into English*. Cambridge: Macmillan.

Cicero, Marcus Tullius (1824), *De Legibus*. Frankfurt am Main: Broenner.

—(1841), *Treatise on the Laws* (trans. Francis Barham), *Political Works of Marcus Tullius Cicero*, vol. 2. London: Edmund Spettigue.

Clark, Terry N. (1969), 'Introduction', in Terry N. Clark (ed.), *Gabriel Tarde on Communication and Social Influence*. Chicago: University of Chicago Press, pp. 1–69.

Cloak, F. Ted. (1975), 'Is a cultural ethology possible?'. *Human Ecology*, 3, (3), 161–82.

Cohen, Fred (1984), 'Computer viruses – theory and experiments', in James H. Finch and E. Graham Dougall (eds), *Computer Security: A Global Challenge: Proceedings of the Second IFIP International Conference on Computer Security*. Amsterdam: Elsevier, pp. 143–9.

Cohen, Lazarus (1825), *New System of Astronomy*. London: Letts.

Cohen, Ted (1978), 'Metaphor and the cultivation of intimacy'. *Critical Inquiry*, 5, (1), 3–12.

Colebrook, Claire (2008), *Milton, Evil and Literary History*. London: Continuum.

Comrie, Bernard (2005), 'Writing systems', in Martin Haspelmath, Matthew S. Dryer, David Gil and Bernard Comrie (eds), *The World Atlas of Language Structures*. Oxford: Oxford University Press, pp. 568–71.

Conrad, Lawrence I. and Wujastyk, Dominik (eds) (2000), *Contagion: Perspectives from Pre-Modern Societies*. Aldershot: Ashgate.

'Contagion' (1989), in *Oxford English Dictionary* (2nd edn). Oxford: Oxford University Press.

'Contagion' (2007), in *American Heritage Medical Dictionary*. Boston: Houghton Mifflin.

'Contamination' (1989), in *Oxford English Dictionary* (2nd edn). Oxford: Oxford University Press.

Coogan, Robert (1992), *Erasmus, Lee and the Correction of the Vulgate: The Shaking of the Foundations*. Geneva: Droz.

Cook, Robin (1995), *Contagion*. New York: Putnam.

Cooke, Jennifer (2009), *Legacies of Plague in Literature, Theory and Film*. Houndmills: Palgrave Macmillan.

Cressy, Serenus (1668), *The Church-History of Brittany from the Beginning of Christianity to the Norman Conquest*: s. n.

Cullen, Ben (2000), *Contagious Ideas: On Evolution, Culture, Archaeology, and Cultural Virus Theory*. Oxford: Oxbow.

Darwin, Charles (1859), *On the Origin of Species by Means of Natural Selection*. London: John Murray.

Davis, Cynthia J. (2002), 'Contagion as metaphor'. *American Literary History*, 14, (4), 828–36.

Dawkins, Richard (1976), *The Selfish Gene*. Oxford: Oxford University Press.

—(1978), 'Reply to Fix and Greene'. *Contemporary Sociology*, 7, (6), 709–12.

—(1982), *The Extended Phenotype: The Gene as the Unit of Selection*. Oxford: Freeman.

—(1993), 'Viruses of the mind', in Bo Dahlborn (ed.), *Dennett and his Critics: Demystifying Mind*. Oxford: Blackwell, pp. 13–27.

De Bruyn, Theodore S. (1988), 'Pelagius's interpretation of Rom. 5: 12–21'. *Toronto Journal of Theology*, 4, 30–43.

de Man, Paul (1978), 'The epistemology of metaphor'. *Critical Inquiry*, 5, (1), 13–30.

Defoe, Daniel (1790), 'Preface', in *Serious Reflections of Robinson Crusoe* (vol. 3). London: J. Walter, pp. i–viii.

—(1974 [1722]), *Due Preparations for the Plague*, in George Atherton Aitken (ed.), *Romances and Narratives by Daniel Defoe* (vol. 15). New York: AMS Press.

—(1998 [1722]), *A Journal of the Plague Year*. Oxford: Oxford University Press.

Deignan, Alice (2008), 'Corpus linguistics and metaphor', in Raymond W. Gibbs, Jr. (ed.), *The Cambridge Handbook of Metaphor and Thought*. Cambridge: Cambridge University Press, pp. 280–94.

Deleuze, Gilles (1962), *Nietzsche et la philosophie*. Paris: Presses Universitaires de France.

—(2004 [1968]), *Difference and Repetition* (trans. of *Différence et répétition*, trans. Paul Patton). London: Continuum.

Deleuze, Gilles and Guattari, Félix (1987 [1980]), *A Thousand Plateaus: Capitalism and Schizophrenia* (trans. of *Mille plateaux, v. 2 of Capitalisme et schizophrénie*, trans. Brian Massumi). Minneapolis: University of Minnesota Press.

Dennett, Daniel (1991), *Consciousness Explained*. Boston: Little, Brown.

—(1996), *Darwin's Dangerous Idea: Evolution and the Meanings of Life*. New York: Simon and Schuster.

Derrida, Jacques (1972), *Marges de la philosophie*. Paris: Minuit.

—(1981 [1972]), *Dissemination* (trans. of *La Dissémination*, trans. Barbara Johnson). London: Athlone.

—(1982 [1972]), *Margins of Philosophy* (trans. of *Marges de la philosophie*, trans. Alan Bass). Brighton, Sussex: Harvester.

—(1993 [1989]), 'The rhetoric of drugs: An interview' (trans. of 'Rhetorique de la drogue'). *Differences*, 5, (1), 1–25.

—(1994), 'The spatial arts: An interview with Jacques Derrida', in Peter Brunette and David Wills (eds), *Deconstruction and the Visual Arts*. Cambridge: Cambridge University Press, pp. 9–32.

Despine, Prosper (1870), *De la contagion morale*. Marseille: Étienne Camoin.

Distin, Kate (2005), *The Selfish Meme: A Critical Reassessment*. Cambridge: Cambridge University Press.

Doukas, John (1989), 'Contagion effect on sovereign interest rate spreads'. *Economics Letters*, 29, (3), 237–41.

Douthwaite, John (2011), 'Conceptual metaphor and communication: An Austinian and Gricean analysis of Brian Clark's *Whose Life Is It Anyway?*', in Monika Fludernik (ed.), *Beyond Cognitive Metaphor Theory: Perspectives on Literary Metaphor*. New York: Routledge, pp. 137–57.

Drost, Mark P. (1986), 'Nietzsche and mimesis'. *Philosophy and Literature*, 10, (2), 309–17.

Drout, Michael D. C. (2006), *How Tradition Works: A Meme-based Cultural Poetics of the Anglo-Saxon Tenth Century*. Tempe: Arizona Center for Medieval and Renaissance Studies.

Dumas, Georges (1911), 'Contagion mentale'. *Revue Philosophique*, 71, 225–44; 384–407.

Durkheim, Émile (1962 [1897]), *Suicide: A Study in Sociology* (trans. of *Le Suicide: étude de sociologie*, trans. John. A Spaulding and George Simpson). Glencoe, IL: Free Press.

Ebrard, N. (1870), *Du suicide considéré aux points de vue médical, philosophique, religieux et social*. Avignon: Seguin Ainé.

Edwards, Sebastian (2000), 'Contagion'. *The World Economy*, 23, (7), 873–900.

Eichengreen, Barry and Portes, Richard (1987), 'The anatomy of financial crises', in Richard Portes and Alexander K. Swoboda (eds), *Threats to International Financial Stability*. Cambridge: Cambridge University Press, pp. 10–66.

Eichengreen, Barry, Rose, Andrew K. and Wyplosz, Charles (1996), 'Contagious Currency Crises'. NBER Working Paper No. 5681.

Eikon Basilike, The Pourtraicture of His Sacred Majestie in his Solitudes and Sufferings (1648). London: s. n.

Else, Gerald F. (1958), ' "Imitation" in the fifth century'. *Classical Philology*, 53, (2), 73–90.

Erasmus, Desiderius (1518), 'Quo pacto posis adulatorem ab amico di gnoscere, Plutarchi Erasmo interprete', in *Institutio principis Christiani*. Basel: Frobenius, pp. 260–312.

—(1536), *Adagiorum chiliades*. Basel: Frobenius.

—(1982), *Adages I i 1 to I v 100* (trans. Margaret Mann Phillips), *Collected Works of Erasmus*, vol. 31. Toronto: University of Toronto Press.

—(1989), *Adages I vi 1 to I x 100* (trans. R. A. B. Mynors), *Collected Works of Erasmus*, vol. 32. Toronto: University of Toronto Press.

—(1994 [1516]), *Annotations on Romans* (trans. John B. Payne, Albert Rabil, Robert D. Sider and Warren S. Smith), *Collected Works of Erasmus*, vol. 56. Toronto: University of Toronto Press.

—(2005), *Adages III iv to IV ii 100* (trans. Denis Drysdall), *Collected Works of Erasmus*, vol. 35. Toronto: University of Toronto Press.

—(2006), *Adages IV iii 1 to V ii 51* (trans. John N. Grant and Betty I. Knott), *Collected Works of Erasmus*, vol. 36. Toronto: University of Toronto Press.

Eriksson, Kai (2005), 'Foucault, Deleuze, and the ontology of networks'. *European Legacy*, 10, (6), 595–610.

Esquirol, Étienne (1838), *Maladies mentales considérées sous les rapports médical, hygiénique et médico-légal* (vol. 1). Paris: Baillière.

Euripides (1828), *Bacchae* (trans. Ian Johnston). Arlington, VA: Richer Resources.

Fauconnier, Gilles and Turner, Mark (1996), 'Blending as a central process of grammar', in Adele Goldberg (ed.), *Conceptual Structure, Discourse, and Language*. Stanford: Center for the Study of Language and Information (CSLI), pp. 113–29.

—(1998), 'Conceptual integration networks'. *Cognitive Science*, 22, (2), 113–87.

—(2002), *The Way We Think: Conceptual Blending and the Mind's Hidden Complexities*. New York: Basic.

Featley, Daniel (1626), *A Second Parallel together with a Writ of Error Sued against the Appealer*. London: Robert Milbourne.

Fee, Elizabeth (1989), 'Henry E. Sigerist: From the social production of disease to medical management and scientific socialism'. *Milbank Quarterly*, 67, (1), 127–50.

Fiore, Peter Amadeus (1981), *Milton and Augustine: Patterns of Augustinian Thought in Paradise Lost*. Pennsylvania: Pennsylvania State University Press.

Flanagan, Robert J., Holt, Charles C. and Bosworth, Barry (1976), 'Wage interdependence in unionized labor markets'. *Brookings Papers on Economic Activity*, 3, 635–81.

Forceville, Charles (1996), '(A)symmetry in metaphor: The importance of extended context'. *Poetics Today*, 16, (4), 677–708.

'Foreign Furor for Investments' (1890, 13 September), *Iron and Machinery World*, 68, 9–10.

Forth, Christopher E. (2001), 'Moral contagion and the will: The crisis of masculinity in *fin-de-siècle* France', in Alison Bashford and Claire Hooker (eds), *Contagion: Historical and Cultural Studies*. London: Routledge, pp. 61–75.

Foucault, Michel (1984), 'Space, knowledge, and power. Interview with Paul Rabinow', in Paul Rabinow (ed.), *The Foucault Reader*. New York: Pantheon, pp. 239–56.

Frazer, James George (1905), *Lectures on the Early History of the Kingship*. London: Macmillan.

—(1911–15), *The Golden Bough: A Study in Magic and Religion* (3rd edn). London: Macmillan.

Freud, Sigmund (1919 [1913]), *Totem and Taboo: Resemblances between the Psychic Lives of Savages and Neurotics* (trans. of *Totem und Tabu: Einige Übereinstimmungen im Seelenleben der Wilden und der Neurotiker*, trans. A. A. Brill). New York: Moffat, Yard and Company.

—(1921), *Massenpsychologie und Ich-Analyse.* Leipzig: Internationaler Psychoanalytischer.

—(1922 [1921]), *Group Psychology and the Analysis of the Ego* (trans. of *Massenpsychologie und Ich-Analyse*, trans. James Strachey). London: International Psycho-analytical Press.

Fulke Greville, Lord Brooke (1870), *Works in Verse and Prose Complete* (vol. 4). C. Tiplady and Son [Printed for private circulation].

Fuller, Thomas (1655), *The Church-history of Britain from the Birth of Jesus Christ until the Year MDCXLVIII* (vol. 1). London: John Williams.

Gai, Prasanna and Kapadia, Sujit (2010), 'Contagion in Financial Networks'. *Bank of England Working Papers*, 383, www.bankofengland.co.uk/publications/workingpapers/wp383.pdf.

Galloway, Alexander R. and Thacker, Eugene (2007), *The Exploit: A Theory of Networks.* Minneapolis: University of Minnesota Press.

Gauden, John (1642), *Three Sermons Preached Upon Severall Publike Occasions.* London: R. Bishop for Andrew Crook.

Gebauer, Gunter and Wulf, Christoph (1995 [1992]), *Mimesis: Culture – Art – Society* (trans. of *Mimesis*, trans. Don Reneau). Berkeley: University of California Press.

Genette, Gérard (1982a [1966]), 'Figures' (trans. Alan Sheridan), in *Figures of Literary Discourse.* New York: Columbia University Press, pp. 45–60.

—(1982b [1970]), 'Rhetoric restrained' (trans. of 'La rhétorique restreinte', trans. Alan Sheridan), in *Figures of Literary Discourse.* New York: Columbia University Press, pp. 103–26.

Genter, Dedre and Jeziorski, Michael (1993), 'The shift from metaphor to analogy in Western science', in Andrew Ortony (ed.), *Metaphor and Thought* (2nd edn). Cambridge: Cambridge University Press, pp. 447–80.

Gerlach, Stefan and Smets, Frank (1994), 'Contagious Speculative Attacks'. Basle: Bank for International Settlements – Monetary and Economic Department.

Gibbon, Edward (1788), *History of the Decline and Fall of the Roman Empire* (vol. 6). London: A. Strahan and T. Cadell.

—(1796), *Miscellaneous Works of Edward Gibbon, Esquire. With Memoirs of His Life and Writings, Composed by Himself* (vol. 1). London: A. Strahan, T. Cadell, Jr. and W. Davies.

Gilbert, D. L. (ed.) (1868), *Oeuvres de La Rochefoucauld* (vol. 1). Paris: Hachette.

Gilbert, Pamela K. (1997), 'Ingestion, contagion, seduction: Victorian metaphors of reading'. *LIT: Literature Interpretation Theory*, 8, (1), 83–104.

—(2008), *Cholera and Nation: Doctoring the Social Body in Victorian England.* Albany: State University of New York Press.

Gilliam, Terry (1995), *Twelve Monkeys* [Film].

Gilman, Ernest B. (2009), *Plague Writing in Early Modern England.* Chicago: University of Chicago Press.

Girard, René (1974), 'The plague in literature and myth'. *Texas Studies in Literature and Language*, 15, (5), 833–50.

—(1977 [1970]), 'Dionysus and the violent genesis of the sacred' (trans. of 'Dionysos et la genèse violente du sacré', trans. Sandor Goodhart). *Boundary 2*, 5, (2), 487–506.

—(2005 [1972]), *Violence and the Sacred* (trans. of *La violence et le sacré*, trans. Patrick Gregory). London: Continuum.

Gladwell, Malcom (2000), *The Tipping Point: How Little Things Can Make a Big Difference*. Boston: Little, Brown.

Gleick, James (2011), *The Information: A History, A Theory, A Flood*. New York: Pantheon.

Glick, Reuven and Rose, Andrew K. (1999), 'Contagion and trade: Why are currency crises regional?', in Pierre-Richard Agénor, Marcus Miller, David Vines and Axel Weber (eds), *The Asian Financial Crisis: Causes, Contagion and Consequences*. Cambridge: Cambridge University Press, pp. 284–306.

Golden, Leon (1975), 'Plato's concept of *Mimesis*'. *British Journal of Aesthetics*, 15, (2), 118–31.

Goldstein, Jan (1984), ' "Moral contagion": A professional ideology of medicine and psychiatry in eighteenth- and nineteenth-century France', in Gerald L. Geison (ed.), *Professions and the French State, 1700–1900*. Philadelphia: University of Pennsylvania Press, pp. 181–222.

Gordon, Robert J. (1975), 'The demand for and supply of inflation'. *Journal of Law and Economics*, 18, (3), 807–36.

Gould, Stephen Jay (2002), *The Structure of Evolutionary Theory*. Harvard: Harvard University Press.

Grafen, Alan (2006), 'The intellectual contribution of *The Selfish Gene* to evolutionary theory', in Alan Grafen and Mark Ridley (eds), *Richard Dawkins: How a Scientist Changed the Way We Think*. Oxford: Oxford University Press, pp. 66–74.

Graham, Tyler (1998), 'St Augustine's novelistic conversion'. *Contagion: Journal of Violence, Mimesis, and Culture*, 5, 135–54.

Green, Joshua and Jenkins, Henry (2011), 'Spreadable media: How audiences create value and meaning in a networked economy', in Virginia Nightingale (ed.), *The Handbook of Media Audiences*. Oxford: Wiley-Blackwell, pp. 109–27.

Greene, Penelope J. (1978), 'From genes to memes? [Rev. of *The Selfish Gene*]'. *Contemporary Sociology*, 7, (6), 706–9.

Greenstone, Gerry (2009), 'A commentary on cholera: The scourge that never dies'. *BCMJ*, 51, (4), 164–7.

Grigsby, Bryon Lee (2004), *Pestilence in Medieval and Early Modern English Literature*. New York: Routledge.

Gunders, John and Brown, Damon (2010), *The Complete Idiot's Guide to Memes*. New York: Alpha.

Hamilton, James and Hamilton, Lawrence (1981), 'Models of social contagion'. *Journal of Mathematical Sociology*, 8, (1), 133–60.

Hamilton, William D. (1977), 'The play by nature [Rev. of *The Selfish Gene*]'. *Science*, 196, (4291), 757–9.

Hamlin, Christopher (1998), *Public Health and Social Justice in the Age of Chadwick: Britain, 1800–1854*. Cambridge: Cambridge University Press.

Hannaway, Caroline (1994), 'Environment and miasmata', in W. F. Bynum and Roy Porter (eds), *Companion Encyclopedia of the History of Medicine* (vol. 1). London: Routledge, pp. 292–308.

Hardt, Michael and Negri, Antonio (2000), *Empire*. Cambridge, MA: Harvard University Press.

Haroutunian, Lulu M. (1964), 'Camus and the white plague'. *MLN*, 79, (3), 311–15.

Hatfield, Elaine, Cacioppo, John T. and Rapson, Richard L. (1994), *Emotional Contagion*. Cambridge: Cambridge University Press.

Hayles, N. Katherine (1999), *How We Became Posthuman: Virtual Bodies in Cybernetics, Literature, and Informatics*. Chicago: University of Chicago Press.

Healy, Margaret (1993), 'Discourses of the plague in early modern London', in J. A. I. Champion (ed.), *Epidemic Disease in London*. London: University of London Centre for Metropolitan History, pp. 19–34.

Hecquet, Phillipe (1733), *Naturalisme des convulsions dans les maladies de l'épidémie convulsionnaire*. Soleure: Andreas Gymnicus.

Hegel, Georg Wilhelm Friedrich (2001 [1807]), *Spirit: Chapter Six of Hegel's Phenomenology of Spirit* (trans. of *Phänomenologie des Geistes*, trans. Hegel Translation Group). Indianapolis: Hackett.

Heidegger, Martin (1961), *Nietzsche*. Pfullingen: Neske.

Heil, John Paul (2005), *The Rhetorical Role of Scripture in 1 Corinthians*. Atlanta: Society of Biblical Literature.

Herder, Johann Gottfried von (1968 [1784–91]), *Reflections on the Philosophy of the History of Mankind* (trans. of *Ideen zur Philosophie der Geschichte der Menscheit*, trans. T. O. Churchill). Chicago: University of Chicago Press.

Heyd, Michael (2005), 'Original sin, the struggle for stability, and the rise of moral individualism in late seventeenth-century England', in Philip Benedict and Myron P. Gutmann (eds), *Early Modern Europe: From Crisis to Stability*, Newark: University of Delaware Press, pp. 197–233.

Heylighen, Francis and Chielens, Klaas (2009), 'Evolution of culture, memetics', in Robert A. Meyers (ed.), *Encyclopedia of Complexity and Systems Science*. Berlin: Springer-Verlag, pp. 3205–20.

Hippocrates (1923a), 'Breaths' (trans. W. H. S. Jones), in *Hippocrates* (vol. 2). London: Heinemann, pp. 219–53.

—(1923b), 'The sacred disease' (trans. W. H. S. Jones), in *Hippocrates* (vol. 2). London: Heinemann, pp. 127–83.

—(1931), 'Nature of man' (trans. W. H. S. Jones), in *Hippocrates* (vol. 4). London: Heinemann, pp. 1–41.

Hobbes, Thomas (1651), *Leviathan, or The Matter, Forme, and Power of a Common Wealth, Ecclesiasticall and Civil*. London: Andrew Crooke.

Hoffman, Robert R. (1980), 'Metaphor in science', in Richard P. Honeck and Robert R. Hoffman (eds), *Cognition and Figurative Language*. Hillsdale, NJ: Lawrence Erlbaum, pp. 393–423.

Hofstadter, Douglas R. (1983), Metamagical themas: Virus-like sentences and self-replicating structures. *Scientific American*, 248, 14–22.

Hofstadter, Douglas R. and Dennett, Daniel (eds) (1981), *The Mind's I: Fantasies and Reflections on Self and Soul*. Brighton: Harvester.

Holland, Philemon (trans.) (1911 [1603]), *Plutarch's Moralia: Twenty Essays*. London: J. M. Dent. Rpt. of Holland, Philemon, trans. (1603). *Plutarch's Moralia*. London: Arthur Hatfield.

Holmes, Jonathan and Streete, Adrian (2005), 'Introduction', in *Refiguring Mimesis: Representation in Early Modern Literature*. Hatfield, Hertfordshire: University of Hertfordshire Press, pp. 1–13.

Hospital, Janette Turner (2003), *Due Preparations for the Plague*. New York: W. W. Norton.

Hoyle, Leigh (2010), *Genes, Memes, Culture, and Mental Illness: Toward an Integrative Model*. New York: Springer.

Hull, David (2000), 'Taking memetics seriously: Memetics will be what we make it', in Robert Aunger (ed.), *Darwinizing Culture: The Status of Memetics as a Science*. Oxford: Oxford University Press, pp. 43–67.

Hull, Michael F. (2005), *Baptism on Account of the Dead (1 Cor 15:29): An Act of Faith in the Resurrection*. Leiden: Brill.

Hume, David (1825 [1754–5]), *The History of England from the Invasion of Julius Caesar, to the Revolution in 1688* (vol. 6). London: Jones and Company.

Hutcheon, Linda and Hutcheon, Michael (1996), *Opera: Desire, Disease, Death*. Lincoln: University of Nebraska Press.

Irigaray, Luce (1999 [1983]), *The Forgetting of Air in Martin Heidegger* (trans. of *L'oubli de l'air chez Martin Heidegger*, trans. Mary Beth Mader). London: Athlone.

—(2004), *Luce Irigaray: Key Writings*. London: Continuum.

Isidore of Seville, St (2006), *The Etymologies of Isidore of Seville* (trans. Stephen A. Barney, W. J. Lewis and Oliver Berghof). Cambridge: Cambridge University Press.

Jameson, Horatio Gates (1855), *A Treatise on Epidemic Cholera*. Philadelphia: Lindsay and Blakiston.

Jan, Steven B. (2007), *The Memetics of Music: A Neo-Darwinian View of Musical Structure and Culture*. Aldershot: Ashgate.

Jeffreys, Mark (2000), 'The meme metaphor'. *Perspectives in Biology and Medicine*, 43, (2), 227–42.

Johnson, Mark (1981), 'Introduction: Metaphor in the philosophical tradition', in Mark Johnson (ed.), *Philosophical Perspectives on Metaphor*. Minneapolis: University of Minnesota Press, pp. 3–47.

Johnson, Samuel (1749), *The Vanity of Human Wishes: The Tenth Satire of Juvenal, Imitated by Samuel Johnson*. London: R. Dodsley.

—(1755), *A Dictionary of the English Language in which the Words are Deduced from their Originals, Illustrated in their Different Significations by Examples by the Best Writers*. London: W. Strahan.

—(1759), *The History of Rasselas, Prince of Abissinia* (2nd edn, vol. 1). London: R. and J. Dodsley.

Jolly, Paul (1869), 'Introduction a l'étude de la philosophie dans ses rapports avec l'hygiène et la médecine: – imitation'. *L'Union Médicale*, 7, (28–9), 349–58, 369–77.

Jonsson, Stefan (2006), 'The invention of the masses: The crowd in French culture from the revolution to the commune', in Jeffrey T. Schnapp and Matthew Tiews (eds), *Crowds*. Stanford, CA: Stanford University Press, pp. 47–76.

Kant, Immanuel (1996 [1871]), *Critique of Pure Reason* (trans. of *Kritik der reinen Vernunft*, trans. Werner S. Pluhar). Indiana: Hackett.

Kaufman, Charlie (2008), *Synecdoche, New York* [Film].

Keesing, Roger M. (1985), 'Conventional metaphors and anthropological metaphysics: The problematic of cultural translation'. *Journal of Anthropological Research*, 41, (2), 201–17.

Keller, Evelyn Fox (2000), *The Century of the Gene*. Cambridge: Harvard University Press.

Kerényi, Carl (1976), *Dionysos: Archetypal Image of Indestructible Life* (trans. Ralph Manheim). Princeton: Princeton University Press.

Kinnunen, Jussi (1996), 'Gabriel Tarde as a founding father of innovation diffusion research'. *Acta Sociologica*, 39, (4), 431–42.

Kinzelbach, Annemarie (2006), 'Infection, contagion, and public health in late medieval and early modern German imperial towns'. *Journal of the History of Medicine and Allied Sciences*, 61, (3), 369–89.

Kirby, John T. (1997), 'Aristotle on metaphor'. *American Journal of Philology*, 118, (4), 517–54.

Koch, Tom (2005), *Cartographies of Disease: Maps, Mapping, and Medicine*. Redlands: ESRI.

Kofman, Sarah (1972), *Nietzsche et la métaphore*. Paris: Payot.

—(1993 [1972]), *Nietzsche and Metaphor* (trans. Duncan Large). London: Athlone.

Kolb, Robert W. (2011a), 'Introduction', in Robert W. Kolb (ed.), *Financial Contagion: The Viral Threat to the Wealth of Nations*. Hoboken: John Wiley, pp. xiii.

—(2011b), 'What is *Financial Contagion*', in Robert W. Kolb (ed.), *Financial Contagion: The Viral Threat to the Wealth of Nations*. Hoboken: John Wiley, pp. 3–10.

Koller, Hermann (1954), *Die Mimesis in der Antike*. Berne: Francke.

Krell, David Farrell (1998), *Contagion: Sexuality, Disease, and Death in German Idealism and Romanticism*. Bloomington: Indiana UP.

Kremer-Marietti, Angèle (trans.) (1969 [1873]), 'Introduction théorétique sur la vérité et le mensonge au sens extra-moral', in *Le Livre du philosophe: études theoretiques [By Friedrich Nietzsche]*. Paris: Aubier-Flammarion.

Kronenfeldner, Maria (2011), *Darwinian Creativity and Memetics*. Durham: Acumen.

'Krumm' (1857), in *Flügel's Complete Dictionary of the Germana and English Languages* (new edn, vol. 2). London: Whittaker and Co.

Kuper, Adam (2000), 'If memes are the answer, what is the question?', in Robert Aunger (ed.), *Darwinizing Culture: The Status of Memetics as a Science*. Oxford: Oxford University Press, pp. 175–88.

La Rochefoucauld, François de (1664), *Sentences et maximes morales*. Paris: Claude Barbin.

Lacan, Jacques (2006 [1961]), 'Metaphor of the subject' (trans. of 'La métaphore du sujet', trans. Bruce Fink), in *Écrits*. New York: Norton, pp. 755–8.

Lakoff, George (1993), 'The contemporary theory of metaphor', in Andrew Ortony (ed.), *Metaphor and Thought* (2nd edn). Cambridge: Cambridge University Press, pp. 202–51.

Lakoff, George and Johnson, Mark (1980), *Metaphors We Live By*. Chicago: University of Chicago Press.

—(1999), *Philosophy in the Flesh: The Embodied Mind and its Challenge to Western Thought*. New York: Basic.

—(2003), 'Afterword, 2003', in *Metaphors We Live By* (rev. edn). Chicago: University of Chicago Press, pp. 243–76.

Lakoff, George and Turner, Mark (1989), *More than Cool Reason: A Field Guide to Poetic Metaphor*. Chicago: University of Chicago Press.

Lamarck, Jean-Baptiste (1914 [1809]), *Zoological Philosophy: An Exposition with Regard to the Natural History of Animals* (trans. of *Philosophie Zoologique*, trans. Hugh Elliot). London: Macmillan.

Lamb, Marion J. (2011), 'Attitudes to soft inheritance in Great Britain, 1930s–1970s', in Snait B. Gissis and Eva Jablonka (eds), *Transformations of Lamarckism: From Subtle Fluids to Molecular Biology*. Cambridge, MA: MIT Press, pp. 109–20.

Large, Duncan (1993), 'Translator's introduction', in Sarah Kofman (ed.), *Nietzsche and Metaphor*. London: Athlone, pp. vii–xlv.

Latour, Bruno (1993 [1991]), *We Have Never Been Modern* (trans. of *Nous n'avons jamais été modernes: Essai d'anthropologie symétrique*, trans. Catherine Porter). Cambridge, MA: Harvard University Press.

—(2002), 'Gabriel Tarde and the end of the social', in Patrick Joyce (ed.), *The Social in Question: New Bearings in History and the Social Sciences*. London: Routledge, pp. 117–32.

—(2005), *Reassembling the Social: An Introduction to Actor-Network Theory*. Oxford: Oxford University Press.

Lawtoo, Nidesh (2009), 'Nietzsche and the psychology of mimesis: From Plato to the *Führer*', in Herman W. Siemens and Vasti Roodt (eds), *Nietzsche, Power and Politics: Rethinking Nietzsche's Legacy for Political Thought*. Berlin: Walter de Gruyter, pp. 667–93.

Le Bon, Gustave (1895), *Psychologie des foules*. Paris: Félix Alcan.

—(2002 [1895]), *The Crowd: A Study of the Popular Mind* (trans. of *La psychologie des foules*, trans. unknown). New York: Dover.

Leavy, Barbara F. (1992), *To Blight With Plague: Studies in a Literary Theme*. New York: New York University Press.

Levy, David A. and Nail, Paul R. (1993), 'Contagion: A theoretical and empirical review and reconceptualization'. *Genetic, Social, and General Psychology Monographs*, 119, (2), 233–84.

Lewin, Roger (1981), 'Lamarck will not lie down'. *Science*, 213, (4505), 316–21.

Lewis, Charlton T. and Short, Charles (1879), *A Latin Dictionary*. Oxford: Clarendon.

Liddell, Henry George and Scott, Robert (1846), 'mímhma', in *A Greek–English Lexicon*. New York: Harper and Brothers, p. 936.

—(1940), *A Greek–English Lexicon*. Oxford: Clarendon.

Locke, John (1693), *Some Thoughts Concerning Education*. London: A. and J. Churchill.

—(1959 [1690]), *An Essay Concerning Human Understanding* (vol. 2). New York: Dover.

Lottman, Herbert R. (1979), *Albert Camus: A Biography*. London: Weidenfeld and Nicolson.

Lucas, Prosper (1833), *De l'imitation contagieuse ou de la propagation sympathique des névroses et des monomanies*. Paris: Didot le Jeune.

Lupton, Deborah (1994), 'Panic computing: The viral metaphor and computer technology'. *Cultural Studies*, 8, (3), 556–68.

Lynch, Aaron (1996), *Thought Contagion: How Belief Spreads through Society: The New Science of Memes*. New York: Basic Books.

Lynch, Patrick (1995), *Carriers*. New York: Villard.

Maasen, Sabine and Weingart, Peter (2000), *Metaphors and the Dynamics of Knowledge*. London: Routledge.

McClelland, J. S. (1989), *The Crowd and the Mob: From Plato to Canetti*. London: Unwin Hyman.

MacCormac, Earl R. (1985), *A Cognitive Theory of Metaphor*. Cambridge, MA: MIT Press.

McDonald, Bruce (2008), *Pontypool* [Film].

McDougall, William (1920), *The Group Mind*. New York: G. P. Putnam's Sons.

McGrath, Alister E. (2004), *Dawkins' God: Genes, Memes, and the Meaning of Life*. Oxford: Wiley Blackwell.

MacPhail, Theresa Marie (2004), 'The viral gene: An undead metaphor recoding life'. *Science as Culture*, 13, (3), 325–45.

Madan, Francis Falconer (1950), *A New Bibliography of the Eikon Basilike of King Charles the First*. Oxford: Oxford Bibliographical Society.

Magner, Lois N. (1992), *A History of Medicine*. New York: Dekker.

—(2009), *A History of Infectious Diseases and the Microbial World*. Westport: Praeger.

Mailhot, Laurent (1973), *Albert Camus: Ou L'Imagination du Désert*. Montréal: Les Presses de L'Université de Montréal.

Malik, Kenan (1996), *The Meaning of Race: Race, History and Culture in Western Society*. New York: New York University Press.

Mann, Thomas (1990 [1912]), *Death in Venice* (trans. of *Der Tod in Venedig*, trans. H. T. Lowe-Porter), in John Wain (ed.), *Oxford Library of Short Novels*, vol. 3. Oxford: Clarendon.

Marsden, Paul (1998), 'Memetics and social contagion: Two sides of the one coin?'. *Journal of Memetics*, 2, www.cfpm.org/jom-emit/1998/vol2/marsden_p.html.

—(2000), 'Forefathers of memetics: Gabriel Tarde and the Laws of Imitation'. *Journal of Memetics*, 4, www.cfpm.org/jom-emit/2000/vol4/marsden_p.html.

Martin, Robert Montgomery (1835), *History of the British Colonies* (vol. 5). London: James Cochrane and Co.

Massey, Arthur (1933), *Epidemiology in Relation to Air Travel*. London: H. K. Lewis.

Masson, Paul (1999), 'Contagion: Monsoonal effects, spillovers and jumps between multiple equilibria', in Pierre-Richard Agénor, Marcus Miller, David Vines and Axel Weber (eds), *The Asian Financial Crisis: Causes, Contagion and Consequences*. Cambridge: Cambridge University Press, pp. 265–80.

Mayr, Ernst (1980), 'Prologue: Some thoughts on the history of the evolutionary synthesis', in Ernst Mayr and William B. Provine (eds), *The Evolutionary Synthesis: Perspectives on the Unification of Biology*. Harvard: Harvard University Press, pp. 1–48.

'Meme' (2001), in *Oxford English Dictionary* (3rd edn). Oxford: Oxford University Press.

Métreaux, Alexandre (1982), 'French crowd psychology: Between theory and ideology', in William R. Woodward and Mitchell G. Ash (eds), *The Problematic Science: Psychology in Nineteenth-century Thought*. New York: Praeger, pp. 276–99.

Midgley, Mary (1979), 'Gene-juggling [Rev. of *The Selfish Gene*]'. *Philosophy*, 54, 439–58.

Mill, John Stuart (1848), *Principles of Political Economy with Some of their Applications to Social Philosophy* (vol. 2). Boston: Charles C. Little and James Brown.

Miller, Hugh T. (2002), 'Idea contagion', in *Postmodern Public Policy*. Albany: State University of New York Press, pp. 33–49.

Milton, John (2005 [1667]), *Paradise Lost*. Oxford: Oxford University Press.

Mitchell, Peta (2008), *Cartographic Strategies of Postmodernity: The Figure of the Map in Contemporary Theory and Fiction*. London: Routledge.

—(2011), ' "The stratified record upon which we set our feet": The spatial turn and the multilayering of history, geography, and geology', in Michael Dear, Jim Ketchum, Sarah Luria and Douglas Richardson (eds), *GeoHumanities: Art, History, Text at the Edge of Place*. London: Routledge, pp. 71–83.

Monod, Jacques (1970), *Le hasard et la nécessité: essai sur la philosophie naturelle de la biologie moderne*. Paris: Seuil.

—(1972), *Chance and Necessity: An Essay on the Natural Philosophy of Modern Biology* (trans. of *Le hasard et la nécessité: essai sur la philosophie naturelle de la biologie moderne*). New York: Vintage.

Montaigne, Michel de (1588 [1580]), *Essais de Michel Seigneur de Montaigne* (5th edn): Abel L'Angelier.

—(1842 [1580]), *The Complete Works of Michael De Montaigne* (trans. Charles Cotton). London: John Templeman.

Moreau de Tours, Paul (1875), *Contagion du suicide à propos de l'épidémie actuelle*. Paris: s. n.

Morgan, Marjorie (1994), *Manners, Morals, and Class in England, 1774–1858*. New York: St. Martin's.

Morris, Martina (2004a), 'Editor's introduction', in Martina Morris (ed.), *Network Epidemiology: A Handbook for Survey Design and Data Collection*. Oxford: Oxford University Press.

— (ed.) (2004b), *Network Epidemiology: A Handbook for Survey Design and Data Collection*. Oxford: Oxford University Press.

Morse, Stephen A. (2006), 'Historical perspectives of microbial bioterrorism', in Burt Anderson, Herman Friedman and Mauro Bendinelli (eds), *Microorganisms and Bioterrorism*. New York: Springer, pp. 15–29.

Moulthrop, Stuart (1997), 'No war machine', in Joseph Tabbi and Michael Wutz (eds), *Reading Matters: Narratives in the New Media Ecology*, Ithaca: Cornell University Press, pp. 269–92.

Murphy, Ann V. (2007), 'Beyond performativity and against 'identification': Gender and technology in Irigaray', in Maria Cimitile and Elaine P. Miller (eds), *Returning to Irigaray: Feminist Philosophy, Politics, and the Question of Unity*. Albany: State University of New York Press, pp. 77–92.

Nicoll, Henry J. (1886), *Landmarks of English Literature*. New York: Appleton.

Nietzsche, Friedrich (1903), 'Über Wahrheit und Lüge im aussermoralischen Sinne', in Ernst Holzer and August Horneffer (eds), *Nietzsche's Werke (Grossoktavausgabe)* (2nd edn, vol. 10). Leipzig: C. G. Naumann, pp. 189–207.

—(1911 [1873]), 'On truth and lies in a nonmoral sense' (trans. Maximilian A. Mügge), in Oscar Levy (ed.), *The Complete Works of Friedrich Nietzsche: Early Greek Philosophy and Other Essays* (vol. 2). New York: Macmillan, pp. 171–92.

—(1979a [1872]), 'The philosopher: Reflections on the struggle between art and knowledge' (trans. of 'Der letzte Philosoph. Der Philosoph. Betrachtungen über den Kampf von Kunst und Erkenntniss'), in Daniel Breazeale (ed.), *Philosophy and Truth: Selections from Nietzsche's Notebooks of the Early 1870s*. Sussex: Harvester, pp. 3–58.

—(1979b [1873]), 'On truth and lies in a nonmoral sense' (trans. of 'Über Wahrheit und Lüge im aussermoralischen Sinne'), in Daniel Breazeale (ed.), *Philosophy and Truth: Selections from Nietzsche's Notebooks of the Early 1870s*. Sussex: Harvester, pp. 79–97.

Nolan, Christopher (2010), *Inception* [Film].

Nutton, Vivian (1983), 'The seeds of disease: An explanation of contagion and infection from the Greeks to the Renaissance'. *Medical History*, 27, 1–34.

—(2000), 'Did the Greeks have a word for it? Contagion and contagion theory in Classical Antiquity', in Lawrence I. Conrad and Dominik Wujastyk (eds), *Contagion: Perspectives from Pre-Modern Societies*. Aldershot: Ashgate, pp. 137–62.

Nye, Robert A. (1975), *The Origins of Crowd Psychology: Gustave Le Bon and the Crisis of Mass Democracy in the Third Republic*. London: Sage.

O'Neill, Sean and Hamilton, Fiona (August 2011), 'Mob Mentality Turns Contagious'. *The Australian*, p. 13.

Oliver, Kelly (2001), *Witnessing: Beyond Recognition*. Minneapolis: University of Minnesota Press.

Orléan, André (1989), 'Mimetic contagion and speculative bubbles'. *Theory and Decision*, 27, (1–2), 63–92.

Otto, Walter Friedrich (1965 [1933]), *Dionysus: Myth and Cult* (trans. of *Dionysos: Mythos und Kultus*, trans. Robert B. Palmer). Bloomington: Indiana University Press.

Ovid (2004), *Metamorphoses* (trans. David Raeburn). London: Penguin.

Parikka, Jussi (2005a), 'Digital monsters, binary aliens – computer viruses, capitalism and the flow of information'. *Fibreculture*, 4, www.four.fibreculturejournal.org/fcj-019-digital-monsters-binary-aliens-computer-viruses-capitalism-and-the-flow-of-information/.

—(2005b), 'The universal viral machine: Bits, parasites and the media ecology of network culture'. *CTheory*,(td029), www.vxheavens.com/lib/mjp02.html.

—(2007a), 'Contagion and repetition: On the viral logic of network culture'. *Ephemera*, 7, (2), 287–308.

—(2007b), *Digital Contagions: A Media Archaeology of Computer Viruses*. New York: Peter Lang.

Parikka, Jussi and Sampson, Tony D. (2009), *The Spam Book: On Viruses, Porn, and Other Anomalies from the Dark Side of Digital Culture*. Cresskill, NJ: Hampton.

Parker, Robert (1983), *Miasma: Pollution and Purification in Early Greek Religion*. Oxford: Clarendon.

Pascuzzi, Maria (2005), *First and Second Corinthians*. Collegeville, MN: Liturgical Press.

Peacham, Henry (1593), *The Garden of Eloquence* (revised edn). London: H. Jackson.

Pelagius (2002), *Pelagius's Commentary on St Paul's Epistle to the Romans* (trans. Theodore De Bruyn). Oxford: Oxford University Press.

Pelling, Margaret (1978), *Cholera, Fever and English Medicine, 1825–65*. Oxford: Oxford University Press.

—(2001), 'The meaning of contagion: Reproduction, medicine and metaphor', in Alison Bashford and Claire Hooker (eds), *Contagion: Historical and Cultural Studies*. London: Routledge, pp. 15–38.

Pernick, Martin S. (2002), 'Contagion and culture'. *American Literary History*, 14, (4), 858–65.

Perry, George L. (1975), 'Determinants of wage inflation around the world'. *Brookings Papers on Economic Activity*, 2, (403–47).

Petersen, Wolfgang (1995), *Outbreak* [Film].

Pettersson, Bo (2011), 'Literary criticism writes back to metaphor theory: Exploring the relation between extended metaphor and narrative in literature', in Monika Fludernik (ed.), *Beyond Cognitive Metaphor Theory: Perspectives on Literary Metaphor*. New York: Routledge, pp. 94–112.

Pfister, Michael (2005), 'Aufklärung als Ansteckung', in Mirjam Schaub, Nicola Suthor and Erika Fischer-Lichte (eds), *Ansteckung: Zur Körperlichkeit eines ästhetischen Prinzips*. München: Wilhelm Fink, pp. 263–74.

Phillips, David P. (1980), 'Airplane accidents, murder, and the mass media: Towards a theory of imitation and suggestion'. *Social Forces*, 58, (4), 1001–24.

Pilkington, Mary (1797), *The Force of Example, or, the History of Henry and Caroline*. London: E. Newbery.

Pinker, Steven (2007), *The Stuff of Thought*. Camberwell, Vic: Allen Lane.

Pires de Oliveira, Roberta (2001), 'Language and ideology: An interview with George Lakoff', in René Dirven, Bruce Hawkins and Esra Sandikcioglu (eds), *Language and Ideology: Theoretical Cognitive Approaches*. Amsterdam: John Benjamins, pp. 23–47.

Pitcher, A. R. (November 1976), 'Claim [Letter to the Editor]'. *New Scientist*, 72, 355.

Plato (1973), *The Republic and Other Works* (trans. B. Jowett). New York: Anchor.

—(1995), *Phaedrus* (trans. Alexander Nehamas and Paul Woodruff). Indianapolis: Hackett.

Plutarch (1888), 'Quomodo adulator ab amico internoscatur', in Gregorius N. Bernardakis (ed.), *Moralia* (vol. 1). Leipzig: Teubner, pp. 118–80.

—(1960), *Plutarch's Moralia* (trans. Frank Cole Babbitt, vol. 3). Harvard: Harvard University Press.

Potolsky, Matthew (2006), *Mimesis*. New York: Routledge.

Primaudaye, Pierre de La (1577), *L'Académie Françoise* (new revised edn). Paris: Guillaume Chaudière.

Rancour-Laferriere, Daniel (1981), 'Preliminary remarks on literary memetics', in Karl Menges and Daniel Rancour-Lafferiere (eds), *AXIA: Davis Symposium on Literary Evaluation*. Stuttgart: Akademischer Verlag Hans-Dieter Heinz, pp. 77–87.

Ranger, Terence and Slack, Paul (eds) (1992), *Epidemics and Ideas: Essays on the Historical Perception of Pestilence*. Cambridge: Cambridge University Press.

Ray, Darrel W. (2009), *The God Virus: How Religion Infects Our Lives and Culture*. Kansas: IPC Press.

Rees, Brinley Roderick (1991), *Pelagius: Life and Letters*. Woodbridge: Boydell.

Rees, Joan (1971), *Fulke Greville, Lord Brooke*. Berkeley: University of California Press.

Resnik, Salomon (2001), *The Delusional Person: Bodily Feelings in Psychosis*. London: H. Karnac.

Reynolds, Anthony (2000), 'Unfamiliar methods: Blumenberg and Rorty on metaphor'. *Qui Parle*, 12, (1), 77–103.

Richards, Ivor A. (1924), *Principles of Literary Criticism* (2nd edn). London: Routledge & Kegan Paul.

—(1936), *The Philosophy of Rhetoric*. London: Oxford University Press.

Richardson, Samuel (1742), *Pamela; or, Virtue Rewarded* (6th edn, vol. 4). London: Printed for S. Richardson.

Ricoeur, Paul (1973), 'Creativity in language: Word, polysemy, metaphor'. *Philosophy Today*, 17, (2), 97–111.

—(1975), *La métaphore vive*. Paris: Seuil.

—(1986 [1975]), *The Rule of Metaphor: Multi-disciplinary Studies of the Creation of Meaning in Language* (trans. of *La métaphore vive*, trans. Robert Czerny, Kathleen McLaughlin and John Costello). London: Routledge.

Robinson, Douglas (2008), *Estrangement and the Somatics of Literature: Tolstoy, Shklovsky, Brecht*. Baltimore: Johns Hopkins.

Rodgers, Joseph L. and Rowe, David C. (1993), 'Social contagion and adolescent sexual behavior: A developmental EMOSA model'. *Psychological Review*, 100, (3), 479–510.

Rose, Nick (1998), 'Controversies in meme theory'. *Journal of Memetics*, 2, www.cfpm.org/jom-emit/1998/vol2/rose_n.html.

Rose, Nikolas (2007), *The Politics of Life Itself: Biomedicine, Power, and Subjectivity in the Twenty-First Century*. Princeton: Princeton University Press.

Rosenberg, Charles E. (1992), *Explaining Epidemics and Other Studies in the History of Medicine*. Cambridge: Cambridge University Press.

Rosenberg, Charles E. and Golden, Janet (eds) (1997), *Framing Disease: Studies in Cultural History*. New Brunswick: Rutgers University Press.

Rousseau, Jean-Jacques (1781), 'Essai sur l'origine des langues', in *Collection complète des oeuvres de J. J. Rousseau* (vol. 16). Geneva: s. n., pp. 211–325.

—(1866 [1762]), *Émile ou de l'éducation*. Paris: Garnier Frères.

—(1938 [1762]), *Emile, or Education* (trans. Barbara Foxley). London: J. M. Dent and Sons.

—(1966 [1781]), 'Essay on the origin of languages' (trans. John H. Moran and Alexander Gode), in *On the Origin of Language: Two Essays*. Chicago: University of Chicago Press, pp. 1–74.

Russell, Rollo (1892), *Epidemics, Plagues, and Fevers: Their Causes and Prevention*. London: Edward Stanford.

Sampson, Tony (2004), 'A virus in info-space'. *M/C: A Journal of Media and Culture*, 7, (3), www.journal.media-culture.org.au/0406/07_Sampson.php.

—(2007), 'The accidental topology of digital culture: How the network becomes viral'. *Transformations*, 14, www.transformationsjournal.org/journal/issue_14/article_05.shtml.

—(2011), 'Contagion theory beyond the microbe'. *CTheory*, Theory Beyond the Codes no. 14, www.ctheory.net/articles.aspx?id=675.

Saramago, José (2007 [2004]), *Seeing* (trans. of *Ensaio sobre a Lucidez*, trans. Margaret Jull Costa). Orlando: Harcourt.

Sarasin, Philipp (2008), 'Vapors, viruses, resistance(s): The trace of infection in the work of Michel Foucault', in S. Harris Ali and Roger Keil (eds), *Networked Disease: Emerging Infections in the Global City*. Malden: Blackwell, pp. 267–80.

Saunders, Anthony (1987), 'The interbank market, contagion effects and international financial crises', in Richard Portes and Alexander K. Swoboda (eds), *Threats to International Financial Stability*. Cambridge: Cambridge University Press, pp. 196–232.

Savage, Robert (2010), 'Translator's afterword', in Hans Blumenberg (ed.), *Paradigms for a Metaphorology*. Ithaca: Cornell University Press, pp. 133–46.

Savile, Henry (trans.) (1598), *The Ende of Nero and Beginning of Galba. Fower Bookes of the Histories of Cornelius Tacitus and The Life of Agricola* (2nd edn). London: Edmund Bollifant, for Bonham and John Norton.

Schaub, Mirjam, Suthor, Nicola and Fischer-Lichte, Erika (eds) (2005), *Ansteckung: Zur Körperlichkeit eines ästhetischen Prinzips*. München: Wilhelm Fink.

Scheler, Max (1970 [1923]), *The Nature of Sympathy* (trans. of *Wesen und Formen der Sympathie*, trans. Peter Heath). London: Routledge and Kegan Paul.

Schell, Heather (1997), 'Outburst! A chilling true story about emerging-virus narratives and pandemic social change'. *Configurations*, 5, (1), 93–133.

Schmid, Hans B. (2009), 'Evolution by imitation: Gabriel Tarde and the limits of memetics', in *Plural Action: Essays in Philosophy and Social Science*. Berlin: Springer-Verlag, pp. 197–214.

Secor, Marie and Walsh, Lynda (2004), 'A rhetorical perspective on the Sokal Hoax: Genre, style, and context'. *Written Communication*, 21, 69–91.

Seneca, Lucius Annaeus (1620), *Lucius Annaeus Seneca Works, both Moral and Natural, Translated into English* (trans. Thomas Lodge). London: William Stansby.

—(1786), *The Epistles of Lucius Annaeus Seneca* (trans. Thomas Morell, vol. 2). London: W. Woodfall.

—(1825), *L. Annaei Senecae ad Lucilium epistolae selectae*, in Augustus Pauly (ed.). Stuttgart: J. B. Metzleri.

Serres, Michel (1982 [1980]), *The Parasite* (trans. of *Le parasite*, trans. Lawrence R. Schehr). Baltimore, MD: Johns Hopkins University Press.

Sheehan, Evan Louis (2006), *The Mocking Memes: A Basis for Automated Intelligence*. Bloomington: AuthorHouse.

Shennan, Stephen (2002), *Genes, Memes and Human History: Darwinian Archaeology and Cultural Evolution*. London: Thames and Hudson.

Siegfried, André (1965 [1960]), *Routes of Contagion* (trans. of *Itinéraires de contagions: Epidémies et idéologies*, trans. Jean Henderson and Mercedes Clarasó). New York: Harcourt, Brace, and World.

Sigerist, Henry E. (1938), 'The history of medical history', in James Alexander Miller (ed.), *Milestones in Medicine: Laity Lectures of the New York Academy of Medicine*. New York: D. Appleton-Century, pp. 163–84.

Sighele, Scipio (1891), *La folla delinquente: Studio di psicologia collettiva*. Torino: Fratelli Bocca.

—(1892), *La foule criminelle: Essai de psychologie collective* (trans. of *La folla delinquente: Studio di psicologia collettiva*, trans. Paul Vigny). Paris: Félix Alcan.

Simon, Mallory (September 2011), 'A Greek tragedy: How the debt crisis spread like a virus in *Contagion*'. *CNN*. www.news.blogs.cnn.com/2011/09/19/a-greek-tragedy-how-the-debt-crisis-spread-like-a-virus-in-contagion/.

Sloterdijk, Peter (2009 [2002]), *Terror from the Air* (trans. of *Luftbeben*, trans. Amy Patton and Steve Corcoran). Los Angeles: Semiotext(e).

Slutkin, Gary (August 2011), 'Rioting is a disease spread from person to person. The key is to stop the infection'. *Observer*, p. 18.

Smith, William (1868), *Dictionary of the Bible* (vol. 1). New York: Hurd and Houghton.

Snooks, Graeme Donald (2003), *The Collapse of Darwinism, or the Rise of a Realist Theory of Life*. Oxford: Lexington.

Snowden, Frank M. (1995), *Naples in the Time of Cholera*. Cambridge: Cambridge University Press.

Sobolev, Dennis (2008), 'Metaphor revisited'. *New Literary History*, 39, (4), 903–29.

Soderbergh, Steven (2011), *Contagion* [Film].

Sokal, Alan and Bricmont, Jean (1998), *Intellectual Impostures: Postmodern Philosophers' Abuse of Science*. London: Profile.

Sontag, Susan (1983 [1978]), *Illness as Metaphor*. Harmondsworth: Penguin.

Souter, Alexander (c. 1906), *The Commentary of Pelagius on the Epistles of Paul: The Problem of its Restoration*. London: Oxford University Press.

Spariosu, Mihai (1984), 'Plato's *Ion*: Mimesis, poetry and power', in Ronald Bogue (ed.), *Mimesis in Contemporary Theory* (vol. 2). Philadelphia: John Benjamins, pp. 13–26.

—(1989), *Dionysus Reborn: Play and the Aesthetic Dimension in Modern Philosophical and Scientific Discourse*. Cornell: Cornell University Press.

Sperber, Dan (1996), *Explaining Culture: A Naturalistic Approach*. Oxford: Blackwell.

Steele, Edward J. (Ted) (1981), *Somatic Selection and Adaptive Evolution: On the Inheritance of Acquired Characters*. Chicago: University of Chicago Press.

Steele, Edward J. (Ted), Lindley, Robyn A. and Blanden, R. V. (1998), *Lamarck's Signature: How Retrogenes are Changing Darwin's Natural Selection Paradigm*. Sydney: Perseus.

Stephenson, Neal (1992), *Snow Crash*. New York: Bantam.

Stewart, Dugald (1827), *Elements of the Philosophy of the Human Mind* (vol. 3). Philadelphia: Carey, Lea and Carey.

Stockwell, Peter (2002), *Cognitive Poetics*. London: Routledge.

Storm, William (1998), *After Dionysus: A Theory of the Tragic*. Ithaca: Cornell University Press.

Swiggers, Pierre (1984), 'Cognitive aspects of Aristotle's theory of metaphor'. *Glotta*, 62, (1–2), 40–5.

Tacitus, Cornelius (1850), *The Histories of Caius Cornelius Tacitus*. New York: Appleton and Company.

Taine, Hippolyte A. (1870), *De l'intelligence*. Paris: Hachette.

—(1878a), *Les origines de la France contemporaine: La Révolution, tome I*. Paris: Hachette.

—(1878b), *"Les Origines de la France Contemporaine": The Revolution, vol. 1* (trans. John Durand). London: Daldy, Isbister and Co.

—(1881a), *Les origines de La France contemporaine: La Révolution, tome II: La conquéte Jacobine*. Paris: Hachette.

—(1881b), *"Les Origines de la France Contemporaine": The Revolution, vol. 2* (trans. of *Les Origines de La France Contemporaine: La Révolution, Tome II: La Conquéte Jacobine*, trans. John Durand, 2nd edn). London: Sampson Low, Marston, Searle, and Rivington.

Tanaka, Yuzuru (2004), *Meme Media and Meme Market Architectures: Knowledge Media for Editing, Distributing, and Managing Intellectual Resources*. Hoboken: Wiley IEEE.

Tarde, Gabriel (1886), *La criminalité comparée*. Paris: Félix Alcan.

—(1890), *La philosophie penale*. Paris: A. Storck and G. Masson.

—(1893), 'Monades et science sociale [Monadologie et sociologie]'. *Revue Internationale de Sociologie*, 1, 157–73.

—(1895), 'Monadologie et sociologie', in *Essais et mélanges sociologiques*. Paris: A. Storck and G. Masson, pp. 309–89.

—(1903 [1890]), *The Laws of Imitation* (trans. of *Les lois de l'imitation: étude sociologique*, trans. Elsie Clews Parsons). New York: Henry Holt.

—(1907 [1898]), *Social Laws: An Outline of Sociology* (trans. of *Les lois sociales: esquisse d'une sociologie*, trans. Howard C. Warren). New York: Macmillan.

Tatem, Andrew J., Rogers, David J. and Hay, S. I. (2007), 'Global transport networks and infectious disease spread', in Simon I. Hay, Alastair J. Graham and David J. Rogers (eds), *Global Mapping of Infectious Diseases: Methods, Examples and Emerging Applications*. London: Elsevier, pp. 294–335.

Taussig, Frank W. (1911), *Principles of Economics* (vol. 1). New York: Macmillan.

Taylor, Alfred Edward (1928), *A Commentary on Plato's Timaeus*. Oxford: Clarendon.

Teh, J. Shin and Rubin, Harvey (2009), 'Global diseases: The role of networks in the spread and prevention of infection', in Paul R. Kleindorfer and Yoram Wind (eds), *The Network Challenge: Strategy, Profit, and Risk in an Interlinked World*. Upper Saddle River, NJ: Pearson, pp. 471–94.

Thacker, Eugene (2004), 'Foreword: Protocol is as protocol does', in Alexander R. Galloway (ed.), *Protocol: How Control Exists after Decentralization*. Cambridge, MA: MIT Press, pp. xi–xxii.

—(2005), 'Living dead networks'. *Fibreculture*, 4, www.four.fibreculturejournal.org/fcj-018-living-dead-networks/.

—(2009), 'The shadows of atheology: Epidemics, power and life after Foucault'. *Theory, Culture & Society*, 26, (6), 134–52.

'The Fire This Time' (August 2011), *The Economist*. www.economist.com/node/21525945.

Thomson, E., Rev. (1855), 'Moral education'. *Ladies' Repository*, 15, 11–14; 92–6.

Thorne, James P. (1982), 'George Lakoff and Mark Johnson, *Metaphors We Live By*'. *Journal of Linguistics*, 19, (1), 245–8.

Thrift, Nigel (2008), *Non-Representational Theory: Space, Politics, Affect*. Abingdon, Oxon: Routledge.

Thucydides (2006), *The History of the Peloponnesian War* (trans. Richard Crawley). New York: Barnes and Noble Classics.

Toews, David (2003), 'The new Tarde: Sociology after the end of the social'. *Theory, Culture and Society*, 20, (5), 81–98.

Tolstoy, Leo Nikolayevich (1898 [1897]), *What is Art?* (trans. of *Chto takoe iskusstvo?*, trans. Charles Johnston). Philadelphia: Henry Altemus.

Travis, John. (September 2011). 'Don't call it viral marketing: The story behind *Contagion*'s microbial billboard'. *Science Insider*. www.news.sciencemag.org/scienceinsider/2011/09/dont-call-it-viral-marketing-the.html?ref = hp.

Tullie, George (1684), 'How to know a flatterer from a friend', in Matthew Morgan (ed.), *Plutarch's Morals: Translated from the Greek by Several Hands* (vol. 2). London: John Gellibrand, pp. 1–85.

Turner, Mark (1992), 'Language is a virus'. *Poetics Today*, 13, (4), 725–36.

van Ginneken, Jaap (1985), 'The 1895 debate on the origins of crowd psychology'. *Journal of the History of the Behavioral Sciences*, 21, 375–82.

—(1992), *Crowds, Psychology, and Politics, 1871–99*. Cambridge: Cambridge University Press.

van Loon, Joost (2002), 'A contagious living fluid: Objectification and assemblage in the history of virology'. *Theory, Culture & Society*, 19, (5–6), 107–24.

Vandenbroucke, Jan P. (2004), 'Changing images of John Snow in the history of epidemiology', in Alfredo Morabia (ed.), *A History of Epidemiologic Methods and Concepts*. Basel: Birkhäuser Verlag, pp. 141–8.

Veness, Hugh (1971), 'The psychology of crowd behaviour: A review of Freud's theories in the light of contemporary historical research'. *Australian and New Zealand Journal of Psychiatry*, 5, 199–205.

Vico, Giambattista (1984 [1725]), *The New Science of Giambattista Vico* (trans. of *Principi di Scienza Nuova d'intorno alla Comune Natura delle Nazioni*, trans. Thomas Goddard Bergin and Max Harold Fisch). Ithaca: Cornell University Press.

Vigouroux, Auguste and Juquelier, Paul (1905), *La contagion mentale*. Paris: Octave Doin.

Vinten-Johansen, Peter, Brody, Howard, Paneth, Nigel, Rachman, Stephen and Rip, Michael (2003), *Cholera, Chloroform, and the Science of Medicine: A Life of John Snow*. Oxford: Oxford University Press.

Vrettos, Athena (1995), *Somatic Fictions: Imagining Illness in Victorian Culture*. Stanford: Stanford UP.

Wald, Priscilla (2008), *Contagious: Cultures, Carriers, and the Outbreak Narrative*. Durham: Duke University Press.

Watts, Sheldon (1997), *Epidemics and History: Disease, Power and Imperialism*. New Haven: Yale.

Watts, William (trans.) (1631), *Saint Augustine's Confessions Translated*. London: John Norton.

Weinstein, Arnold (2003), 'Afterword: Infection as metaphor'. *Literature and Medicine*, 22, (1), 102–15.

Weinstock, Jeffrey A. (1997), 'Virus culture'. *Studies in Popular Culture*, 20, (1), www.pcasacas.org/SiPC/20.1/weinstock.htm.

'Wiede' (1857), in *Flügel's Complete Dictionary of the Germana and English Languages* (new edn, vol. 2). London: Whittaker and Co.

Wilcher, Robert (1991), 'What was the King's Book for?: The evolution of "Eikon Basilike"'. *Yearbook of English Studies*, 21, 218–28.

Wills, Garry (2002), 'Augustine's pears and the nature of sin'. *Arion*, 10, (1), 57–66.

Wisecup, Kelly (2008), ' "Let's get semiotic": Recoding the self in Neal Stephenson's *Snow Crash* (1992)'. *Journal of Popular Culture*, 41, (5), 854–77.

Wolfe, Alan (1993), *The Human Difference: Animals, Computers, and the Necessity of Social Science*. Berkeley: University of California Press.

Wujastyk, Dominik and Conrad, Lawrence I. (2000), 'Introduction', in Lawrence I. Conrad and Dominik Wujastyk (eds), *Contagion: Perspectives from Pre-Modern Societies*. Aldershot: Ashgate, pp. ix–xviii.

Yates, Frances A. (1988), *The French Academies of the Sixteenth Century*. London: Routledge.

Younge, Richard (1638), *The Drunkard's Character, Or, A True Drunkard with Such Sinnes as Raigne in Him*. London: R. Badger.

—(1655), *Armour of Proof, or A Soveraign Antidote against the Contagion of Evil Company*. London: James Crump.

Zilinskas, Raymond A. (2011), 'Contagion: A movie pandemic versus the reality of public health'. *WMD Junction*, www.cns.miis.edu/wmdjunction/110923_contagion.htm.

Index

www.ingramcontent.com/pod-product-compliance
Lightning Source LLC
Chambersburg PA
CBHW050441280326
41932CB00013BA/2196